Searching for Paradise

Searching for Paradise

Economic Development and Environmental Change in the Mountain West

Douglas E. Booth

ROWMAN & LITTLEFIELD PUBLISHERS, INC.
Lanham • Boulder • New York • Oxford

ROWMAN & LITTLEFIELD PUBLISHERS, INC.

Published in the United States of America
by Rowman & Littlefield Publishers, Inc.
A Member of the Rowman & Littlefield Publishing Group
4720 Boston Way, Lanham, Maryland 20706
www.rowmanlittlefield.com

12 Hid's Copse Road
Cumnor Hill, Oxford OX2 9JJ, England

British Library Cataloguing in Publication Information Available

Library of Congress Cataloging-in-Publication Data

Booth, Douglas E.
  Searching for paradise : economic development and environmental change
in the mountain West / Douglas E. Booth.
      p. cm.
Includes bibliographical references and index.
  ISBN 0-7425-1875-2 (alk. paper) — ISBN 0-7425-1876-0 (pbk.: alk. paper)
  1. Economic development—Environmental aspects—West (U.S.) 2.
Urban-rural migration—Environmental aspects—West (U.S.) 3. West
(U.S.)—Population—Environmental aspects. 4. Landscape
protection—West (U.S.) 5. Biological diversity conservation—West
(U.S.) I. Title.
  TD195 .E25 B66 2002
  333. 7'2'0978—dc21

                                                                2002001881

Printed in the United States of America

♾ ™ The paper used in this publication meets the minimum requirements of American
National Standard for Information Sciences—Permanence of Paper
for Printed Library Materials, ANSI/NISO Z39.48–1992.

To my mountain West backpacking partner, Bob Koch, who has an amazing ability to find humor and irony in all of life's experiences.

Contents

Illustrations

TABLES

FIGURES

Preface

Since relocating to the heartland from the Pacific Northwest some thirty years ago, I have found it more convenient to backpack and travel in the Rocky Mountain states than to return every year to the land of my birth. Over the years I have noticed the mountain valleys and foothill ridge tops filling up with new residential development. This has caused me to wonder about the forces behind this residential expansion and the consequences for the local natural environment. At the same time, as an academic economist, my primary concern in my research and teaching has been the relationship between economic growth and environmental change. Some researchers have suggested that the relationship between the two is weakened in more affluent and sophisticated economies because growth tends to be driven by information and services that, at first glance, appear to place more limited material demands on our natural resource base than the more industrially oriented economies of the past. One interesting consequence of modern technology is that we are increasingly free to live where we want. Information can be produced almost anywhere and is easily transmitted. We don't necessarily need to live in an urban setting anymore to earn a living or enjoy the benefits of the modern consumer economy. This raises the possibility that the longstanding trend of population migration to the suburbs is being carried beyond urban boundaries to relatively remote areas of great natural beauty such as the mountain West. If this population spreading is indeed driven by affluence and new kinds of technology, and if it is causing additional stresses to the native flora and fauna of the mountain West, then we cannot say with certainty that the link between economic growth and environmental change has been severed. The primary goal of this book is to shed light on this important issue.

If population spreading to the mountain West is having significant environmental consequences, the question arises as to whether visitors and residents, both new and old, want to do anything to alter existing trends. Do we want the mountain West flora and fauna preserved for our own benefit or for its own sake? How should the preservation be accomplished? A second goal of this book is to summarize some of the existing thinking on this issue. Americans have a long-standing ambivalence about urban life. Nonetheless, if we want to conserve the biological diversity that remains in our natural and seminatural landscapes, we may need to improve the attractiveness of our cities to get at least some people to reconsider their desire to move ever outward from our urban centers. Moreover, those of us who still choose to live in a rural setting may have to consider doing so at higher population densities than we are accustomed to if we want to preserve the natural landscape.

Many have helped me either directly or indirectly to do the work behind this book. Let me begin by thanking Marquette University and its College of Business Administration for not only affording me the time for research and writing, but also for providing me travel money to visit land trusts and conduct interviews in the mountain West. Numerous individuals have helped me as well. I want to offer special thanks to Lucy Blake, president of the Sierra Business Council, for allowing me to use data from their survey of Sierra Nevada voters. Two individuals at the Colorado Natural Heritage Program were especially helpful, Susan Spackman and Mike Wunder. Let me also thank the Montana and California Natural Heritage Programs for their assistance. Everyone who took the time to respond to my experts' survey on rare and imperiled species deserves my gratitude as do all participants in my land trust interviews. An anonymous reviewer helped me to sharpen my thinking on a number of issues. Although we have never met, I owe special thanks to Thomas Michael Power for the inspiration his work has provided me. Naturally, none of these people can be blamed for any remaining flaws and errors in this work. Finally, let me thank my wife, Carol, and my two sons, Edward and Jeremy, for putting up with my grumpiness when things weren't going well or the computer crashed.

1

〜

The "Suburbanization" of the Mountain West

No one who has traveled in the mountain West during the past thirty years will fail to notice the changes that have taken place. Homes, some large and luxurious, are springing up with increasing regularity on the valley bottoms, along rivers and streams, and on mountain ridge lines. The mountain West is becoming more crowded even though the traditional economy—based on timber, mining, and agriculture—is in decline. Continued population growth and housing development in the face of this decline suggests that the source of economic expansion is in a state of transformation. The traveler may wonder how those who have moved to remote areas are able to earn a living. The more environmentally sensitive traveler may wonder what the new basis of development means for the landscape and its native plants and animals. Certainly the old economy is implicated in threats to the natural environment. What about the new economy? The perceptive traveler may also wonder whether this new development is in a sense self-spoiling. The obvious attraction of the mountain West is its wealth of unspoiled vistas and beautiful landscapes. Is development spoiling the fundamental attraction of the area by filling up the landscape with housing? Will those who have come for the beautiful views ultimately be disappointed? How will they react politically? Will they push for controls on further growth and shut the door to newcomers in an attempt to save the landscape from further ruin?

These are the kinds of questions that are addressed in the pages to follow. The central hypothesis offered here is that the modern settlement of the mountain West is an extension of the longstanding trend in urban population decentralization that has manifested itself in the spreading of population from large urban centers into suburbs. Migration to the rural mountain West is simply the next

1

step after suburbanization and is a response to rising affluence and technological trends that increase the ease and reduce the cost of both communications and transportation. Technology and affluence enable population decentralization, but human desire drives it. The outward movement away from cities in the United States seems to be motivated by values that are essentially rural in origin. Since our values ultimately determine what we want in life and, more specifically, where we want to live, understanding values that seem to motivate population movement away from cities is a reasonable point-of-entry into the larger topic of population-spreading to remote areas of the mountain West. Thus we begin by addressing the underpinnings of the urban population decentralization process. This will set the stage for the central topic of the book.

THE RURAL IDEAL AND THE ATTRACTION OF THE SUBURBS

Americans have always felt ambivalent about their cities. Cities are essential, as Jane Jacobs so eloquently argues, for the creation of material abundance.[1] The industrial revolution and its accompanying transformation of material living standards took place in cities. The proximity afforded by cities is the life's blood of an industrial and free-market economy. The complex interactions of city life are the roots of technological and scientific innovation. The creation of wealth to this point in our economic history has been an essentially urban affair.

The Jeffersonian vision of a democratic society, on the other hand, presumed that small landowning farmers, not city dwellers, would serve as society's political and cultural backbone. The Jeffersonian vision was profoundly rooted in John Locke's theory of property, a theory specifically developed to throw off the yoke of property ownership based on the divine right of kings. Property ownership in feudal Europe flowed from the crown. All property was ultimately God's to be endowed by God's agent, the king. In simple terms, the Lockian view states that whoever is the first person to work the land and embody labor in it may obtain it. Locke begins with the notion that all men have a natural right to the property of their person and thus to the property of whatever they create. By extension, what one removes from nature and mixes with labor is property as well. Land that is worked in agricultural production thus becomes individual property.[2] Given the settlers' desire for independence from the British crown, and the abundance of uncultivated land on the American continent, the Lockian view of property must have been quite appealing to Jefferson. Just as the pre-feudal German freeman was responsible for the settlement and cultivation of much of northern Europe on the basis of individual property,[3] so was the individual settler in the United States. According to Jefferson, "Cultivators of the earth are the most valuable citizens. They are the most vigorous, the most independent, the most virtuous, and they are tied to their country and wedded to it liberty and interest by the most lasting bonds."[4]

By contrast, Jefferson also wrote that "The mobs of great cities add just so much to the support of pure government, as sores do to the strength of the human body."[5] Jefferson early on expressed rural values and antiurban sentiments that remain influential in American culture to this day. The Jeffersonian view provided the ideological underpinning for the Homestead Act and its 160-acre offer to anyone who would take up residence and improve the land. According to Jefferson, where society chooses not to otherwise allocate land for public ends, "each individual of society may appropriate to himself such lands that he finds vacant, and occupancy will give him title."[6]

The reality of land allocation turned out to be quite different. The best of the public lands often went to railroad corporations, pushing the small landholder onto less desirable tracts.[7] In order to develop the western landscape on a large scale, transportation was a necessity. To stimulate the construction of rail lines, the federal government offered railroad corporations generous land grants. The requirements of large-scale development came into conflict with the ideal of a nation of small landowners.

Jefferson's antipathy to cities was rooted in his distaste for anything industrial. He wanted manufacturing to remain a European endeavor and hoped that Americans could keep their rural ways.[8] Contrary to the Jeffersonian vision, industrial production and cities became the basis for economic expansion. Cities in nineteenth-century America, essential as they were to economic progress, were tinged not only by the pollution and unhealthy conditions created in a newly industrializing society, but also by the corruption of city government political machines. The good and moral life in this country in the eyes of many citizens was to be found in a rural setting, not an urban one. The rural ideal, as Sam B. Warner articulates, includes enjoyment of the pleasures of family life, the security of small communities, and a proximity to the world of nature.[9] Since this ideal was impossible to obtain in an urban society, it was sought through location on the urban fringe by those who could afford it as soon as transportation technology made it possible to do so. Warner documents the first wave of suburbanization occurring in Boston in the last half of the nineteenth century. The old walking city of an approximate two-mile radius became a ten-mile radius city in 1900 with the middle- and upper-income earners concentrated in the new suburbs of the outer rings and the members of the lower-paid working classes crowded into the tenements of the old walking city. Outward expansion of the city's boundaries was enabled by the construction of a street railway system and the extension of municipal services to the newly developing areas. Achieving the rural ideal through suburbanization turned out to contain an internal contradiction. Any connections to nature were soon lost as the urban edge migrated farther out and construction took place on undeveloped land. The pleasures of family life in suburban havens could be obtained in the newly developing areas of the city, but the suburbs never really established their own commercial and community centers, and the interactions of community life integral to the rural ideal were seldom achieved. Retailing remained essentially a central city function concentrated at the urban center and along streetcar lines.

A much more optimistic vision of the potential of urban life and its significance for the economy is offered by Jane Jacobs. In Jacobs's view it is the city, not the countryside, that is ultimately responsible for economic progress. Economies grow not by producing more of the same, but by adding new kinds of work, and new work often springs from the old.[10] It is the proximity and interactions of city life that drive economic expansion. Businesses that start new industries require a variety of producers' goods and services that can only be found in cities. It is among these suppliers that new ideas and technologies are often incubated. These same new industries must also be able to draw upon labor with a diversity of skills that can only be found in cities. For Jacobs it is the city that drives development in the countryside, not the other way around. This is a view largely confirmed in William Cronon's *Nature's Metropolis*, where the central role played by the city of Chicago in the development of the American West is carefully documented.[11]

Jacobs argues as well that the diversity and sociality of well-designed cities can make them attractive and enriching places to lives.[12] Neighborhoods with a diversity of economic activities, short blocks, buildings of different ages, and sufficient population density offer a rich and interesting street life and ample opportunities for economic, social, and cultural fulfillment. The environmental problems initially associated with industrialization have largely been overcome in cities as a consequence of solutions enabled by economic growth and innovation.[13] Nonetheless, through suburbanization, Americans have for the most part turned their backs on cities. The outward movement described by Warner for Boston has continued despite improvements in the environment of the industrial city. The suburbs have proven to be an incredible magnet. Because the countryside beyond seems to be gaining similar magnetic powers, it behooves us to have a better understanding of the whole suburbanization process. If the city is our ultimate source of economic riches, why do we turn away from it? Why now are we in increasing numbers moving away from urban areas and seeking the good life in the countryside?

THE PROCESS OF SUBURBANIZATION

Anthony Downs claims that the dominant suburban vision prevailing today includes five key elements: ownership of detached single-family homes on spacious lots; ownership of automotive vehicles; work in low-rise workplaces with convenient parking; residences in small communities with strong local governments; and an environment free from signs of poverty.[14] This view of suburban life is supported by an urban historian, Kenneth T. Jackson, who lists low residential density, homeownership, a correlation of income and distance from the urban center, and a relatively lengthy trip to work as the central features of suburban living.[15] These descriptions are consistent with Warner's rural ideal—enjoyment of family life, small communities, and proximity to nature—sought by the participants in the first wave of suburbanization in the nineteenth century.[16] The character of the modern desire for suburban living does not appear to have changed dramatically in the last century.

What has changed are the enabling conditions. In the walking city, suburban living was largely precluded by the need to be within walking distance of the urban center, no more than two or three miles. In fifty years the electric streetcar expanded Boston's urban radius from three to ten miles. By 1900 a six-mile commute would require about an hour from home to office.[17] The streetcar enabled those who could afford it to move to the urban periphery. This new technology facilitated the outward movement of residential activity, but left the spatial economics of business largely unchanged. Close proximity to customers and other businesses was required because communication was largely limited to office boys carrying notes. Moreover, goods could only be moved through the congested streets of the city by handcarts and wagons at a relatively high cost. Manufacturing thus huddled close to railheads and ports to limit the costs of moving goods within the city, and offices congregated together for ease of communication. The result was that everyone had to commute to the urban center for employment. Under the new pattern of settlement in the streetcar city, the working class lived in high densities in and about the confines of the old walking city, the more prosperous middle class lived in lower densities somewhat farther out, and the richest class lived in the lowest densities on the urban periphery.[18] At first the newly developing areas were happy to be annexed to the central city, but soon suburban residents wanted independence from the central cities they no longer controlled politically, and they wanted independent determination of their own level of municipal services while avoiding the burdens of central city problems and taxes.[19]

The movement of the relatively prosperous to the urban periphery was, perhaps, inevitable given the nature of the nineteenth-century American city.[20] While cities at the time may indeed have had some of the amenities and features described by Jane Jacobs, these were largely offset in the eyes of the middle class by the forces of industrialization and immigration. Industrialization meant dirty, smoky, gritty cities while immigration, essential for the manning of the industrial system, created overcrowded ghettos repulsive to middle-class sensibilities.[21] In this setting, the suburb provided a peaceful haven from the apparent chaos of the central city. Though the central city and the proximity it afforded was the real source of economic wealth, those who benefited most from it were the first to leave.

To augment the urban land supply, the streetcar took advantage of the mathematical relationship between the radius and the area of the circle with area increasing in proportion to the square of the radius from the center of the city.[22] As the feasible commute expanded from roughly two to six miles for a streetcar system oriented on the urban center as spokes on a wheel, the possible area for urban development increased roughly ninefold. The streetcar brought relatively cheap land on the urban boundary within the sphere of urban development making possible suburban development at relatively low densities.

The motor vehicle expanded the supply of land within the sphere of urban influence even more dramatically by not only reducing commuting times to the urban center, but more importantly by disconnecting work from the urban center. Trucks allowed for the movement of goods within an urban area at much reduced costs.[23] This was especially the case once the interstate highway system was developed with spokes running through old urban centers and radial spurs connecting different suburban locations. Any activity depending on truck transportation could now advantageously locate near interstate junctions and have access to the whole metropolitan area as well as interurban shipping routes while avoiding the congestion of the old central city. The untying of work from the urban center allowed urban areas to be almost boundless. The average commute today is 9.2 miles and takes 22 minutes in contrast to the one hour commute required to cover six miles on the streetcar.[24] Reduced commuting time alone would expand the urban boundary substantially for a core dominated urban area where commuting is from the urban periphery to the center. However, with the suburbanization of employment, the nine mile average commute is more typically between residence and work within the suburban circle. This arrangement allows for the outward movement of work and residence in tandem, bringing potentially vast amounts of rural land into the realm of urban development. Apart from physical barriers, the supply of urban land is limited only by the extent of the urban expressway system. The motor vehicle essentially eliminated constraints on the outward march of urban development.

Numerous other trends aided and stimulated the suburbanization of businesses and residences. The telephone, like the truck, extended communication between businesses and reduced the need for close proximity. With the growth of auto-accessible suburban shopping malls, suburban residents no longer relied on downtown retailing and could live in more distant locations and continue to have access to urban consumption opportunities. The switch to the motor vehicle wasn't simply a matter of consumer choice but was enabled by an incredible public investment in expressways and highways, brought forth in no small measure through the lobbying efforts of a powerful collection of major industries.[25] After World War II, the suburban dream of a detached, single-family dwelling was no longer confined to the relatively wealthy but could now be afforded by the more prosperous segments of the working class with the help of relatively low-cost VA and FHA insured mortgage loans. Homeownership blossomed as a result to the detriment of the older central cities lacking substantial supplies of single-family dwellings that qualified for VA or FHA assistance.[26] Moreover, because of annexation law reforms resulting in the need for local resident approval, suburban residents could avoid annexation by the central city and establish separate municipal jurisdictions instead. This not only prevented the high tax costs associated with central city problems, but it also allowed for the local control of zoning and the use of exclusionary practices, such as minimum lot size requirements, that would keep economically burdensome and undesirable low-income residences out. The end result was to confine the poor to the older, filtered down housing in the central city and create economically and socially homogeneous suburban communities.

THE SUBURBAN DREAM UNFULFILLED

As Sam Bass Warner observed early on, the suburban dream contains inherent flaws and contradictions. Suburban expansion destroyed any sense of connection to the rural landscape. The suburbs generally became independent political jurisdictions, but not intimate, close-knit communities. Of the three components of the rural ideal articulated by Warner, only the pleasure of family life in detached homes was assured in the turn-of-the-century suburbs.[27] In the modern suburb, the security of homeownership in detached homes on relatively large lots and the desire for control over local schools and land use generally prevail, but suburban expansion has brought increasing costs for public facilities, increasing traffic congestion, growing pollution problems, and losses of open space.[28] Such problems have resulted in a reaction against growth in some communities and, for some individuals, a search for more pleasant surroundings beyond urban boundaries.

The initial wave of suburbs that developed after World War II were largely bedroom communities. Residents commuted to the central city for work. In this setting, the essentials of the suburban dream—quiet neighborhoods of single-family homes on large lots in a semi-rural setting—were not hard to maintain. More recently, the suburbs have been transformed. With the construction of large shopping malls, office complexes, and industrial parks, most employment in urban areas is now found in the suburbs.[29] Many suburbs currently have a sufficient density of office space and employment to be urban centers in their own right. In *Edge City: Life on the New Frontier* (1991), a book that has received much attention, Joel Garreau documents the development of new centers of employment in the suburbs and coined the phrase "edge cities" to describe them.[30] Most suburban residents today commute to other suburbs or edge cities for their employment rather than the central city. As a consequence of this trend, suburbs have taken on increasingly urban characteristics including more congestion, noise, pollution, and crime. Quiet bedroom communities in semi-rural settings have been transformed into what are essentially cities, but they are cities that retain quintessentially suburban qualities, the primary one being auto dependence. Moving from one point to another in suburban space mandates the use of the automobile. For this reason, traffic in suburbs is a constant problem despite the relatively large amount of land devoted to highways and streets.

While the economic diversity and increased services associated with the growth of edge cities have brought benefits to many, suburban residents have not always been pleased with the expansion of their own communities. Many suburban residents have revolted against growth. Between 1971 and 1986, more than 150 antigrowth measures appeared on local ballots.[31] A number of surveys have found significant local support for measures to limit local growth including construction moratoriums, ceilings on building permits, open space zoning, environmental impact statement requirements, development fees to cover the cost of public facilities, and minimum lot size requirements.[32] Support for antigrowth measures in local municipalities could be motivated by the desires of the affluent to keep those with lower incomes out of their communities, or it could be a simple reaction by local residents to a deteriorating quality of life associated with rapid local growth. Since the essential determinants of support for growth control are perceptions of rapid growth and perceptions of decline in the local quality of life, and since socioeconomic status is rarely a determinant of support for growth controls, supporters of growth controls seem to be responding primarily to perceptions of community decline.[33] Surprisingly, while perceptions of rapid growth influence support for growth controls, rapid growth itself does not. Even more surprising, local growth controls seem to have little effect on growth itself.[34] In short, growth controls don't work! The consequences of growth cannot be avoided within the urban setting. The only option left to avoid the problems of growth is to move still farther out beyond urban boundaries.

BEYOND THE SUBURBS: POPULATION EXPANSION IN THE SIERRA NEVADAS

If the suburbs have lost their luster, then one option is to move beyond them. California has been on the leading edge of the antigrowth revolt and it may also be taking a leadership position in a new trend of population spreading to landscapes of natural beauty beyond the urban fringe. An example of this phenomenon is the recent rapid growth of population in and near the Sierra Nevada Mountains.

The Sierra Nevada has a lengthy and colorful history of modern human exploitation beginning with the mid-nineteenth century gold rush era. The Sierra Nevada ecosystem has been dramatically reshaped by grazing, mining, logging, fire suppression, water diversions, and hydroelectric projects.[35] While the natural beauty of the area has been recognized from the earliest days of European settlement, only in recent decades has transportation and communication technology made living and recreating in the Sierra Nevada possible for those not engaged in the extractive industries. The Sierra Nevada economy has undergone a transition from dependence on the material riches of the mountain landscape to one that is increasingly dependent on its scenic and ecological values. This transition is manifested in a doubling of population (figure 1.1) between 1969 and 1994 in a 16 county area that encompasses most of the Sierra Nevada Mountains. The growth has been even more rapid in the rural counties (134 percent) than the two urban counties (82 percent), Fresno and Kern.[36]

Population growth in the Sierra Nevada is most likely occurring for the same reasons that many rural counties in the United States are experiencing a growth renaissance. Such counties are usually centers of retirement or outdoor recreation, or are adjacent to metropolitan areas. Counties with these characteristics have generally experienced relatively rapid growth in the period 1970–1990.[37] Communities in counties such as El Dorado, Nevada, and Placer are within commuting distance of Sacramento and are on the receiving end of the outward spread of population from the Sacramento metro area. The decentralization of urban employment away from the central city to the outer suburban ring has increased the accessibility of urban employment from rural counties. Moreover, incomes for many are increasingly footloose by virtue of a growing retirement age population and substantial capital gains in the California urban housing market as well as the stock market. Given the strong preferences Americans seem to have for rural settings, and given their antipathy to high-density urban living and the crime and traffic congestion it brings,[38] it is not surprising that those who are free to choose their residential location unencumbered by economic necessity

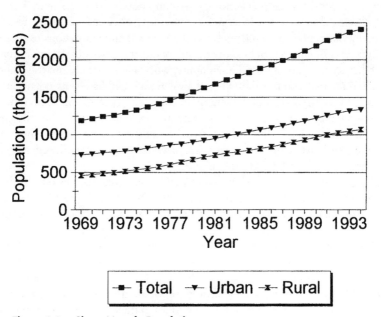

Figure 1.1: Sierra Nevada Population

are increasingly selecting Sierra Nevada counties as their place of residence. New technologies (such as overnight delivery, the fax, the modem, cellular phones, and satellite television transmission) have the effect of further disconnecting economic activity from urban centers and increasing the comforts of life in relatively remote Sierra Nevada locations.[39]

New development in the Sierra Nevada is heavily concentrated in formerly unincorporated rural foothill areas near the old "gold rush" era communities. New residents apparently desire lots sufficient in size to shield them from their neighbor with an intervening landscape of open space and woodlands. While there are a few high-income "gated community" developments and also some moderate-income subdivisions found on the periphery of established municipalities, the development process has occurred primarily through the incremental construction of individual homes as opposed to multiunit subdivisions common in urban areas. Minimum rural lot sizes set by local government to allow for on-site septic systems and well water vary from one to five acres.[40]

Why have so many citizens chosen to live in the Sierra Nevada Mountains? One source of information on this issue is a recent survey conducted for the Sierra Nevada Business Council. To gauge public attitudes on issues related to growth in the Sierra Nevada, the Sierra Business Council undertook a survey in November 1995 of 1,000 randomly selected registered voters in the 16 counties of the Sierra Nevada.[41] The survey focused on reasons for living in the Sierra Nevada, views on threats to Sierra Nevada communities from growth, and attitudes toward land use measures to control local population growth and housing development. The rural ideal of living close to nature in a small community is alive and well in the responses offered by Sierra Nevada residents (table 1.1). The dominant reasons respondents live in their communities include the quality of life, the quality of the environment, the ability to be a part of a small community with beauty and charm, the ability to live in a rural area, and the ability to get away from urban life. Respondents are less concerned with the quality of the schools, the availability of affordable housing, and the obtainability of cultural resources and activities than they are with the beauty and quality of the landscape and the character of their communities. The respondents are clearly attracted by that which is unavailable to them in an urban setting. The rural is clearly preferred to the urban.

While at first glance the Sierra Nevada may seem like paradise itself, the development process is beginning to take its toll. The primary threat to open space and natural habitat from population expansion in rural Sierra Nevada counties is the phenomenon of sprawl associated with low-density housing development. The first negative consequence of this development pattern to be noticed by local residents is probably increased traffic. Not far behind are declines in open space and natural areas, and a loss of the rural features that originally attracted local residents. Less noticeable and more subtle manifestations of such a decentralized development pattern include the loss and fragmentation of wildlife habitat, septic system failure and groundwater contamination, groundwater shortages, increased air pollution emissions from traffic congestion, and increased fire

Table 1.1. Reasons Sierra Nevada Residents Have Chosen to Live in Their Community: Percent of Respondents

Reason for Living in the Community	Major Reason	Moderate Reason	Minor Reason
Quality of life	76.2	9.6	12.1
Quality of the schools	34.5	13.1	43.2
Availability of affordable housing	29.3	22.0	44.0
Quality of the environment	71.0	15.1	11.9
Cultural resources and activities	24.8	21.0	50.8
Live in a small community	73.0	12.4	12.6
Beauty and charm of community	80.9	9.9	7.6
Lower cost of living	21.6	20.1	56.0
Move away from urban, city life	80.9	5.5	11.6
Live in a rural area	77.8	10.7	9.7
Closer access to developed recreation	34.6	18.2	44.5
Closer access to outdoor recreation	48.0	19.7	30.3

Note: The remaining respondents expressed no opinion or did not answer.

risk and more troublesome fire management in a landscape that mixes residences and wildlands. Specific habitat types at lower elevations, such as blue oak woodlands, are threatened to a greater extent by development because they are poorly represented in protected lands under public ownership. Not only is habitat lost by development, but it is also cut up into smaller patches that may be insufficient in size to support certain species. Moreover, residents introduce domestic pets into the local environment that prey on birds and small mammals, some of which may be rare to begin with. The mere presence of residential development increases pressure to suppress fires in landscapes that may actually require periodic fire to support a full complement of native plant and animal species.[42]

Sam Bass Warner's rural ideal would likely find considerable support among recent migrants to the Sierra Nevada Mountains. Nonetheless, there are inklings already that some localities are taking on characteristics not unlike those found in the suburbs. Indeed, the possibility clearly exists that development in mountainous areas has the potential to spoil the landscape and create what residents have come to escape.

PLAN FOR THE BOOK

Cities historically have been and continue to be central to the process of material wealth creation. Without cities we couldn't be nearly so prosperous as we are. Yet most of us no longer desire to live in central cities, and at least some of us are beginning to reject life in the suburbs surrounding central cities. Just as affluence and new technologies enabled us to pursue the suburban dream, they may now be allowing some of us to pursue our dreams of forgoing urban life entirely.

Whether the growth of population in the mountain West is a continuation of trends that led to suburbanization needs further analysis and justification. This is the task of the next two chapters where population and income data for rural mountain counties in California, Colorado, and Montana will be used to shed light on the population-spreading process.

Unfortunately, population-spreading has the potential to spoil the attractions of the landscape in the first place as well as to create problems for local native species and local ecological communities. Some have suggested that this new form of growth—manifested in the construction of new housing on relatively large plots of land, increased commercial activity, expanded road construction, and local population growth—is relatively benign in terms of its impact on local populations of native plants and animals and naturally occurring ecosystems. While the ecological effects of the extractive industries operating historically in the mountain West has been quite intensively studied, not much is known about the ecological effects of new forms of economic expansion based on retirement and capital income or income earned in a service-oriented economy. In chapter 4 the ecological effects of the traditional mountain West extractive economy are reviewed along with what little is known about the ecological effects of new trends in development driven by population spreading. The basic thesis of this discussion is that environmental effects of human activity tend to be cumulative, meaning that the impact of the new economy will add to that of the old. In chapter 5 the results of a survey of experts on threats from new forms of development to rare and imperiled species in California, Colorado, and Montana will be presented and discussed to offer further judgements on whether the latest forms of economic development are ecologically harmful or not.

Population expansion in the Sierra Nevada Mountains, as we have seen, may well be degrading the open spaces and natural communities that attract new residents in the first place. As suburban population expansion has fostered antigrowth revolts, so might population growth in the mountain West. In chapter 6 I explore further the willingness of residents in rapidly growing Sierra Nevada counties to undertake measures that will restrict growth using survey data. Is growth itself leading to sentiments for restricting further growth? This chapter will demonstrate that voters in the Sierra Nevada mountains strongly support measures that control growth and development.

What is the actual political response to population and economic growth in rural counties of the mountain West? While local governments still have much to do to regulate growth and land use in the rural mountain West, one relatively powerful response appears to be the blossoming of new land trusts—voluntary nonprofit organizations that seek to protect lands from development by obtaining conservation easements or land ownership. In chapter 7 the extent of land trust activity for the purpose of protecting open space, native species, and natural habitat in the mountain West is surveyed and analyzed with the goal of determining whether such activity is in turn driven by threats from local economic growth. Case studies of land trust activity in Colorado and Montana will be presented to illustrate the forces that stimulate land conservation efforts.

In chapter 8 the ethical question of whether life in cities is essential for the conservation of biological life in wilderness landscapes is raised. Will the continued spreading of human population into relatively wild landscapes ultimately be harmful to native plant and animal biodiversity? If the answer to this questions is yes, and if the conservation of biological diversity is accepted as a moral imperative, then somehow we will need to make cities attractive places to live to forestall the excessive spreading of human population into landscapes needed for biological conservation. How this can be accomplished, and how the effects of population spreading to rural areas can be mitigated by various kinds of land use controls is taken up in the final chapter.

NOTES

1. Jane Jacobs, *The Economy of Cities* (New York: Vintage Books, 1970).

2. This theory is discussed rather nicely in Eugene Hargrove's article, "Anglo-American Land Use Attitudes," *Environmental Ethics* 2 (1980): 121–148.

3. As Hargrove ("Anglo-American Land Use Attitudes") notes, in a strict sense the freeman did not own his land, but in practical sense he held it without any necessary obligations to an overlord.

4. Merrill D. Peterson, *The Portable Thomas Jefferson* (New York: The Viking Press, 1975), 383–384.

5. Peterson, *The Portable Thomas Jefferson*, 216–217.

6. Peterson, *The Portable Thomas Jefferson*, 18.

7. Roy Robbins, *Our Landed Heritage: The Public Domain, 1776–1936* (Lincoln: University of Nebraska Press, 1976).

8. Peterson, *The Portable Thomas Jefferson*, 216–217, 383–384.

9. Sam B. Warner Jr., *Street Car Suburbs: The Process of Growth in Boston, 1870–1900* (New York: Atheneum, 1974).

10. Jacobs, *The Economy of Cities*.

11. William Cronon, *Nature's Metropolis: Chicago and the Great West* (New York: W. W. Norton, 1991).

12. Jane Jacobs, *The Death and Life of Great American Cities* (New York: Vintage Books, 1961).

13. Jacobs, *The Economy of Cities*, 103–121.

14. Anthony Downs, *New Visions for Metropolitan America* (Washington D.C.: The Brookings Institution, 1994), 6.

15. Kenneth T. Jackson, *Crabgrass Frontier: The Suburbanization of the United States* (New York: Oxford University Press, 1985), 6–10.

16. Warner, *Street Car Suburbs*.

17. Warner, *Street Car Suburbs*, 2, 52.

18. Warner, *Street Car Suburbs*, 34, 52–56.

19. Warner, *Street Car Suburbs*, 163–166; Jackson, *Crabgrass Frontier*, 147–155.

20. In *Crabgrass Frontier*, Jackson argues that apart from American and British cities the more common pattern is for the rich to live at the core and the poor on the periphery. Industrialization and the rural ideal interact to turn the more common pattern on its head (43).

21. Jackson, Crabgrass Frontier, 69–70; Warner, Street Car Suburbs, 162.

22. Warner, Street Car Suburbs, 129.

23. Warner, Street Car Suburbs, 183.

24. Warner, Street Car Suburbs, 10.

25. Warner, Street Car Suburbs, 163–170, 248.

26. Warner, Street Car Suburbs, 204–233.

27. Warner, Street Car Suburbs, 153–166.

28. Mark Baldassare, The Growth Dilemma (Berkeley, CA: University of California Press, 1986), 1–32; Downs, New Visions for Metropolitan America.

29. Baldassare, The Growth Dilemma.

30. Joel Garreau, Edge City: Life on the New Frontier (New York: Doubleday, 1991).

31. Mark Baldassare, "Suburban Support for No Growth Policies: Implications for the Growth Revolt," Urban Affairs 12 (1990): 197–206.

32. Baldassare, "Suburban Support for No Growth Policies;" Baldassare and W. Protash, "Growth Controls, Population Growth, and Community Satisfaction," American Sociological Review 47 (1982): 339–346; Baldassare and Georjeanna Wilson, "Changing Sources of Suburban Support for Local Growth Controls," Urban Studies 33 (1986): 459–471; Don E. Albrecht et al., "Constituency of the Antigrowth Movement: A Comparison of Urban Status Groups," Urban Affairs Quarterly 21 (1986): 607–616; Roland Anglin, "Diminishing Utility: The Effect on Citizen Preferences for Local Growth," Urban Affairs Quarterly 25 (1990): 684–696; and C. Connerly and James E. Frank, "Predicting Support for Local Growth Controls," Social Science Quarterly 67 (1986): 572–585.

33. Baldassare and Wilson, "Changing Sources of Suburban Support for Local Growth Controls," 459–471.

34. John R. Logan and Min Zhou, "Do Suburban Growth Controls Control Growth?" American Sociological Review 54 (1989): 461–471.

35. Timothy P. Duane, "Human Settlement: 1850–2040" in Status of the Sierra Nevada, Volume II: Assessment and Scientific Basis for Management Options, Sierra Nevada Ecosystem Project, Final Report to Congress, (Davis, Calif.: Centers for Water and Wildland Resources, University of California, Davis, 1996), 235–360.

36. All population data used in this study were taken from U.S. Department of Commerce, Bureau of Economic Analysis, Regional Economic Information System, 1969–97, CD-ROM (Washington, D.C., 1997).

37. William H. Frey and Alden Speare Jr. "The Revival of Metropolitan Population Growth in the United States: An Assessment of Findings From the 1990 Census," Population and Development Review 18 (1992): 129–146; Glenn V. Fuguitt and Calvin L. Beale, "Recent Trends in Nonmetropolitan Migration: Toward a New Turnaround?" Growth and Change 27 (1996): 156–174.

38. T. W. Ilvento and A. E. Luloff, "Anti-Urbanism and Nonmetropolitan Growth: A Reevaluation," Rural Sociology 47 (1982): 220–233.

39. Duane, "Human Settlement: 1850–2040."

40. Duane, "Human Settlement: 1850–2040."

41. The survey was conducted by J. Moore Methods, Inc. (Sierra Business Council, Sacramento, Calif.: 1997). Of the 1,000 respondents sampled, 982 responses were used for analysis.

42. Duane, "Human Settlement: 1850–2040."

2

≈

Economic Trends in the Mountain Counties: Rural-Urban Convergence

Over the last half-century, population spreading in the United States has manifested itself primarily as a movement from central city to suburb within metropolitan areas. The motivations and economic changes driving this movement are those already discussed in chapter 1. Before investigating whether the movement of population to rural areas is an extension of the suburbanization process, we need to familiarize ourselves with economic trends in rural mountain counties to establish whether rural growth is indeed occurring at a greater rate than regional growth in general and to determine what kinds of income and employment are providing the economic foundation for rural growth. Moreover, a topic of special interest will be whether the composition of the rural economy is becoming more like that of a large metropolitan urban economy. If an economically footloose population is spreading to rural areas and bringing income and employment with it, the rural economy is likely to exhibit a compositional structure that is increasingly like an urban economy. The traditional rural economy, with its dependence on extractive industries, is likely to have a less diverse industry composition than an urban economy with its greater diversity of economic activity. Conversely, a rural economy based on population spreading and footloose income is likely to include more diverse kinds of employment. Migrants from urban areas are likely to bring a greater diversity of jobs with them, and relatively affluent families moving to the rural West will likely demand roughly the same diversity of goods and services they did in an urban setting. Comparatively affluent middle-class families, disproportionately employed in services and the professions, have been on the leading edge of the suburbanization movement. If they are also a significant force in the spreading of population to rural areas, then the rural economy can be expected to become more like the urban economy in terms of the diversity of economic activity.

15

Up to the 1970s, very little spreading of population occurred beyond metropolitan boundaries. Since the 1970s, population migration to rural areas with significant natural amenities has accelerated,[1] especially in the rural counties of the mountain West. In California, Colorado, and Montana, population in rural mountain counties as a group (table 2.1) grew 93 percent between 1969 and 1997, while the population of the three states as a whole expanded by 64 percent (figure 2.1).[2] Because Denver's metropolitan population is heavily concentrated on the edge of the Rocky Mountains, it will be used as a benchmark for comparison to the rural mountain counties. The Denver area urban population expanded by 75 percent between 1969 and 1997, 18 percentage points below the expansion rate for rural mountain counties. Population growth in the Denver metropolitan area was more rapid in the early 1970s than in the rural mountain counties, but by the mid-1970s Denver metro growth was falling behind rural mountain county growth (figure 2.1).

The relative performance of real per capita income for urban and rural areas, however, is the opposite of the pattern of population growth (figure 2.2). Real per capita income in 1982–84 dollars is higher and grows more rapidly in the Denver metropolitan area than in the rural mountain counties. The outward movement of population from urban centers has yet to reverse the gap between urban and rural incomes. Despite this income disparity, the rural mountain county growth rate exceeds our metropolitan Denver urban benchmark.[3] Even though rural living may require some economic sacrifice, rural mountain counties have clearly gained in popularity as a place to live.

Table 2.1. Mountain West Counties

California	Colorado		Montana	
Alpine	Archuleta	La Plata	Beaverhead	Lincoln
Amador	Chaffee	Mesa	Bighorn	Madison
Butte	Clear Creek	Mineral	Broadwater	Meagher
Calaveras	Conejos	Moffat	Carbon	Mineral
Eldorado	Costilla	Montezuma	Cascade	Missoula
Inyo	Custer	Montrose	Deerlodge	Park
Lassen	Delta	Ouray	Flathead	Pondera
Madera	Dolores	Park	Gallatin	Powell
Mariposa	Eagle	Pitkin	Glacier	Ravalli
Mono	Fremont	Rio Blanco	Golden Val.	Sanders
Nevada	Garfield	Rio Grande	Granite	Silver Bow
Placer	Gilpin	Routt	Jefferson	Stillwater
Plumas	Grand	Saguache	Judith Basin	Sweet Grass
Shasta	Gunnison	San Juan	Lake	Teton
Sierra	Hinsdale	San Miguel	Lewis/Clark	Wheatland
Siskiyou	Huerfano	Summit		
Tehama	Jackson	Teller		
Trinity	Lake			
Tulare				
Tuolumne				

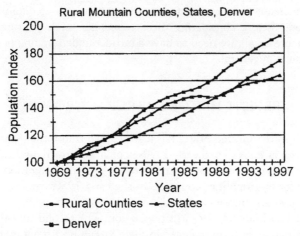

Figure 2.1:   Population Growth Index

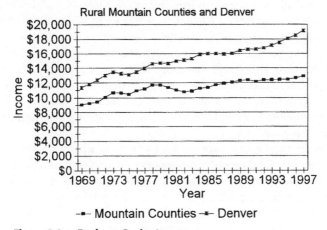

Figure 2.2:   Real per Capita Income

Historically, the residents of rural mountain counties relied heavily on the extractive industries, such as lumber and mining, for their income. Because of employment declines in these industries over the last fifteen years, they can hardly be the source of recent population expansion. Rather, rural counties appear to be undergoing an economic transformation based on new sources of income. The attraction of the mountain West is no longer access to extractable resources, but the beauty of the landscape and the abundance of outdoor recreation opportunities it affords. While tourism undoubtedly generates employment in mountain counties, anecdotal evidence suggests that relatively footloose income is the real driving force behind local economic expansion. Migration to a rural mountain county may simply be the next step after suburbanization in response to technological trends that increase the ease and reduce the cost of both communications and transportation.[4] Before considering these economic trends for rural mountain counties in more detail, we need to have a broader understanding of rural development patterns in general.

RECENT HISTORY OF RURAL GROWTH

Rural growth in the United States has featured two transformations in the past 30 years. In the late 1960s and early 1970s population growth and net migration rates accelerated in nonmetropolitan counties, with net migration rates rising above those for metropolitan counties. In the early 1980s, net migration rates in nonmetropolitan counties dropped below those of metropolitan counties and most nonmetropolitan counties lost population. The second transformation in nonmetropolitan growth commenced in the mid-1980s with net migration rates bottoming out in 1986, rising into positive territory by 1990, and exceeding the rate for metropolitan counties shortly thereafter. Moreover, a majority of nonmetropolitan counties gained population in the early 1990s. While 1990s gains in net migration and population are highest among counties adjacent to metropolitan areas, other nonmetropolitan counties are not far behind. Counties serving as destinations for retirement-age migrants or containing high levels of recreation-oriented economic activity experienced the highest rates of population growth in the early 1990s among nonmetropolitan counties.[5] In this period of time, the amenities of rural life appear to be an increasingly attractive force in location decisions.

Research on the first transformation focused on whether a temporary shift away from growth dominance by metropolitan counties occurred, or whether a new, comparatively permanent trend of population movement away from metropolitan areas was taking place. Proponents of the latter view suggested that the movement to rural areas was driven by longstanding desires to live at low densities in smaller communities with access to scenic and recreational amenities, and, moreover, that the fulfillment of those desires was enabled by the increasing affluence of retirees and the increasing mobility of information-age businesses that are able to operate at some distance from urban centers.[6] Previously, most people were tied to cities for economic reasons; recently, more are free to realize the rural ideal through their choice of where to live.

Advocates of the view that the 1970s rural upsurge was temporary and the result of period-specific phenomenon point to rising energy costs in the latter half of the 1970s, stimulating oil and gas exploration in the rural West and South. They argue that the energy crisis and globalization of the economy caused a restructuring of rustbelt manufacturing that hurt employment in large metropolitan areas and that an influx of college-bound baby boomers caused a swelling of rural college town populations. With the collapse of oil and gas expansion and completion of economic restructuring by the 1980s, large metropolitan areas were poised to regain their position of leadership in population growth.[7] The bloom appeared to be off the rural rose. The problem with this view is its failure to account for the resurgence of nonmetropolitan growth in the 1990s.[8]

Recent research on rural growth focuses on the nature of preferences for rural locations and on actual employment and industry location trends in nonmetropolitan counties. Urban dwellers frequently express a strong aversion to living in urban settings, particularly large metropolitan areas, according to some of the early survey research on the subject.[9] In other words, Jeffersonian antiurban sentiments are widely held and continue to be a part of our cultural heritage. However, Don A. Dillman (1979) argues that locational preferences have never been a very good predictor of rural-urban migration patterns. Economic necessity traditionally drove migration from rural areas to urban centers, not deep-seated locational preferences. Contrary to this traditional pattern, research on migration in the 1970s suggests that locational preference satisfaction played a role in the first nonmetropolitan turnaround. Amenities were found to be an important determinant of migration among counties, especially for middle-aged and older individuals,[10] and urban-rural migration in the period was driven more by environmental push-and-pull considerations than employment seeking.[11] Some chose to live in rural areas in order to escape the tensions and problems of urban life. Recent survey research on 15 high-amenity counties that contain or are adjacent to federally designated wilderness areas found that amenities and the quality of life were more important as determinants of in-migration than economic concerns such as employment.[12] In sum, locational choice involves two dimensions. Both opportunities for earning income and local amenities enter into subjective evaluations of different places to live in the residential location decision. In the past, income has played the dominant role in such a decision; more recently, amenities have become more important, possibly because of the increased mobility of income-earning opportunities.

Current research on nonmetropolitan and rural employment patterns has basically two strands. One involves analysis of statistical data on employment trends, while the other is somewhat more speculative and anecdotal and suggests that new technologies—the personal computer, faxes, modems, the Internet, overnight delivery, and satellite television—are enabling more businesses and individuals to chose rural locations. Research addressing employment trends in the late 1970s found little to support the view that nonmetropolitan counties were gaining employment from high-technology industries.[13] However, research on trends in the 1980s suggests that high-technology industries are spinning off some of their manufacturing operations to nonmetropolitan counties and that freestanding (nonbranch) plants are choosing to locate in counties more distant from metropolitan areas than branch plants.[14] Because services, such as computer software design, capable of being delivered electronically in the information age, are likely to be more footloose than manufacturing where the physical transportation of inputs and outputs is required, service industry expansion could well be the driving force behind nonmetropolitan growth. A study of service employment, however, found that producer-oriented services, such as business consulting, continue to be heavily concentrated in large metropolitan areas in 1984.[15] This conclusion is supported for the Pacific Northwest region in research by William B. Beyers and others who find little evidence of decentralization in producer services.[16] Producer services are providers of inputs to other businesses and are not necessarily tied to a local market. For this reason, producer services are potentially a basic industry that produces for export. A nonbasic industry, on the other hand, is one that serves a strictly local market. In a world of economic specialization, in order to have the income to import goods and services, a local economy needs to have basic industries that sell to the outside world. Basic industry expansion, consequently, is a traditional vehicle for local economic expansion.

Research with a more local focus paints a vibrant picture of rural growth. In his work on the Yellowstone region, Thomas M. Power suggests that economic expansion is being driven by footloose investment and retirement income, self-employment, and local services such as auto repair, house maintenance, and health care.[17] He finds the traditional export-oriented extractive sector to be a declining source of income and employment, and he argues that local services constitute an expanding share of economic activity and can foster local economic expansion as a result of a shift toward locally supplied goods and services. In work on the same region, Raymond Rasker and his colleagues argue that footloose information age entrepreneurs producing goods or services for export outside the region are locating in the Yellowstone area in order to enjoy access to the abundance of local amenities.[18] With modern low-cost communications technology and rapid shipment by truck on the interstate highway system, even manufacturing can locate in relatively remote rural areas. What are usually referred to as local market services in the information age could easily serve both a regional clientele as well as customers outside the local area. A neighborhood business could be both basic and nonbasic at the same time. A local specialty retailer, for example, could sell to a larger market through the Internet by advertising through the mail and by using overnight package delivery. An investment advisor can serve both a local market and customers outside the region. In an era when the production and communication of information is an increasingly important part of all areas of economic life, economic activity is no longer necessarily tied to large urban centers.

Scholars are largely in agreement that rural growth is amenity driven. This certainly is the case for migration to rural counties of the Sierra Nevada according to the survey research discussed in chapter 1. The negative consequences of urban sprawl may also be a driving force behind rural expansion. Some are migrating to rural areas to escape the congestion and environmental degradation associated with suburban growth much as earlier generations sought to escape environmental and social deterioration in the central city by moving to the suburbs. The economic foundation of migration to rural areas is not yet fully understood. What is the role of retirement income? How important is the growth of local services in the economy? Are export-oriented, footloose service jobs permitting movement to rural areas? These questions remain to be answered. The first step in attempting to answer them for rural counties of the mountain West is to investigate recent employment and income trends.

EMPLOYMENT AND INCOME
TRENDS IN THE MOUNTAIN WEST

What sectors of the rural economy have been expanding in relative terms and what sectors have been shrinking relatively? How well do different sectors perform compared with the benchmark Denver urban economy? Is there convergence in the compositional structure of the rural economy toward that of the urban economy? To answer these questions, a simple scheme for presenting employment data in relative terms is needed. The approach adopted here is to consider the amount of employment in key sectors (one-digit industries) per thousand population. This kind of data tells us at a glance how many jobs are available by sector relative to the population as a whole and allows for easy rural-urban comparisons. Income is not only earned through participation in productive activity, but is also received from the ownership of capital and from transfer payments, mainly Social Security. Consequently, considering income sources in relative terms is essential for a complete picture. This is accomplished by comparing trends in the relative shares of earned income (wage, salary, and proprietor's income), income from capital, and transfer payment income for the benchmark Denver metro and the rural mountain economies.

Rural Employment Trends in the Extractive Industries

The extractive industries in the rural mountain West were once the mainstay of the local economy. They provided the basic industry employment upon which the rest of the local economy was built. In recent years, this has clearly changed. In the mountain counties, farm employment per thousand population has declined from 63 to 37, a 41 percent reduction (figure 2.3). Farming is clearly a shrinking piece of the economic pie in the mountain counties, offering a much reduced share of local employment opportunities.

Another key extractive industry, mining, cannot be easily analyzed at the county level because much of the data for counties with relatively small employment levels is not reported to avoid disclosure for individual firms. We can, however, look at the state-level trends for mining employment, most of which

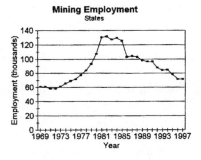

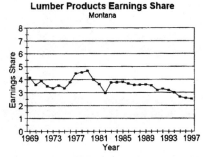

Figure 2.3:   Extractive Industry Trends

occurred in mountain counties. Mining employment peaked in 1982 at approximately 132,000 in the three states considered here (California, Colorado, and
Montana) and declined to 71,000 by 1997, a drop of 46 percent (figure 2.3).
Clearly, mining is no longer leading the economic charge in rural mountain
counties.[19]

The lumber industry also cannot be easily analyzed at the county level because
of disclosure problems. The lumber industry has declined, however, and this can
be illustrated by looking at the lumber industry earnings share for Montana, the
state that is most economically dependent on lumber among the three states (fig-

ure 2.3). From its peak of 4.7 percent in 1979, the share of lumber industry earnings for Montana fell steadily to 2.5 percent in 1997. The lumber industry, as with the other extractive sectors in the mountain West, is no longer an engine of economic growth in the rural economy.

The decline of the extractive economy is of great significance in the rural mountain West. It was the extractive sector that fostered historical booms in population and the local economy, and it was the decline of these industries that brought forth subsequent economic and population busts. Moreover, the current population boom in many mountain counties cannot be connected in any way to the extractive sector because of its shrinkage. As Thomas M. Power puts it, those who look to the extractive industries as a source of local prosperity are essentially looking in the economic "rearview mirror."[20] To explain current rural expansion, we must look elsewhere.

Rural and Urban Employment Trends

If the number of employees per thousand population is rising for a particular industry, that industry is experiencing relative expansion. That is, the number of jobs available in that industry relative to population is growing, and the industry is acting as an engine of employment growth. Moreover, the number of employees per thousand population for rural and urban areas will reflect fundamental differences between rural and urban economies. By looking at comparative data on employment per thousand population for rural mountain counties and for the benchmark Denver metropolitan area, those sectors acting as engines of growth can be discovered and key differences and similarities between the rural and urban economy in the mountain West can be established.

Let's begin by considering trends and differences in aggregate employment per thousand population before looking at employment for each major industry. Average employment per thousand population is clearly less for rural counties than for the benchmark urban metropolitan economy (figure 2.4A). For rural counties this figure rises from 407 in 1969 to 595 in 1997 while the same figure increases in the Denver metro area from 474 to 715 in the same period. The percentage increase for rural counties is about 46 percent while the same figure for the benchmark metro area is slightly less at 42 percent. Between 1985 and 1997, the period of the rural growth turnaround described above, the gap between rural and urban employment per thousand shrinks with an increase of 112 in rural counties and 56 in the Denver metro area. In terms of the employment-population ratio, rural counties are presently becoming more like the benchmark urban economy. Although they have yet to rise to the level of Denver, employment opportunities have been rising relatively more rapidly in mountainous rural counties than in the Denver area. Not only are rural mountain areas gaining in appeal as a place to live, the ability to earn a living in such areas appears to be improving.

Shrinkage in rural-urban differences is apparent in other employment trends as well. Although manufacturing employment per thousand is significantly higher in the Denver metro area relative to the rural counties (52 versus 35), since 1985 the gap has closed (figure 2.4A). From 1985 on, manufacturing employment per thousand continued its recovery from the 1982 recession in the rural counties, rising from a low of around 25 per thousand to a high of 35, while it faltered in the Denver metro area, declining from about 58 in 1982 to 52 in 1997. Consequently the rural-urban gap has shrunk, although manufacturing is clearly not acting as a major engine of economic expansion in rural areas over the long run since employment per thousand has yet to attain its previous 1969 peak. In the manufacturing sector, urban and rural areas appear to be slowly converging in terms of their employment-population ratio. In relative terms, rural mountain areas are increasingly attractive to manufacturing.

Construction employment per thousand in rural and urban areas are similar in magnitude, although rural employment appears to be less volatile and has a stronger growth trend (figure 2.4A). Construction employment in rural areas appears to have increased from around 20 to around 40 per thousand over the twenty-eight-year period. Growth in construction activity in rural areas is clearly contributing to rural economic expansion and causing a relative convergence in the ratio of rural to urban construction activity as measured by employment-population ratios. If population is spreading to rural areas and inducing a housing boom, a convergence of rural and urban construction activity relative to population would be expected.

Transportation and utility employment is higher in the Denver metro area than rural mountain counties as is employment in the wholesale trade sector (figure 2.4B). Because of greater reliance on public transportation systems in urban areas, transportation employment is likely to be relatively larger in urban than rural areas. Also, urban areas are critical hubs in regional transportation systems and would likely contain higher transportation sector employment levels for this reason. A similar phenomenon may explain relatively higher urban employment for utilities as well. Major utility facilities, such as electric generating plants, are often located at the hub of larger utility network grids, and these hubs are usually found in large urban centers. Wholesale trade employment would also tend to be relatively higher in an urban area such as Denver because of its critical role as a regional transportation hub. Locating wholesale business activity in Denver, as opposed to a rural location outside the hub, would likely result in lower shipping costs. Locating a trucking distribution center at the Denver airport, for instance, would reduce the costs of package handling and transshipment as opposed to locating such a center in a rural area. In the latter case, packages passing through the airport would have to be handled twice instead of once for the Denver airport location. In recent years, wholesale trade employment per thousand has remained relatively flat in both rural counties and the Denver metro area while trans-

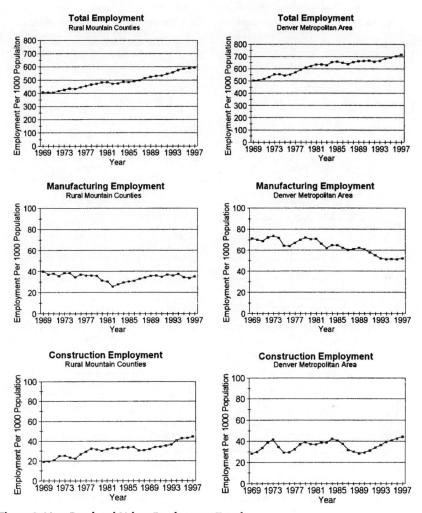

Figure 2.4A: Rural and Urban Employment Trends

portation and utility employment has expanded somewhat in the Denver metro area and has remained flat in rural mountain counties. For these two sectors, rural-urban convergence is not occurring and is unlikely to occur in the near future.

The dominant engines of growth in both rural mountain counties and the Denver metro area are retail trade and services employment. Each of these sectors has experienced substantial growth since 1969 in both rural and urban areas (figures 2.4B, 2.4C). The magnitude of employment per thousand population in

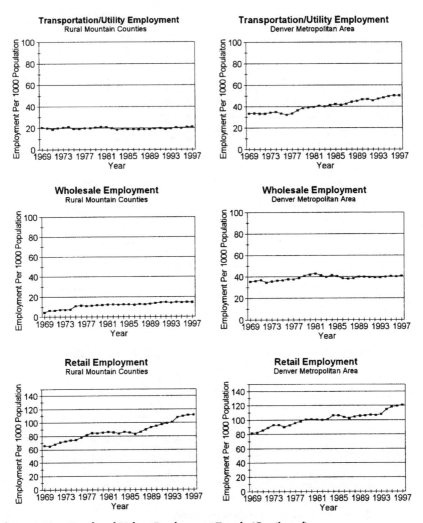

Figure 2.4B: Rural and Urban Employment Trends (Continued)

each sector is somewhat higher in the Denver metro area, but rural counties have closed the gap with Denver in recent years. Between 1985 and 1997 the rural increase in retail employment per thousand population was 26.4, while a similar figure for the Denver metro area was 15.2. Those moving to rural mountain areas apparently have the wherewithal to support expansion of local retail activity. Comparable figures for the expansion of services employment per thousand are respectively 70.8 for the rural counties and 62.5 for Denver. Services employment growth in both locations is so large that it accounts for most of the expan-

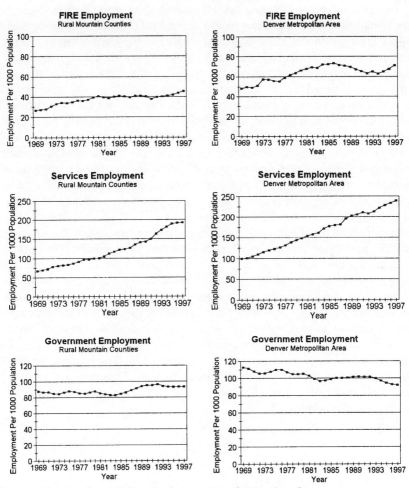

Figure 2.4C:　Rural and Urban Employment Trends (Continued)

sion in employment per thousand population between 1969 and 1997. Clearly, both rural and urban areas are becoming heavily service-oriented in terms of employment opportunities, suggesting that a service economy in both rural and urban areas appears to be the wave of the future. Because services are often labor and information intensive, they have a significant chance for survival at rural locations. Informational services, whose content is entirely data, can be produced and transported to customers from remote locations. Given the relative rise of services in rural mountain county employment, information-based service activity is likely to occur with increasing frequency in rural locations.

Trends in finance, insurance, and real estate employment (FIRE) and government employment complete the picture for our rural-urban comparison (figure 2.4C). FIRE per thousand is significantly higher in the Denver metro area than rural counties, as should be expected (71 versus 45 per thousand). Denver continues to be a major center of financial activity. Since 1985, however, the rural-urban gap has closed slightly with a modest increase of 4.5 per thousand for FIRE in rural areas and a slight decrease of 1.5 per thousand in the Denver metro area. FIRE has contributed modestly to rural growth as a consequence of a mild upward trend to its employment-population ratio. The government employment-population ratio for rural mountain counties and the Denver area have almost converged with the Denver metro area ratio falling and the rural ratio rising. An upward trend in government employment would be expected in rural areas as a consequence of population spreading if new residents demand improvements in local government services.

In sum, rural counties are becoming more like our benchmark Denver metropolitan area in most sectors. Employment growth in rural counties is being driven primarily by the expansion of the retail and service industries. The amount of growth per thousand population in these sectors and for employment in total has been greater on average for rural counties than for the Denver area since the beginning of the rural growth turnaround in 1985 (figure 2.5). Both employment and population expansion are clearly spreading beyond urban boundaries and the compositional structure of rural employment appears to be becoming more urban-like, at least at the level of aggregation considered here. Employment opportunities are clearly on the rise in the rural mountain West. Those who want to live in a rural mountain setting are increasingly able to do so while, at the same time, finding a way of earning a living.

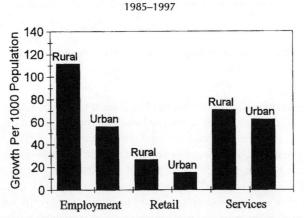

Figure 2.5:   Employment Growth Per 1,000 Population

Rural and Urban Income Trends

Although the relative mix of employment for rural areas seems to be converging with the combination found in the Denver metropolitan area, income trends are following a divergent path. Per capita income, as already noted in figure 2.2 is significantly higher and growing relatively faster in the Denver metropolitan area than in the average rural county. Moreover, the distribution of income by source in rural areas is also diverging from the urban pattern (figures 2.6, 2.7). Earned income in the form of wages, salaries, and proprietors' income is a decreasing share of total income in both rural and urban areas, but the decline in the share for the average rural county is substantially greater than our Denver benchmark. From 1969 to 1997 the earned income share fell in the Denver metro area from 76.6 percent to 72.0 percent while for rural areas the same figure fell from 72.0 percent to 58.3 percent. The earned income share has dropped dramatically in rural areas. The income share that increased by the largest amount is transfer income, most of which is Social Security income received by retirees. The transfer income share in the average rural county increased from 12.7 percent to 21.2 percent between 1969 and 1997, an amount that is much greater than the increase from 8.1 percent to 11.1 percent experienced in the Denver metro area. The final share of income by type is dividend, interest, and rental income, and includes an imputation of rental income from owner-occupied housing. In short, this is income from capital exclusive of capital gains (referred to as dividend income). The dividend income share has increased for the average rural county from 15.3 percent in 1969 to 20.6 percent and for the Denver metropolitan area from 15.4 percent to 16.8 percent.

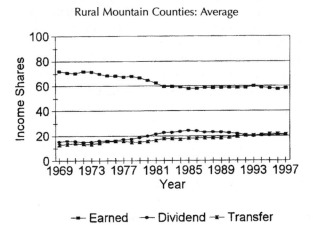

Figure 2.6:   Income Shares

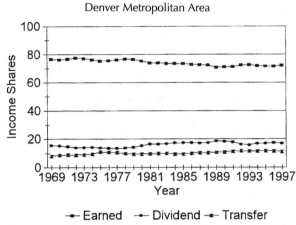

Figure 2.7:   Income Shares

Strong growth of transfer income in the rural counties is partly responsible for the relatively slow growth in real per capita income. For 1997 the transfer income share across sample counties has a strong negative correlation with per capita income while the earned income share and the dividend share are positively correlated with per capita income.[21] This suggests that an increase of the transfer income share reduces per capita income while an increase in earned and dividend income shares has the opposite effect. The relative growth of the transfer income share also suggests that the proportion of retirees living in rural counties is rising. The spread of population to rural counties is, at least in part, driven by retirees who choose to settle in or near mountainous areas known for their natural beauty. The growing share of both dividend and transfer income suggests that these forms of footloose income may well be contributing to rural economic expansion. Income from labor is growing in the rural mountain West, but it is growing somewhat more slowly than transfer and dividend income. The growth of retirement income is placing a drag on the growth of per capita income in rural counties relative to the Denver metro area. This is preventing the rural-urban convergence of per capita income that we see in other economic trends.

CONCLUSION

According to the data, population is spreading into the rural counties of the mountain West at a relatively rapid rate. Employment is expanding even more rapidly than population and is driven primarily by the expansion of retail and services. Moreover, the composition of employment in rural counties is becoming more like that found in our benchmark Denver metropolitan area. While all types of income are spreading into mountain counties, relatively more footloose transfer and dividend income is expanding somewhat faster to rural areas than earned income. Rural growth is thus being fueled in part by income that is not tied to employment.

While these trends are compatible with the thesis that population spreading into rural counties is comparable to historical patterns of suburbanization, they don't prove the point. One could argue, for example, that retirees are responsible for population spreading and that employment is simply following to serve them. The next chapter will offer an approach that provides a clearer test of the thesis that recipients of earned income are also spreading to rural mountain counties independently of retirees.

NOTES

1. Glenn V. Fuguitt and Calvin L. Beale, "Recent Trends in Nonmetropolitan Migration: Toward a New Turnaround?" *Growth and Change* 27 (1996): 156–174.

2. These three states are chosen for analysis because they have been the focus of much research and anecdotal discussions of growth in the mountain West. See Thomas M. Power, "Ecosystem Preservation and the Economy in the Greater Yellowstone Area," *Conservation Biology* 5 (1991): 395–404 and *Lost Landscapes and Failed Economies: The Search for Value of Place* (Washington, D.C.: Island Press, 1996); Ray Rasker and Dennis Glick, "Footloose Entrepreneurs: Pioneers of the New West?" *Illahee* 10 (1994): 34–43; Sierra Nevada Ecosystem Project, Final Report to Congress, *Status of the Sierra Nevada, Volume I: Assessment Summaries and Management Strategies* (Davis, Calif.: Centers for Water and Wildland Resources, University of California, Davis, 1996); Richard L. Knight, "Field Report from the New American West" in *Wallace Stegner and the Continental Vision: Essays on Literature, History, and Landscape*, ed. Curt Meine (Washington, D.C.: Island Press, 1997), 181–200; and Richard L. Knight, George N. Wallace, and William E. Riebsame, "Ranching the View: Subdivisions versus Agriculture," *Conservation Biology* 9 (1995): 459–461. All counties that include a significant proportion of their land area in the Rocky Mountains and adjacent mountainous landscapes or the Sierra Nevada and Cascade Mountains were chosen for study with the exception of those that were judged to be a part of a major metropolitan area. Because they are heavily urbanized and have most of their population located in the San Joaquin Valley, Fresno and Kern County in the Southern Sierras are excluded from the sample. In Colorado the sample includes all the mountainous counties except those in the Colorado Springs, Denver, Boulder, and Fort Collins areas. The Fort Collins-Boulder-Denver area is fast becoming a large metropolitan complex, and the county that includes Colorado Springs is mostly in the Great Plains. In Montana, the sample includes all Rocky Mountain counties. The data source for income, population, and employment in this study is the U.S. Department of Commerce (1997) unless otherwise noted.

3. This comparison does not consider differences in living costs between rural and urban areas.

4. For a discussion of the decline of remoteness in the information age and related issues, see Harlan Cleveland, "The Twilight of Hierarchy: Speculations on the Global Information Society," *Public Administration Review* 45 (1985): 185–195.

5. Fuguitt and Beale, "Recent Trends in Nonmetropolitan Migration"; and Kenneth M. Johnson and Calvin L. Beale, "The Recent Revival of Widespread Population Growth in Nonmetropolitan Areas of the United States," *Rural Sociology* 59 (1994): 655–667.

6. Fuguitt and Beale, "Recent Trends in Nonmetropolitan Migration."

7. William H. Frey and Alden Speare Jr., "The Revival of Metropolitan Population Growth in the United States: An Assessment of Findings from the 1990 Census," *Population and Development Review* 18 (1992): 129–146.

8. Fuguitt and Beale, "Recent Trends in Nonmetropolitan Migration."

9. Larry G. Blackwood and Edwin H. Carpenter, "The Importance of Anti-Urbanism in Determining Residential Preferences and Migration Patterns," *Rural Sociology* 43 (1978): 31–47; Don A. Dillman, "Residential Preferences, Quality of Life, and the Population Turnaround," *American Journal of Agricultural Economics* 61 (1979): 960–966; and T. W. Ilvento and A. E. Luloff, "Anti-Urbanism and Nonmetropolitan Growth: A Reevaluation," *Rural Sociology* 47 (1982): 220–233.

10. David E. Clark and William J. Hunter, "The Impact of Economic Opportunity, Amenities, and Fiscal Factors on Age-Specific Migration Rates," *Journal of Regional Science* 32 (1992): 349–365.

11. James D. Williams and Andrew J. Sofranko, "Motivations for the Inmigration Component of Population Turnaround in Nonmetropolitan Areas," *Demography* 16 (1979): 239–255.

12. Christiane von Reichert and Gundar Rudzitis, "Multinomial Logistic Models Explaining Income Changes of Migrants to High-Amenity Counties," *The Review of Regional Studies* 22 (1992): 25–42; Gundars Rudzitis and Harley E. Johansen, "How Important Is Wilderness? Results from a United States Survey," *Environmental Management* 15 (1991): 227–233; and "Migration into Western Wilderness Counties: Causes and Consequences," *Western Wildlands* 15 (1989): 19–23.

13. James P. Miller, "The Product Cycle and High Technology Industry in Nonmetropolitan Areas, 1976–1980," *The Review of Regional Studies* 19 (1989): 1–12.

14. David L. Barkley, "The Decentralization of High-Technology Manufacturing to Non-Metropolitan Areas," *Growth and Change* 19 (1988): 13–30; David L. Barkley and John E. Keith, "The Locational Determinants of Western Nonmetro High Tech Manufacturers: An Econometric Analysis," *Western Journal of Agricultural Economics* 16 (1991): 331–344; and Stephen M. Smith and David L. Barkley, "Local Input Linkages of Rural High-Technology Manufacturers," *Land Economics* 67 (1991): 472–485.

15. James P. Miller and Herman Bluestone, "Prospects for Service Sector Employment Growth in Non-Metropolitan America," *The Review of Regional Studies* 18 (1988): 28–41.

16. William B. Beyers, "Trends in Service Employment in Pacific Northwest Counties: 1974–1986," *Growth and Change* 22 (1991): 27–50. Still another study finds that the relative concentration of managerial and professional occupations in metropolitan areas has actually increased relative to nonmetropolitan areas. See Thomas J. Kirn, Richard S. Conway Jr., and William B. Beyers, "Producer Services Development and the Role of Telecommunications: A Case Study in Rural Washington," *Growth and Change* 21 (1990): 33–50.

17. Power, "Ecosystem Preservation and the Economy in the Greater Yellowstone Area" and *Lost Landscapes and Failed Economies.*

18. Rasker and Glick, "Footloose Entrepreneurs"; Jerry D. Johnson and Raymond Rasker, "Local Government: Local Business Climate and Quality of Life," *Montana Policy*

Review 3 (1993): 11–19; and Ray Rasker, Norma Tirrell, and Deanne Klopfer, *The Wealth of Nature: New Economic Realities in the Yellowstone Region* (Washington, D.C.: The Wilderness Society, 1991).

19. The one-digit agricultural, forestry, and fishing service industry is also fraught with disclosure problems. For this reason, and because of relatively low employment levels in sample counties, it is excluded from consideration here.

20. Power, *Lost Landscapes and Failed Economies*, 9.

21. The respective correlation coefficients are −.73, .52, and .17.

3

Population Spreading in the Mountain West: Mobility and Footloose Income

The casual traveler in the mountain West can hardly avoid noticing the signs of growth. New ranchettes and subdivisions are popping up everywhere, and real estate signs advertising new developments are hard to miss. Growth is reflected as well in the data trends just discussed in chapter 2. Both population and employment are expanding rapidly, the primary engines of employment growth are services and retailing, and transfer and capital investment (dividend) incomes are rising somewhat more rapidly than earned income in rural mountain counties. Population is clearly spreading beyond metropolitan boundaries. The question now to be addressed is whether this process of population spreading is an extension of the longstanding process of population movement from city to suburb.

SUBURBANIZATION AND POPULATION SPREADING

Suburbanization initially featured out-migration of population from city to suburb by working families whose breadwinners commuted from suburb to central city for employment. Eventually, businesses began to suburbanize as well, partly to serve a growing suburban market, and partly to be near their employees. Business suburbanization was also stimulated by freeway construction that connected suburbs with each other as well as the central city in metropolitan areas. This connection increased the accessibility of suburban locations for both manufacturing and wholesale distribution. The favored business site was now a large plot of land on which a large, single-story business facility could be constructed with good freeway access. Products could be manufactured in efficient single-story plants at a suburban location and shipped to markets far and near by truck. The

35

rail and port facilities of the old central city could be avoided as well as the old inefficient multistory plants built in an era of relatively high land prices and belt-driven steam engines. With the automobile becoming the dominant transportation mode, the large suburban shopping center with its freeway access and acres of parking lots became the favored environment for retail shopping, displacing the large downtown department stores as well as the local neighborhood retailing district. So a suburban-style population spreading involves an outward movement of working families from city to suburb as well as an outward movement of employment. The dynamic in many metropolitan areas now appears to be a continuous outward spreading of population to more distant suburbs followed by an outward movement of businesses and employment.[1] Consequently, if population spreading to rural counties of the mountain West is indeed an extension of the suburbanization process, it would have to include a spreading of families dependent on earned income. Sources of earned income would have to be sufficiently footloose in order to survive in rural mountain county locations.

The key location constraint for businesses that serve as sources of earned income is the ease and cost of transportation and communications with customers and suppliers. In a world of costly communication and transportation, centralized business locations with close proximity to customers, suppliers, and labor markets is critical to economic survival. This is why large, densely packed cities were prime centers of economic activity in the nineteenth century when the cost of communicating and moving goods within cities was relatively high. Businesses huddled together at urban centers close to rail lines and ports to communicate more readily and to avoid the costs of moving goods around. As such costs decline, centralized locations become less advantageous and business opportunities less location dependent. If information production and movement have indeed become key functions of the modern economy, then communication costs ought to be of critical importance in business location decisions. But with the kinds of computer and communications technologies we now have, the cost of communication associated with distance has become trivial. In a world of computers, modems, and the Internet, those who produce information can locate almost anywhere and transport their product at an extremely low cost. With such phenomena as overnight delivery and the growing predominance of goods with a high value-to-weight ratio, the cost of transporting goods has also become relatively unimportant. This means that businesses and their employees have more location options. For an increasing array of business activities, remote locations are a possibility. The attractions of such locations are the amenities they offer. In the mountain West, such attractions would include the beauty of the natural landscape and an array of locally available recreational opportunities.

Population growth in rural mountain counties could theoretically be driven by location-dependent economic activity such as the extractive industries, tourism, and vacation home development. In order for the population-spreading hypothesis to be sustained, these traditional sources of growth have to be unimportant.

If they truly prove to be inconsequential, then population expansion would have to be economically based on an influx of residents with mobile forms of income. Obvious candidates are retirees dependent on transfer income and income from financial investments and people below retirement age who have sufficient investment income to live on without working. If population growth is driven entirely by these kinds of footloose income, then the population-spreading process would be qualitatively different from the movement of population from city to suburb.

To evaluate whether population expansion is in fact an extension of population spreading from city to suburb involves several steps. The first step is to judge whether population growth in rural mountain counties is occurring in a wavelike pattern with less remote counties experiencing growth prior to the more remote in a fashion similar to the historical experience in suburbs around urban centers where inner suburbs experienced their development booms prior to those farther out. If this is found to be the case, then the next step is to establish whether or not location dependent activities, such as extractive industries or tourism, are coincidentally causing the observed pattern of population settlement and growth. If location dependent activity can be ruled out, then the underpinning for population growth must be footloose forms of income. The third step is to confirm that the movement of population to rural mountain counties is indeed amenity dependent. Even if we can conclude that amenities are attracting population, it still could be the case that the migration of retirees and wealthy citizens, who are not dependent on earned income, to mountain counties explains the observed population expansion patterns. If so, the suburban extension thesis fails. However, if, in addition, families who rely on earned income are moving to mountain counties and are not in any way dependent on economic activity generated by retirees and the wealthy, then the pattern of settlement is indeed comparable to the suburbanization experience. If this can be shown, then population is spreading beyond suburbs to rural mountain counties and is bringing its means of earning an income with it. Employment follows population and population is attracted to the amenities and beauty of the rural mountain West landscape.

To complete the story of mountain West population growth and economic expansion, employment patterns need to be investigated. Employment and population spreading are likely to be strongly correlated, but at the margin other forces may also influence employment location patterns. For example, certain amenities that are popular with tourists, such as ski areas or national parks, may attract employment that tends to be temporary in nature and does not foster significant population growth. To the extent that property values achieve extraordinary heights in such locations, because of the popularity of second home development or large homes for the relatively affluent, workers in these areas may not be able to afford to reside locally and may have to commute very long distances. While tourism and second home construction might appear at first glance to be an attractive development strategy, the kind of permanent employment it fosters may not be of the sort that results in population expansion and the creation of an economically diverse local community. Moreover, vacation home development occurring on relatively large, valley bottom parcels or along ridge lines may end up spoiling the natural beauty that attracted vacationers and others in the first place. If people are moving to the mountain West to escape the monotony of the modern suburb, they may be disappointed to find that they are simply recreating what they are trying to escape.

The investigation of mountain West growth patterns to follow is a little complex and involved, but the reward should be a comparatively complete and comprehensive picture.

POPULATION DENSITY GRADIENTS
AND POPULATION SPREADING

Studies of suburbanization generally focus on population density as the critical phenomenon requiring explanation.[2] A variable key in urban population density studies is distance to the urban center. A population density gradient that declines as distance increases is present in most metropolitan areas and is conventionally explained as the result of a tradeoff between access to the urban center and lower land prices on the urban periphery (induced by more abundant land supplies). The standard view is that lower land prices on the urban periphery foster the substitution of land for access, resulting in lower population densities further out and construction of housing on larger and larger parcels of land. An alternative explanation is historical: older suburbs closer to the urban center developed when commuting was more costly and density patterns were consequently higher. Newer suburbs further out developed at lower densities in an era of lower commuting costs, longer feasible commuting distances, and expanded land supplies. As the diameter of the circle of feasible commuting around an urban center expands, the amount of land available for development expands by the square of the circle's radius. Therefore, land is available for the construction of more spacious houses. Whatever the actual explanation, suburbanization driven by reduced commuting and transportation costs causes population growth on the periphery and a flattening of the density gradient. Density growth in the suburbs occurs as a wavelike process with population expanding first in the inner suburbs, until vacant land is more-or-less fully developed, and then in more distant suburbs, where undeveloped land is available. The suburban density gradient (excluding the central city) first steepens as the inner suburbs develop and then flattens as growth shifts to the outer suburbs. As employment opportunities expand on the periphery, the attraction of the urban center for employment diminishes, although it doesn't entirely disappear.

The comparable hypothesis to be tested here is whether access to a large regional urban area is a critical variable in the rural residential choice for mountain West counties. Even though rural residents may be sufficiently free to choose their residential or business location for immediate access to rural amenities, they may not want to sever their urban ties entirely. If rural amenities are desired and uniformly available in rural mountain counties, and if urban access is important, then counties closer to major urban centers would be preferred as business and residential locations over more distant ones. However, relative population expansion in the more accessible counties would tend to push land prices up, resulting in a potential tradeoff between lower land prices in more distant counties and closer access in less distant counties. The density gradient would thus be the result of substituting land for access in a manner comparable to that found in urban areas. A density gradient would also reflect a mix of different preferences for access to the urban center. Those residents with a stronger desire for access would settle in nearer counties bidding up land values, and those with a weaker desire for access would choose more distant counties with lower land values. Also, population growth might proceed in a wavelike pattern with more accessible counties filling up first before migration shifts to less accessible counties. If this were the case, the density gradient for rural counties would shift up initially and steepen. Once the more accessible counties fill up, the gradient would shift upward and level off as population growth shifted to the less accessible counties.

To test the density gradient hypothesis and to investigate other possible determinants of population density, employment, and income, I have used the 86 rural mountain counties of California, Colorado, and Montana discussed in chapter 2. A critical feature of these counties is the large amount of public lands in federal ownership contained within their boundaries.[3] For this reason, only a portion of the land in most counties in the sample is available for use by residents and businesses. Consequently, density calculations make sense only for privately owned lands since these are the sole lands available for residential and business development.[4] In estimating the density gradient, the highway mileage from the largest city or town in each county to the closest regional urban center is used as the urban distance measure.[5]

The changing relationship between population density and distance can be observed in two ways. First, sample counties can be ordered according to their distance from a regional urban center, and then average population densities can be calculated for all counties within different distance zones (zero to 200, 200 to 400, 400 to 600, and more than 600 miles). The resulting data is summarized in figure 3.1. Clearly, population density has been growing much more rapidly in the less distant counties, especially for those within the 200-mile distance zone, supporting the premise that population is spreading outward from urban centers to the most accessible counties first.

Another somewhat more sophisticated approach to looking at population density growth patterns is to statistically estimate the population density gradients for different years and consider their growth pattern over time. This can be done using the

Urban Distance Gradient

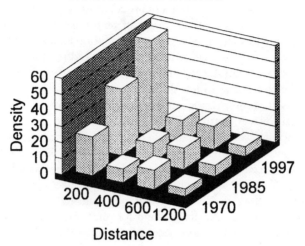

Figure 3.1:   Density and Distance

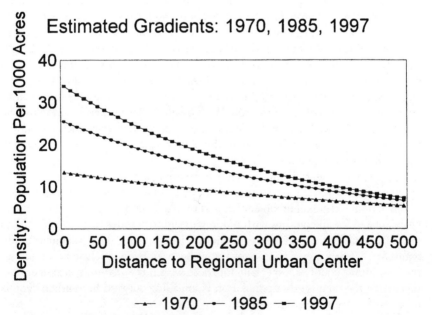

Figure 3.2:   Population Density (in miles)

techniques described in the appendix to this chapter.[6] The end results of this procedure are the density gradients presented in figure 3.2. The estimated density gradients shift upward over time and steepen. Counties that are less distant from urban
centers are experiencing substantially greater population density growth than more
distant counties, again confirming the population-spreading hypothesis.

Two simple conclusions follow from these results: First, because the density
gradient is rising over time, a significant number of people are moving to mountain counties.[7] Second, because counties close to regional urban centers have
higher population densities and are experiencing more growth than those farther
away, freedom to choose where to live is apparently constrained by a desire for
urban center proximity.[8] Population is pushing out into rural counties from large
urban centers in a wavelike pattern comparable to that experienced by suburbs
surrounding central cities after World War II. Unlike suburbs, proximity to urban areas from rural counties for the purpose of daily commuting is ruled out because, with few exceptions, counties in the sample are outside of easy commuting distances to regional metropolitan centers or local metropolitan areas.[9]

For a full justification of the conclusion that footloose income is playing a
role in growth of the mountain West, however, we need to establish whether location dependent or footloose sources of income and employment are driving
variations in population density across counties and population density growth
over time. It is possible that mountain counties are experiencing population
growth because of expansion in local extractive industries, although this seems
unlikely given the aggregate decline in these industries discussed in chapter 2.
It is also possible that population growth can be traced to the growth of tourism,
or second home development. Population density patterns across counties and
growth in population density could conceivably be explained by such location
dependent sources of employment and income. For the population-spreading
hypothesis to stand, the importance of location dependent forms of economic
activity in the determination of population density and its growth over time
must be checked statistically.

THE FAILURE OF LOCATION DEPENDENT EMPLOYMENT
TO DETERMINE POPULATION DENSITY GROWTH

The economy of mountainous counties was traditionally based on location dependent activities that could not easily be moved elsewhere. The extractive industries could not be moved because the object of extraction, minerals or timber, were available locally. Of course businesses in extractive industries will
move if reserves of such commodities are more profitably extracted in other locations. This no doubt accounts for the recent decline in resource extraction activities in mountain counties. If extraction is profitable locally, however, then
local employment will be generated. The processing of extracted commodities

is also likely to take place locally because processing usually involves significant weight loss that reduces transportation costs. If extracted ores are processed outside the local area, the transportation costs would typically be much greater than if ore is processed locally and then transported. Consequently, extractive activity will be location dependent. Because the beauty of the mountain counties is also immobile, mountain, landscape-based tourism will also be location dependent.

Can traditional extractive industries and location dependent tourism be ruled out as determinants of population density and sources of density growth? If so, we must look elsewhere to more modern forms of economic development for an explanation of population growth. The time period 1985–1997 is selected here for analysis of changes in population, employment, and income. At the time the analysis was conducted, 1997 was the latest time period for which data was available, while 1985 appears to be the inflection point beyond which growth accelerates for the population growth curve in figure 2.1. In 1985, population growth accelerated following a period of slow growth lasting from about 1979 to 1984.

For the three sample states as a whole, the mining and lumber industries are not good candidates to be generators of population density or growth. As noted in chapter 2, mining employment fell substantially between 1985 and 1997. Over the same period, the lumber industry income share in the three states dropped from .49 percent to .36 percent.[10] Nonetheless, to be sure that extractive economic activity is not the source of population density growth, the impact of these industries on population density needs to be examined. Because of unreported data, income figures are not available for these industries in all sample counties. Lumber industry data in 1997 is available for 68 of the 86 counties.[11] To evaluate whether the lumber industry is affecting population density and density growth, the relationship between population density and the relative size of the lumber industry measured in terms of the industry's earned income share is considered. The greater the industry's relative importance, the more likely it will affect the level of population density in a county.

According to the data presented in figure 3.3, population density is higher in counties with very low (0–4 percent) lumber industry income shares and lower in counties with high industry income shares (4–22 percent). If anything, the presence of the lumber industry detracts from population density levels to the tune of about 18 per thousand acres. Because of excessive disclosure problems, data for 1985 cannot be used for comparison. Since the lumber industry has a negative effect on population density and is in decline, it certainly seems unlikely it could be fueling population density growth.[12]

The story is essentially the same for the mining industry, as can be seen in figure 3.4. The effect the mining income share on population density is negative in both 1985 and 1997.[13] In both years, the presence of the mining industry reduces population density, and the reduction is slightly greater in 1997 than 1985

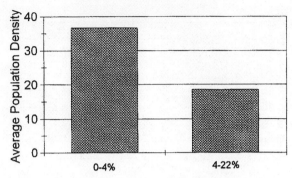

Figure 3.3:   **The Lumber Industry and Population Density: 1997**

(15 per thousand acres versus 10). Counties with more mining activity have a lower population density, and the negative impact of mining on density is increasing somewhat over time. Like the lumber industry, mining has a negative effect on population density and is experiencing employment decline. Consequently, it is highly unlikely that mining can foster a population boom. If anything, both mining and the lumber industry are reducing population in counties where they are heavily concentrated. In the past, both mining and lumber have been the source of population expansion in mountain West counties; today they are a cause of population decline.

In sum, neither lumber nor mining appear to be a driving force in the determination of population density. Most importantly, lumber and mining have a negative, not a positive, impact on population density. Neither the lumber or mining industries substantially alter the basic statistical relationship between population density and distance to a regional metropolitan center.

One other potential stimulus to population density and local population growth is tourism. Unfortunately there is no comprehensive economic measure of tourism, although tourism is apparently a growth industry.[14] The one industry that depends heavily on tourism for which income data are available is hotel and motel services. If income in this sector reflects tourism, and if tourism is a significant economic force in mountain counties, then those counties with a larger share of hotel and motel income should have higher levels of economic activity and more population. It turns out that the hotel-motel industry has a negative effect on population density, as can be seen in figure 3.5, an effect that is slightly greater in 1997 than 1985. In 1997, the reduction in population density from a higher tourism income share is about 20 per thousand acres while it is close to 15 in 1985. So tourism does not seem to be driving population density nor,

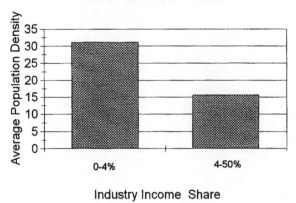

Industry Income Share

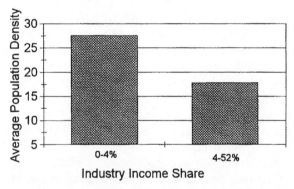

Figure 3.4:   The Mining Industry and Population Density

consequently, population density growth.[15] In fact, its presence causes a downward shift in population density and that downward shift appears to be increasing slightly over time.

Location dependent income sources, such as the extractive industries and
tourism, thus fail as sources of population density and are thus unlikely to be fostering population density growth. The basic relationship between population
density and distance to a metropolitan center is left undisturbed by the presence
of extractive industries or tourism.[16] The key conclusion so far is that the traditional sources of economic and population expansion in mountain counties are
not driving growth currently. This leaves some form of population spreading as
the only possible explanation since there are no other location dependent industries in mountain counties that could serve as generators of growth. The only

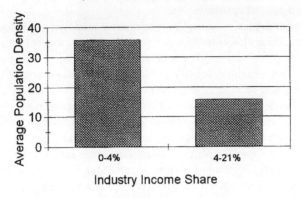

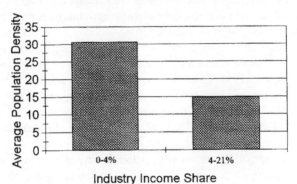

Figure 3.5:   The Hotel-Motel Industry and Population Density

attraction left for mountain West population to consider is the beauty of the landscape itself and the amenities it has to offer.

AMENITIES AS DETERMINANTS OF POPULATION DENSITY

The traditional determinants of population density in rural mountain counties no longer seem to be operative. If this is the case, then what is driving population density patterns in addition to access to major metropolitan areas? What is attracting people to live in the rural counties of the mountain West? The next hypothesis to be addressed is that population densities are affected by a mixture of created and natural amenities.

Amenities having the potential to render some rural mountain counties more attractive than others likely include interstate highways, ski areas, universities or colleges, and national parks and designated wilderness areas.[17] The number of interstate highways, like the distance to regional metropolitan centers, is a measure of accessibility, and more accessible counties are likely to be more attractive to in-migrants than less accessible counties.[18] If lower transportation costs matter in the decision on where to live, then local access to the interstate highway system should influence population density patterns. Anecdotal evidence suggests that ski areas, such as Aspen or Vail, Colorado, are magnets for relatively affluent housing development.[19] Similarly, national parks and designated wilderness areas may be draw in-migrants looking for relatively pristine landscapes.[20] And finally, universities and colleges are not only a direct source of population and employment, but also provide various services and cultural amenities that may be attractive to residents and knowledge intensive businesses.

Three of the amenities—interstates, universities and colleges, and national parks—turn out to have a statistically significant impact on population density while the other two—ski areas and wilderness—don't (see appendix). Interstates have a substantial impact on population density as can be seen in figures 3.6. Counties with interstates have a density of about 12 more per thousand acres in 1985 and 15 more in 1997. According to the statistical analysis in the appendix, another interstate increases population density by 58 percent in 1985 and 53 percent in 1997. Note that effect of interstates on population density doesn't change much between 1985 and 1997. Thus the relative effect of interstates on population density is not changing to any great degree over time.

Universities and colleges affect population density in a fashion similar to interstates. According to the statistical analysis in the appendix, the addition of another university or college at the margin increases population density by 79 percent in 1985 and 74 percent in 1997. Clearly, the presence of higher education institutions matters for population density. This is also reflected in the average density statistics presented in figures 3.7 for counties with and without universities or colleges. Counties with universities or colleges have a greater average population density equal to about 14 per thousand acres in both 1985 and 1987. Again, as in the case of interstates, the relative effect of universities and colleges on population density does not change dramatically over time between 1985 and 1997.

The county land area share in national parks in the statistical analysis of the appendix has a positive and statistically significant effect on population density. However the effect doesn't appear in the average density data for counties with and without parks, probably because other factors that effect population density, such as interstates and colleges and universities, have a more powerful impact on density that overshadows the effect of national

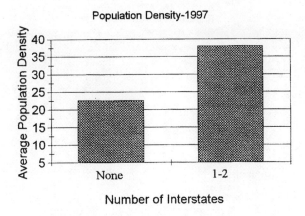

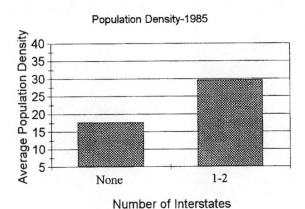

Figure 3.6:   Interstates and Population Density

parks. The average density for counties without parks in 1997 was about 30 per thousand acres and the average density for counties with parks was about 24 per thousand acres. The comparable figures for 1985 are 23 and 19 per thousand acres. Nonetheless, the statistical analysis in the appendix reveals that a one-point increase in the proportion of a county's land area in a national park results in 6 percent increase in population density for both 1985 and 1997. At the margin, the presence of a national park in a county does have a modest positive impact on population. Since national parks occur in the more remote, less populated counties, they likely have diminished population densities because of their low accessibility to regional urban centers. This apparently overpowers the positive marginal impact of national parks on county population.

Population Density-1997

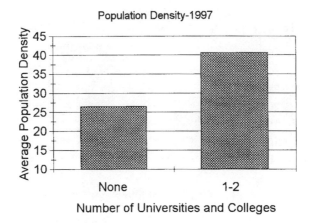

Number of Universities and Colleges

Population Density-1985

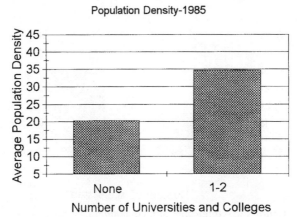

Number of Universities and Colleges

Figure 3.7   Universities and Colleges: Impact on Population Density

Created amenities in the form of interstates and universities and colleges clearly have a positive impact on population density. The presence of national parks also positively affects population density, indicating that pristine landscapes attract residents. The relative impact of these amenities on population density, however, doesn't change much between 1985 and 1997, suggesting that population density growth rates for different counties is unaffected by amenities. Counties are growing because of population spreading, but the presence of amenities is not affecting the relative rate of expansion although counties with amenities have greater densities to begin with and maintain this relative advantage over time. The only factor we have found so far that does differentially affect density growth rates is the distance to the nearest regional urban center.

Counties closer to such urban centers are growing relatively more rapidly than those farther away.

Given that wilderness and ski areas are also potentially attractive amenities, it is a little surprising that they don't attract population disproportionately. Wilderness is a rough proxy for the presence of high quality untouched landscapes while ski areas signify the presence of resort facilities. We will see, however, that both wilderness and ski areas play a somewhat different role in mountain West development. They don't affect population spreading, but they do affect other important phenomena.

VACATION HOMES AND POPULATION DENSITY

Areas with significant natural beauty likely attract substantial numbers of vacation homes that in turn increase local employment to serve vacationing temporary residents. This added employment could increase the number of local residents and therefore local population density. It is at least theoretically possible that vacation home growth is driving population density and its development. We need to determine whether this is in fact occurring.

The proportion of housing units that is second homes can be calculated from the 1990 United States Department of Commerce Census and reflects the relative extent of vacation home activity in a county.[21] According to the data in figure 3.8 and the statistical analysis in the appendix, vacation homes are relatively more concentrated in counties that have lower population densities and less access to urban centers. Moreover, vacation homes also are more heavily concentrated in counties that have wilderness and ski areas. About 20 percent of homes in counties with wilderness areas are vacation homes as opposed to 10 percent for counties without wilderness areas. Similarly, about 20 percent of homes in counties with ski areas are vacation homes as opposed to about 14 percent for counties without ski areas. Ski and wilderness areas attract second homes. Finally, the statistical analysis in the appendix further suggests that vacation homes are less concentrated in counties with good interstate access and universities or colleges. In short, vacation homeowners desire *inaccessibility* above accessibility, proximity to *natural amenities* offered by wilderness areas, and *recreation opportunities* offered by ski areas. Vacation homes can thus be ruled out as a key factor driving population density and its growth since features desired in a county by vacation homeowners are precisely the opposite of those desired by local residents. Vacation homes are concentrated in precisely those locations avoided by most permanent residents. We will return to the consequences of this phenomenon when we discuss the relationship between employment, per capita income, ski areas, wilderness, and vacation homes below. We will see that localities with high levels of income, high ratios of employment to population, ski areas, and designated

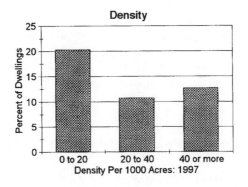

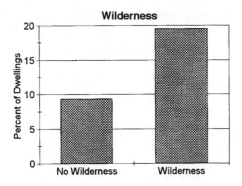

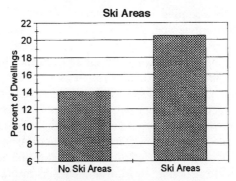

Figure 3.8: Vacation Homes, Population Density, Wilderness, and Ski Areas

wilderness are facing substantial development pressures even though the growth in the number of their permanent residents is not the most rapid among mountain counties.

In sum, the most important variable driving population density and its growth is distance to the closest regional urban center. As distance increases, population density decreases. Population growth is causing the density gradient to shift up and to become steeper. Population growth is proceeding in a wavelike fashion with accessible counties growing relatively more rapidly than the less accessible ones. While accessibility is still desired, population is sufficiently at liberty to move to mountain counties. At the margin, population density is somewhat greater in those counties having interstate highways, universities or colleges, and national park land, but the relative attraction of these amenities does not seem to be changing much over time. The results of the data analysis so far fail to refute the hypothesis that population is spreading to the rural mountain West much like it has spread to urban suburbs historically.

INCOME OVER SPACE AND TIME

Underlying the spread of population to mountain counties is, of course, the spread of income. As noted in chapter 2, the rural counties of the mountain West are not quite keeping up with the benchmark Denver urban area in terms of per capita income growth. This is partly explained by the lower ratio of employment to income in rural counties which is in turn related to a higher and growing rural dependence on retirement transfer income. Transfer income tends to be a drag on per capita income since counties with a higher proportion of this income type incline toward a lower per capita income.[22] Both transfer and retirement income are expanding somewhat more rapidly than earned income, as noted in chapter 2.

While earned income is clearly expanding in mountain West counties, in theory such expansion could be the product of an income multiplier process based on retirement income. If this were the case, then retirement, not population spreading in the classic sense, could explain rural population density growth. Thomas M. Power, Joan Kendall, and Bruce W. Pigozzi, for example, argue that footloose retirement income is a driving force in the growth of rural counties and has a strong income multiplier effect that causes earned income to increase.[23] In this explanation, retirement income is considered basic and the spending by retirees on goods and services generates additional so-called nonbasic income. Nonbasic income is received as earned income by those who work in sectors of the economy serving local residents, and local income in total (basic plus nonbasic) is, consequently, some multiple of basic retirement income. Another retiree brings income into the local community that will be partly spent locally and thus generates additional local income. Retirees who receive transfer and investment income from outside the local community replace the export-oriented extractive industries of the past as the generator of external income needed to finance the purchase of imported goods and services.

To establish whether retirees are the primary source of basic income in the new economy, we need to consider the relationship between the various types of income. If the spatial pattern of earned income and transfer income is the same, then the hypothesis that retirement income is driving aggregate income and population growth cannot be rejected. On the other hand, if earned income has a different relative spatial distribution than transfer income, the hypothesis that a significant number of earned income recipients are spreading to mountain counties independently of retirees cannot be rejected. Simply put, if the spatial pattern of retirement income differs from earned income, retirement income cannot be the total explanation for earned income.

The first step, consequently, is to consider the distribution of income shares according to the distance of counties from regional urban centers. While footloose retirement income is clearly fostering growth in mountain West counties, a negative gradient on distance for the earned income share and the positive gradients for transfer and dividend income shares suggest that some earned income recipients are attracted to mountain counties independently of other forms of income (figures 3.9A and 3.9B). For counties within 200 miles of a regional urban center, the share of earned income was about 63 percent in 1997 while it was about 53 percent for counties 1,200 or more miles from a regional urban center. Conversely, for the transfer income share the same figures were 18 percent and 23 percent. Earned income is distributed across counties differently than transfer and dividend income. This is confirmed by the density gradient data in figures 3.9A and 3.9B as well as by the statistical analysis of income in the appendix. As distance to the nearest regional urban center increases, the share of earned income in the total declines while the share of retirement transfer income increases. Thus retirement income expansion cannot be the only source of growth for earned income. Some part of earned income expansion in rural mountain counties must have another explanation.

These results suggest that transfer and dividend income recipients are relatively more independent in choosing where to live than those who rely on earned income. Disproportionate access to urban centers is clearly not as important to dividend or transfer income recipients as for the population at large. Moreover, transfer and dividend income earners as a group find the less accessible counties relatively more attractive, possibly because they can avoid competition for land with those who get their income from work and locate disproportionately in the more accessible counties. This also suggests that earned income is, at least in part, unrelated to transfer and dividend income and that some earned income recipients are moving to mountain West counties and bringing their income sources with them. As with suburbanization, the spread of population to the rural mountain West is accompanied by a diffusion of employment, and at least some of that employment is independent of the growth of the rural retired population. Footloose earned income is thus part of the explanation for growth in rural mountain counties. Businesses and self-employed

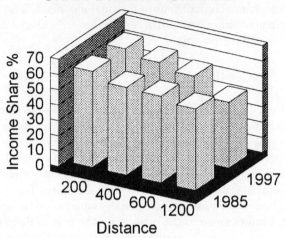

Figure 3.9A: Earned Income Share

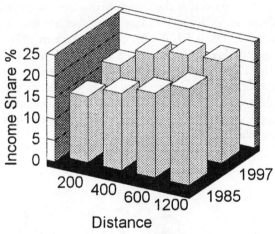

Figure 3.9B: Transfer Income Share

individuals must be sufficiently mobile to be able to disconnect themselves from urban economic centers and move to relatively remote localities. The existence of a population density gradient oriented on large urban centers and the importance of interstate highways in explaining population density suggest that physical access to large centers of economic activity is still important, although access doesn't allow for significant amounts of daily commuting to a place of employment. Relatively new technologies (such as overnight delivery, the fax, the modem, the personal computer, the Internet, and the Worldwide Web) that reduce shipping and communications costs are making it easier to conduct business from relatively remote locations in the rural mountain West by stretching the lines of communication from urban centers that are still critical to the functioning of the regional economy.

INCOME AND POPULATION GROWTH

The spread of population to suburbs around central cities has historically been driven by reduced commuting costs and times, improvements in communications technologies, and growing affluence. The positive effects that the presence of interstate highways and close access to regional urban centers have on population density in the above analysis lend support to the importance of low cost transportation in rural mountain West location decisions. Transportation thus plays a role in both population spreading to the suburbs and to rural areas.

One reason families move to the suburbs is to be able to build bigger houses and own more land. Obviously, fulfilling this desire is relatively expensive. As a result, it is the affluent that have led the movement to the suburbs historically.[24] Is this the case for population spreading to the mountain West? Again, given the cost and size of the homes being constructed in mountain valleys of the West, anecdotal evidence suggests that the answer to this question is yes. Per capita income indeed decreases as distance to large urban centers increases in the same fashion as population (figure 3.10A). Per capita income in 1997 is about $5,500 higher on average for those who live within 200 miles of urban centers than it is for those who live 1,200 miles or more from a regional urban center. As we have already shown, counties closest to regional urban centers are growing relatively more rapidly than those farther out. Affluence and population growth go together. This suggests that affluence is indeed one of the forces behind population spreading to the mountain West.[25]

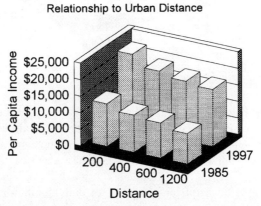

Figure 3.10A: Per Capita Income

The relatively affluent are also attracted to counties having certain other features, such as ski areas and wilderness. Per capita income in counties with ski areas is about $3,900 more than counties without in 1997, and it is about $1,200 more for counties with designated wilderness than counties without (figure 3.10B). So counties with ski and wilderness areas are attracting the relatively more affluent residents. On the other hand, retirement income recipients who depend on transfer payments are avoiding locations with ski areas. The share of 1997 transfer income in counties

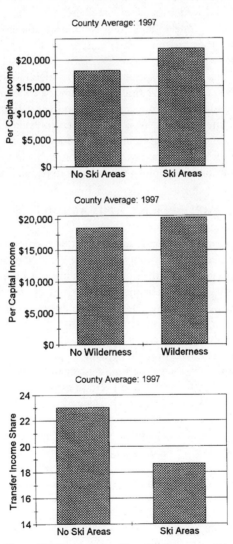

Figure 3.10B: Income, Transfer Payments, Ski Areas, and Wilderness

with ski areas is about 19 percent and in counties without ski areas about 23 percent (figure 3.10B). Less affluent retirees dependent on transfer income are again avoiding locations occupied by more affluent earned income recipients. Retiree transfer income recipients avoid counties with both ski and wilderness areas, while the relatively more affluent seek them out.

Ski areas and wilderness not only attract vacation homes as noted above, but they also attract the relatively wealthy. Because of this combination, environmental problems associated with development are likely to be more extensive in locations with ski areas and wilderness than elsewhere. Both the affluent and second home owners are more prone to build relatively large houses on large parcels of land. In other words, they are more likely to spread out over the landscape than live at high densities within the confines of existing municipal boundaries. Since wilderness and ski areas typically appear adjacent to high mountain valleys, these same valleys are likely to be the victims of low density, widespread development. This issue will be revisited again in chapter 7 when the relationship between land trust formation and the extent of local development pressures is taken up.[26] The relative concentration of vacation homes and the affluent in mountain counties with ski resorts and wilderness areas has another consequence as well, namely a relatively high concentration of employment relative to population.

EMPLOYMENT AND AMENITIES

Employment and population usually grow together but not necessarily in strict proportion. Employment in mountain counties is growing relative to population and the extra employment growth is driven primarily by retail and services sectors of the economy as noted in chapter 2. Growth in and retail and services employment per thousand population for the mountain counties is close in magnitude to the benchmark Denver metro area, although rural figures have grown somewhat more rapidly in recent years helping to close the rural-urban gap. Even though rural and urban trends in the employment-population ratio are similar in the aggregate, an investigation of the forces affecting employment per thousand population in rural areas is worth undertaking to determine if there are unique characteristics of mountain counties, such as amenities, that attract employment to a relatively greater extent than population. Doing so will also help us understand why employment is more heavily concentrated in some mountain counties than population and how this could add to development pressures.

As can be seen in figures 3.11A and 3.11B, amenities such as ski and wilderness areas attract employment to a greater degree than population. Employment is relatively higher in counties with ski areas and wilderness but population is not, as was discovered in the above analysis of population density. Ski areas and wilderness attract employment to a greater degree than they attract population. Much of the higher total employment in counties with ski areas and wilderness occurs because of higher employment in retailing and services. Counties with ski areas have 160 employees per thousand population more than counties without

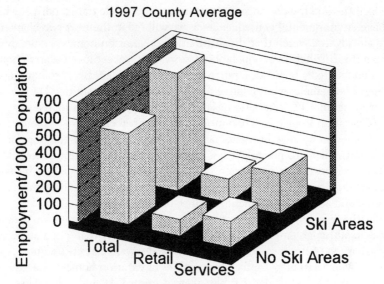

Figure 3.11A: Employment and Ski Areas

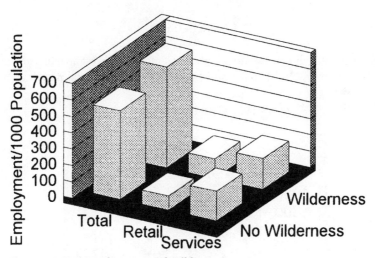

Figure 3.11B: Employment and Wilderness

ski areas, and counties with wilderness have 70 more employees per thousand population than counties without, according to 1997 data. Employment is thus relatively more concentrated in counties with ski facilities and wilderness than is population. This suggests that both retail and services activity are greater in high mountain ski communities near wilderness areas and that they contribute to development pressures. More retail and services will mean the construction of more facilities and the presence of increased motor vehicle traffic, both of which can have environmental consequences as we will see in the next two chapters.

We already discovered that the distribution of vacation homes is quite different from the distribution of population density over space. Since vacation home-owners undoubtedly make local purchases, their presence is likely to have a positive impact on employment relative to population. This is confirmed by the data present in figure 3.12. The ratio of employment to population increases as the share of vacation homes rises. Counties with a 30 percent share or more of vacation homes on average have around 880 employees per thousand population, while counties with 10 percent or less share of vacation homes have around 550 employees per thousand population. Vacation homes not only add to development pressures, but their presence fosters still more economic activity in services and retail and added development pressures in those sectors.

Collectively, population and employment are spreading to mountain counties in tandem, although employment is growing more rapidly than population, and the distribution of employment in space is skewed toward certain amenities, such as ski and wilderness areas, and concentrations of vacation homes. The distribution of more affluent residents is also skewed toward ski and wilderness areas, while the distribution of moderate-income retirees who depend on transfer income is skewed away from these amenities.[27]

CONCLUSION

Is population spreading to counties of the rural mountain West an extension of the suburbanization process? Population is indeed spreading to rural mountain areas,

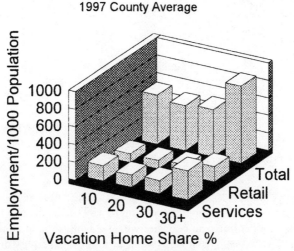

Figure 3.12: Employment and Vacation Homes

and population growth cannot be explained by expansion in the extractive industries that traditionally supported mountain West counties nor by tourism or vacation home development. While population expansion can be partly attributed to
retirees settling in remote mountain counties, this is not the entire story. House-
holds that depend on earned income are increasingly locating in the rural mountain West, particularly in counties that are more accessible to regional urban centers. Retirees are choosing to live in the mountain West in expanding numbers, but
they are more inclined to locate in relatively remote counties and to avoid popular resort communities with ski areas. Earned income is thus, at least partially, independent of retiree income, and some of those who depend on earned income are
moving to the mountain West and bringing their sources of income with them or
are finding employment in businesses whose owners want access to mountain West
amenities or see an advantage in satisfying employee desires for such access. This
population-spreading process, as noted in chapter 1, is apparently motivated by
wants that have traditionally driven suburbanization—to live in small communities; to escape the negative features of urban life such as crime, congestion, and pollution; and to gain access to beautiful rural landscapes.

Economic activity in almost any form in the modern world is seldom free of environmental consequences. The next two chapters will explore whether this general
rule applies to the spreading of population to the mountain West. In particular, the
impact of new forms of development on the diversity of plants and animals that live
in the mountain West will be explored. This will give us insight into the consequences of the new mountain West economy for one key dimension of the natural
environment—biological diversity. After this inquiry, the results of a public opinion
survey in the Sierra Nevada Mountains will be employed to establish whether mountain West residents experiencing the consequences of local growth favor regulatory
measures that would protect open space and natural habitats and thus place limits on
the economic development process. We will see that Sierra Nevada residents are
concerned with the potential for development to spoil the qualities of the natural environment that attracted them to the mountain landscape in the first place.

APPENDIX

Multivariate Regression Analysis

The Statistical Derivation of the Density Gradient

The standard functional form for density equations in the urban economics literature is the following:

(1) $D = e^{(a - bd)}$,

where D equals density, e is the exponential growth factor (2.718), a and b are
constants, and d is the distance variable.[28] With density plotted on the vertical

axis and distance plotted on the horizontal axis, a graph of density would start at a zero distance to the regional urban area and decline at a fixed percentage rate as distance increases as shown in figure 3.2. The relationship, consequently, is presumed to be nonlinear. The coefficient b on the distance variable d in equation (1) is equal to the percentage decline in density per highway mile as distance from the urban center increases.

In order to estimate population density gradients of the kind just described using rural mountain county data, a statistical methodology called multivariate regression analysis must be used. Recognizing that not everyone who reads this book will necessarily be familiar with regression analysis, a brief although incomplete description will be offered before proceeding to the actual analysis. Regression analysis for the uninitiated may seem a bit daunting, but all that it essentially does in its two-dimensional version is to fit a line to a scatter diagram of data with two variables. For the sample of rural mountain counties, for example, the data includes population density D and distance d from the metropolitan center for each county. In a scatter diagram, data is plotted on a two-dimensional graph with density D measured on the vertical axis and distance d measured on the horizontal axis. Such a scatter diagram is presented in figure 3A.1 using 1997 data. Regression analysis provides a method for finding the best fit of a straight line to the data with the dependent variable graphed on the vertical or Y axis and the independent variable graphed on the horizontal or X axis. It basically does this by finding the minimized sum of squared deviations from the line. The estimate points in figure 3A.1 plot out the regression line with the best fit to the data. Given that the basic assumptions of regression analysis hold,[29] statistical judgements can be made

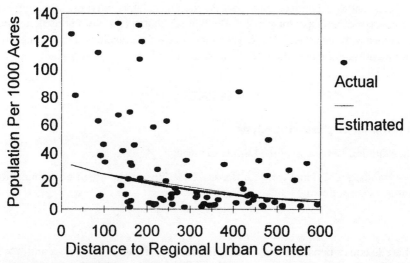

Figure 3A.1:   Population Density: 1997

about the goodness of the line's fit to the data. In particular, whether the slope coefficient for the line is in fact different from zero can be tested statistically. If it is, then the hypothesis that the independent variable affects the magnitude of the dependent variable cannot be rejected.

Multivariate regression analysis estimates a linear equation, but the above density equation (1) is nonlinear. However, it can be converted to a linear equation quite simply by changing both sides of the equation to natural logs as follows:

(2) $\log D = a - b_1 d,$

where a is the constant in the linear equation and b_1 is the slope coefficient and, to repeat, D is population density and d is distance from the regional urban center. Linear regression analysis will allow us to estimate both the constant and the slope and to test for statistical significance. We can go beyond two dimensions by hypothesizing that other independent variables also influence population density in addition to distance. They can be added to the regression equation as follows:

(3) $\log D = a - b_1 d + b_2 x,$

where x represents some other variable that is hypothesized to affect population density D. Again, we can't prove that x affects D, but we can establish whether the hypothesis that it does can be rejected or not. Basically, other variables shift the density gradient up or down, depending on the actual sign of the coefficient.

Population density gradient estimates in table 3A.1 for 1970, 1985, and 1997 do indeed demonstrate that distance to the nearest regional metropolitan center plays a role in locational choice since distance has a negative sign and is a statistically significant determinant of the log of population density.[30] With the dependent variable (population density) in natural logs, the interpretation of the coefficient for distance is the percentage decline in population per highway mile to a regional metropolitan center. In 1970 population density declined by about 18 percent per 100 miles; in 1985 the decline was about 27 percent per 100 miles; and in 1997 the decline was about 30 percent per 100 miles distance according to the regression equation estimates. Population density clearly declines as distance from regional metropolitan centers increase, and the rate of decline is increasing over time, suggesting that counties closer to regional urban centers are growing more rapidly than those that are farther away from such centers.

Density and Location Dependent Industries

Regression analysis reveals that the percentage share of earned lumber industry income at the county level is a negative but not a statistically significant determinant of population density (table 3A.2). The percentage share of lumber industry income has a negative effect on population density, but the amount estimated is not statistically reliable. The regression results indicate that an increase

Table 3A.1.   Regression Equations for Population Density Gradients

Independent Variable or Statistic	Log Population Density		
	1970	1985	1997
Constant	2.59997*	3.23840*	3.52055*
	(11.17)	(13.70)	(14.18)
Distance to Metro Center	−0.00181*	−0.00268*	−0.003062*
	(−2.95)	(−4.29)	(−4.66)
Adjusted R^2	.08	.17	.20
F-statistic	8.67*	18.38*	21.75*

Notes: Figures in parenthesis are t-statistic. An asterisk indicates significance at 95-percent confidence for a two-tailed test. A White Heteroskedasticity Test is negative (White 1980).

in the income share of one percentage point for a county would result in a 1.7 percent decrease in population density. A county that is more dependent on the lumber industry would experience a slightly lower population density than otherwise. Because the figure is comparatively small, population density is not very sensitive to lumber industry income. Consequently, the lumber industry is an unlikely candidate as a driving force behind differences in population density across counties or in the growth of population density.

As in the case of the lumber industry, the percentage share of mining industry earned income for a sample of 58 counties not having data disclosure problems negatively affects population density for 1997, but not quite at a statistically significant level (table 3A.2). For a sample of 75 counties without disclosure problems in 1985, the mining income share also has a negative but not a statistically significant effect on population density (table 3A.2). The negative effect of the mining income share on population density is comparatively modest at -3.7 percent in 1997 and -1.7 percent in 1985 for an increase in the income share by one percentage point.

A population density regression for 1997 finds that the percentage share of hotel and motel income has a negative sign on its coefficient and lacks statistical significance for a sample of 70 counties (table 3A.3), and its inclusion in the regression equation does not significantly affect the population density gradient.[31] An increase in the hotel-motel income share by one percentage point for a county would actually result in a decline in population density by 4.5 percent in 1997.

Finally, for counties within commuting range of urban areas or concentrations of resorts or other local attractions, imported income could be a significant determinant of population density. Where this is the case, local residents would commute to another county for employment. The net percentage share of total personal income imported from (or exported to) locations outside each county (or commuter income) was not found to be a statistically significant determinant of population density in either 1985 or 1997 (table 3A.3) nor did its inclusion affect density gradients significantly. The estimated percentage increase in population density from a one percentage point increase in the imported commuting income share is very small in both 1985 and 1997 (.5 and 1.1 percent respectively) in addition to being statistically unreliable.

Table 3A.2. Regression Equations for Population Density with Extractive Industry Income Shares as Independent Variables

Independent Variable or Statistic	Log Population Density		
	1997	1997	1985
Constant	3.86230*	3.49687*	3.40380*
	(13.71)	(11.00)	(13.16)
Distance to Metro Center	−0.00334*	−0.002544*	−0.00249*
	(−4.68)	(−3.19)	(−3.85)
Share of Lumber Industry Income Percent	-0.01696		
	(−0.59)		
Share of Mining Industry Income Percent		−0.03668	−0.01661
		(−1.95)	(−1.48)
Adjusted R^2	.24	.18	.16
F-statistic	11.81*	7.11*	8.16*
Sample Size	68	58	75

Notes: Figures in parenthesis are t-statistic. An asterisk indicates significance at 95-percent confidence for a two-tailed test. A White Heteroskedasticity Test is negative (White 1980).

Table 3A.3. Regression Equations for Population Density with Tourism and Commuting Measures as Independent Variables

Independent Variable or Statistic	Log Population Density		
	1997	1997	1985
Constant	3.93221*	3.48709*	3.12514*
	(13.44)	(13.47)	(12.09)
Distance to Metro Center	−0.00329*	−0.00301*	−0.00249*
	(−4.78)	(−4.51)	(−3.83)
Share of Hotel-Motel Inc. Percent	−0.04486		
	(−1.26)		
Share of Commuting Inc. Percent		0.00469	0.01057
		(0.63)	(1.07)
Adjusted R^2	.23	.19	.17
F-statistic	11.50*	10.89*	9.78*
Sample Size	70	86	86

Notes: Figures in parenthesis are t-statistic. An asterisk indicates significance at 95-percent confidence for a two-tailed test. A White Heteroskedasticity Test is negative (White 1980). Inc.=income.

Amenities and Population Density

In a modified population density regression equation that includes amenities, the number of interstates and universities or colleges as well as the percentage share of county land in national parks are statistically significant determinants of population density (table 3A.4). One additional interstate (counties typical have zero, one, or two) increases population density at the margin by a rather substantial 58 percent in 1985 and 53 percent in 1994, suggesting that access indeed matters (table 3A.4).[32] The presence of a single university or college increased population density by a substantial 79 percent in 1985 and 74 percent in 1997 (table 3A.4),[33] suggesting that institutions of higher education are indeed magnets for population (the maximum for the sample is two). The national park land share average for the sample is a modest 1.4 percent but it ranges as high as 19 percent and has a standard deviation of 4 percent. While changes in this variable are not theoretically confined to large increments, differences across counties tend to be fairly large. For each one-unit change in the national park percentage land share, population density increased across counties by 6.2 percent in 1985 and 6 percent in 1997 (table 3A.4). The coefficients in the population density equation for the number of ski areas and the share of county land in designated wilderness areas are statistically insignificant in both time periods. This finding is at odds with other research suggesting that wilderness counties are expanding relatively in population and that ski areas have a positive impact on population.[34]

Adding amenity variables to the population density model steepens the slope of the density gradient slightly, and the primary change in regression estimates from 1985 to 1997 is an upward shift and a slight ascent of the gradient from a 31 percent increase in population density per 100 miles to a 35 percent increase. The coefficients on amenities don't change much over time. Population density is growing, but not because of an increase in the attraction

Table 3A.4.   Regression Equations for Population Density and Vacation Home Share Percent with Amenities as Independent Variables

Independent Variable or Statistic	Log Population Density 1997	Log Vacation Home Share 1985	Log Vacation Home Share 1990
Constant	3.30817*	3.05997*	2.28282*
	(11.38)	(11.13)	(10.86)
Distance to Metro Center	−0.00347*	−0.00317*	−0.00007
	(−5.43)	(−5.28)	(−0.14)
Number of Interstates	0.53367*	0.57887*	−0.44850*
	(2.17)	(2.51)	(−2.54)
Number of Ski Areas	0.18350	0.06627	0.31405*
	(1.07)	(0.50)	(3.08)
Universities/Colleges	0.74077*	0.78744*	−0.89217*
	(2.19)	(2.42)	(−3.58)
National Park Land Share Percent	0.06038*	0.06228*	−0.02892
	(1.96)	(2.14)	(−1.30)
Wilderness Land Share Percent	−0.02498	−0.02000	0.04943*
	(−1.33)	(−1.12)	(3.29)
Adjusted R²	.31	.29	.35
F-statistic	7.41*	6.91*	8.57*

Notes: Figures in parenthesis are t-statistic. An asterisk indicates significance at 95-percent confidence for a two-tailed test. A White Heteroskedasticity Test is negative (White 1980).

of any particular amenity since the effects of the independent variables are comparable for 1985 and 1997. Simply put, population is spreading to all rural mountain counties with proportionally greater numbers attracted to counties with amenities. Amenities cause differences in population density across counties, but they do not cause much relative difference over time because of the absence of any dramatic changes in the size of coefficients from 1985 to 1997. The data for the amenities themselves is unchanged between 1985 and 1997 across all counties, except for ski areas that changed slightly (the average decreased from .64 to .56). Because of the steepening of the density gradient, the population growth rate is greater in the more accessible counties closer to metropolitan areas.

Vacation Homes and Population Density

A vacation percentage home share regression equation with amenities as independent variables suggests that the statistical determinants of vacation home activity strongly diverge from the determinants of population density (table 3A.4). Population density is therefore largely unrelated to the relative extent of vacation homes. In fact, vacation home owners seem to avoid locations with substantial population density. Distance to the nearest regional urban center is not as statistically significant an independent variable for the vacation home share regression equation as it is for population density; the number of interstates has a negative and statistically significant effect on the vacation home share while the effect is reversed for population density; the number of ski areas has a statistically significant and positive impact on the vacation home share but an insignificant effect on population density; the impact of colleges and universities on the vacation home share is statistically significant and negative while for population density it is significant and positive; and, finally, the wilderness land share has a positive and statistically significant effect on vacation homes and an insignificant and negative effect on population density (table 3A.4).

Income, Access to Urban Centers, and Amenities

With the exception of the transfer income share, the only statistically significant variable in the income share equations is distance to the nearest regional urban center. The distance gradient for the earned income share is negatively sloped while the gradient is positively sloped for the transfer income share and the dividend income share (tables 3A.5 and 3A.6). Those who get their income from labor are disproportionately attracted to more accessible counties while transfer and dividend income earners are disproportionately attracted to less accessible counties. Moreover, transfer income earners also avoid counties with ski areas and wilderness at statistically significant levels.

Table 3A.5.   Regression Equations for Earned Income and Transfer Income Shares with Amenities as Independent Variables

| | Log Earned Income Share | | Log Transfer Income Share | |
Independent Variable or Statistic	1997	1985	1997	1985
Constant	4.08659*	4.13428*	2.99295*	2.7931*
	(105.72)	(87.89)	(29.39)	(31.81)
Distance to Metro Center	−0.00021*	−0.00047*	0.00047*	0.00059*
	(−2.49)	(−4.59)	(2.10)	(3.06)
Number of Interstates	0.02958	0.01720	0.03325	0.01543
	(0.90)	(0.44)	(0.39)	(0.21)
Nunber of Ski Areas	0.04008	0.03194	−0.27515*	−0.19475
	(1.76)	(1.41)	(−4.59)	(−4.60)
Universities/Colleges	0.04479	0.08497	0.02494	0.03710
	(0.99)	(1.53)	(0.21)	(0.36)
National Park Land Share Percent	−0.00085	0.00320	0.01553	0.00943
	(−0.21)	(0.64)	(1.43)	(1.01)
Wilderness Land Share Percent	−0.00525	0.00239	−0.01201	−0.01160*
	(−0.21)	(0.79)	(−1.82)	(−2.02)
Adjusted R^2	.10	.23	.32	.37
F-statistic	2.49*	5.32*	7.71*	9.31*

Notes: Figures in parenthesis are t-statistic. An asterisk indicates significance at 95-percent confidence for a two-tailed test. A White Heteroskedasticity Test is negative (White 1980).

Table 3A.6.   Regression Equations for Dividend Income Shares and per Capita Income with Amenities as Independent Variables

| | Log Dividend Income Share | | Log Per Capita Income | |
Independent Variable or Statistic	1997	1985	1997	1985
Constant	2.85489*	2.94483*	9.83615*	9.38394*
	(39.82)	(37.27)	(224.68)	(247.48)
Distance to Metro Center	0.00029	0.00064*	−0.00030*	−0.00045*
	(1.83)	(3.69)	(−3.15)	(−5.44)
Number of Interstates	−0.09631	−0.03771	0.003350	0.04224
	(−1.59)	(−0.57)	(0.90)	(1.33)
Number of Ski Areas	0.07963	0.03073	0.14055*	0.06168*
	(1.89)	(0.81)	(5.45)	(3.37)
Universities/Colleges	−0.03561	−0.10817	0.01819	0.00913
	(−0.43)	(−1.16)	(0.36)	(0.20)
National Park Land Share Percent	−0.00479	−0.00435	−0.00008	0.00602
	(−0.63)	(−0.52)	(−0.02)	(1.50)
Wilderness Land Share Percent	0.00770	0.00049	0.00646*	0.00278
	(1.66)	(0.10)	(5.46)	(1.12)
Adjusted R^2	.06	.09	.44	.38
F-statistic	1.92	2.38*	12.01*	9.74*

Notes: Figures in parenthesis are t-statistic. An asterisk indicates significance at 95-percent confidence for a two-tailed test. A White Heteroskedasticity Test is negative (White 1980).

The statistically significant determinants of per capita income for 1985 and 1997 include metro distance, the number of ski areas, and the wilderness land share. To simplify the presentation we will focus only on these variables. Income per capita features a negative metro distance gradient as does population density. For 1985 a 100-mile increase in distance at the margin causes a decline in per capita income of 4.5 percent, and for 1997 the same distance increases cause a decline in per capita income of 3 percent (these are based on the regression co-efficients in table 3A.5). Per capita income is clearly greater for rural counties closer to urban centers.

Per capita income is also attracted over time to counties with ski areas and wilderness. Between 1985 and 1997 the increment to income from one ski area at the margin increased from 6 percent to 14 percent (the regression coefficients in table 3A.6). A one-percentage-point increase in the wilderness land share at the margin would cause per capita income to increase by .65 percent in 1997 (table 3A.6).

Employment and Amenities

The statistically significant determinants of total employment per thousand population include ski areas, wilderness land shares, vacation homes shares, and imported commuting income shares (table 3A.7). Adding another ski area at the margin would have increased employment per thousand by 12 percent in 1997 and 9.5 percent in 1985.[35] Increasing the percentage share of wilderness acres in a county by one point at the margin would have increased employment per thousand by .77 percent in the 1997 regression equation. (The wilderness land share ranges as high as 30 percent.) As suggested in other research, counties with designated wilderness areas are attracting employment to a greater degree than those without wilderness.[36] Increasing the percentage share of vacation homes in the housing stock by one point would have expanded employment per thousand by .5 percent in 1997 and .5 percent in 1985. And increasing the share of commuter income at the margin by one percentage point would have decreased employment by 1.36 percent in 1997 and 1.09 percent in 1985.[37] Commuters reduce the supply of potential employees in the local population and may well purchase goods and services outside their home county to a greater degree than others. Both would tend to depress employment per thousand.

In sum, employment growth appears to be a product of a general simultaneous spreading of population and employment to rural mountain counties. Big differences in employment occur across counties because of amenities, but the coefficients on amenities in regression equations don't differ much between 1985 and 1997. Hence, the relative importance of amenities appears not to be changing over time. Consequently, the main force behind employment growth is population and employment spreading to mountain counties.

Table 3A.7.   Regression Equations for Employment per 1,000 Population with Amenities as Independent Variables

Independent Variable or Statistic	Log Employment per 1,000 Population	
	1997	1985
Constant	6.21600*	5.9991*
	(118.63)	(106.97)
Distance to Metro Center	−0.00010	−0.00003
	(−0.98)	(−0.31)
Number of Interstates	0.02018	0.05269
	(0.50)	(1.38)
Number of Ski Areas	0.12079*	0.09390*
	(4.33)	(4.00)
Universities/Colleges	0.06671	0.04560
	(1.23)	(0.84)
National Park Land Share Percent	−0.00760	−0.00029
	(−1.56)	(−0.06)
Wilderness Land Share Percent	0.00773*	0.00301
	(2.37)	(0.94)
Vacation House Share Percent	0.00511*	0.00579*
	(3.48)	(3.16)
Commuting Income Share Percent	−0.01361*	−0.01094*
	(−9.32)	(−6.19)
Adjusted R^2	.69	.59
F-statistic	25.20*	16.04*
Sample Size	86	86

Notes: Figures in parenthesis are t-statistic. An asterisk indicates significance at 95-percent confidence for a two-tailed test. A White Heteroskedasticity Test is negative (White 1980).

The employment-population ratio for both services and retail employment is affected at statistically significant levels by key amenities and explains much of the impact of amenities on total employment (table 3A.8). Unlike total employment, however, both services and retail employment are positively affected by the presence of interstates at statistically significant levels in 1985 but not in 1997. These two kinds of employment disperse away from counties with interstate access between 1985 and 1997, although the changes to employment as a result of this move are not very large. Ski areas prove to be attractive to services and retail employment relative to population (at statistically significant levels) as they were to total employment in both 1985 and 1997 to about the same degree in both years. Unlike total employment per thousand, the wilderness land share is not quite a statistically significant determinant of services or retail employment, except when the hotel-motel income share is included in the regression equation (reducing the size of the sample because of disclosure issues). The vacation house share is a statistically

Table 3A.8.   Regression Equations for Services and Retail Employment per 1,000 Population with Amenities as Independent Variables

Independent Variable or Statistic	Log Services Employment per 1,000 Population		Log Retail Employment per 1,000 Population	
	1997	1985	1997	1985
Constant	4.82753*	4.32585*	4.27211*	4.10353*
	(44.21)	(37.23)	(37.32)	(32.39)
Distance to Metro Center	−.00030	−0.00034	−.00003	−0.00021
	(−1.42)	(−1.69)	(−0.15)	(−0.93)
Number of Interstates	0.08194	0.17986*	0.12897	0.17948*
	(0.94)	(2.34)	(1.46)	(2.08)
Number of Ski Areas	0.19352*	0.16214*	0.19237*	0.16097*
	(3.28)	(3.48)	(3.15)	(3.04)
Universities/Colleges	0.16757	0.21192*	0.21601	0.15879
	(1.48)	(1.96)	(1.82)	(1.29)
National Park Land Share Percent	0.00578	0.02282*	0.00311*	0.01099
	(1.02)	(2.47)	(0.29)	(1.04)
Wilderness Land Share Percent	0.01266	0.01167	0.01174	−0.00011*
	(1.81)	(1.83)	(1.65)	(−0.01)
Vacation House Share Percent	0.00871*	0.01150*	0.00626*	0.00764
	(2.84)	(3.12)	(1.95)	(1.85)
Commuting Inc. Share Percent	−0.02249*	−0.01051*	−0.00709*	−0.00944*
	(−7.13)	(−3.00)	(−2.22)	(−2.36)
Adjusted R^2	.59	.52	.34	.30
F-statistic	15.81	12.14	6.51	5.53
Sample	84	83	86	86

Notes: Figures in parenthesis are t-statistic. An asterisk indicates significance at 95-percent confidence for a two-tailed test. A White Heteroskedasticity Test is negative (White 1980). Inc.=income.

significant and positive determinant of retail and services employment in 1997. The commuting income share is a negative statistically significant determinant of retail and services employment. In general, the effects of the amenity variables on retail and service employment don't change much between 1985 and 1997, except for the impact of interstates which declines in importance as a determinant of services and retail employment. The conclusion is relatively simple. The growth in service and retail employment between 1985 and 1997 can be attributed primarily to an upward shift in the regression equation. The impact of different amenities on employment changes very little from 1985 to 1997. Amenities matter in determining employment across counties but not over time. Services and retail employment, like employment in total, are growing relative to population because of trends in the larger economy not because of the changing attraction of amenities to any great degree (except for the minor changing impacts of wilderness and interstates noted above).

Table 3A.9. Variable Statistics: Eighty-Six Mountain Counties

	Mean	Standard Deviation	Minimum	Maximum
Population Density 1970	14.39	18.64	0.46	103.14
Population Density 1985	21.96	28.12	0.92	135.67
Population Density 1997	28.11	38.54	0.95	212.40
Employment/1,000 1985	477.74	146.16	211.72	1252.75
Employment/1,000 1997	594.49	221.79	329.28	1551.52
Retail employment/1,000 1985	83.17	42.04	19.46	285.41
Retail employment/1,000 1997	110.24	59.43	29.87	353.33
Services employment/1,000 1985	120.00	77.30	36.00	491.81
Services employment/1,000 1997	185.84	156.43	46.21	1082.58
Per Capita Income 1985	11,323.78	2,192.70	6,845.00	21,968.00
Per Capita Income 1997	19,765.58	5,031.10	12,040.59	49,266.14
Earned Income Share 1985	57.73	10.85	25.94	80.31
Earned Income Share 1997	58.25	9.00	34.72	79.90
Dividend/Interest Income Share 1985	24.27	7.98	11.92	49.84
Dividend/Interest Income Share 1997	20.60	5.72	10.72	36.27
Transfer Income Share 1985	18.01	5.83	3.53	29.56
Transfer Income Share 1994	21.15	7.68	3.87	41.17
Share of Mining Industry Income 1985 Percent (N=75)	6.72	11.61	0.00	52.30
Share of Mining Industry Income 1997 Percent (N=58)	4.00	8.67	0.00	49.64
Share of Lumber Industry Income 1997 Percent (N=68)	3.10	5.14	0.00	22.40
Share of Hotel-Motel Income 1997 Percent (N=70)	2.78	3.85	0.00	21.40
Share of Commuting Income 1985 Percent	4.78	12.60	−22.59	61.47
Share of Commuting Income 1997 Percent	3.63	13.35	−49.74	57.02
Distance to Metro Center (miles)	324.12	195.70	24.00	1,289.00
Number of Interstates	0.37	0.51	0.00	2.00
Number of Ski Areas 1985	0.64	0.93	0.00	4.00
Number of Ski Areas 1997	0.56	0.76	0.00	3.00
Universities/Colleges	0.13	0.37	0.00	2.00
National Park Land Share Percent	1.38	3.98	0.00	19.13
Wilderness Land Share Percent	5.40	6.67	0.00	30.14
Vacation Home Share 1990	16.82	16.25	1.29	71.44

Note: Densities are per 1,000 privately owned acres.

NOTES

1. Kenneth T. Jackson, *Crabgrass Frontier: The Suburbanization of the United States* (New York: Oxford University Press, 1985).

2. Edwin S. Mills and Bruce W. Hamilton, *Urban Economics*, 5th ed. (New York: Harper Collins, 1994), 131–137; and Richard Muth, *Cities and Housing* (Chicago: University of Chicago Press, 1969). The conceptual approach taken in this chapter originates

in an earlier work of mine (Douglas E. Booth, "Spatial Patterns in the Economic Development of the Mountain West," *Growth and Change* 30 [1999]: 384–405).

3. The sample mean for the share of land in federal ownership is 33 percent.

4. All density calculations that follow use county land area minus the land area in federal and state ownership. The data source for county land area is United States Department of Commerce, Bureau of the Census, *County and City Data Book* (Washington, D.C.: U.S. Government Printing Office, 1988); the source for federally owned land area by county is U.S. Bureau of Land Management, "Payments in Lieu of Taxes," Internal Report (1995); and the data sources for state-owned land area by county are data requests from the California State Lands Commission (1998), Colorado Board of Land Commissioners (1998), Colorado State Parks (1998), and Montana Department of Natural Resources and Conservation, Central Land Office (1998).

5. Distances were calculated using Rand McNally's *1995 Road Atlas: Unites States, Canada, Mexico* (Skokie, Ill.: Rand McNally, 1995). For California counties, the closest regional center is San Francisco; for Colorado counties, it is Denver; and for Montana counties, it is either Denver, Seattle, or Salt Lake City, depending on distance.

6. In the main body of this chapter, descriptive data is used to illustrate and support propositions made about economic development trends in the mountain West. Detailed statistical evidence supporting these propositions can be found in a parallel discussion in the appendix. In addition, the appendix addresses certain other issues of general interest but not of great significance for the main argument put forth in this chapter.

7. Individuals dependent on earned income need not literally bring their employment with them in order to move to mountain counties if they are willing to accept a lower rate of pay than they would otherwise earn in a large urban area. The desire to live in localities with significant amenities that improve the quality of life appears to be accompanied by a willingness to accept a lower wage rate according to two studies (Christiane von Reichert and Gundar Rudzitis, "Multinomial Logistic Models Explaining Income Changes of Migrants to High-Amenity Counties," *The Review of Regional Studies* 22 [1992]: 25–42; and Jennifer Roback, "Wages, Rents, and the Quality of Life," *Journal of Political Economy* 90 [1982]: 1257–1278). If this is indeed the case, employers could also be attracted to locate in mountain counties by the lower wage rate.

8. Employers could be trading access to large urban centers for lower wages induced by the desire to live in rural mountain counties. The compromise need not be strictly in terms of wages; it could also occur between access and the ease of recruiting highly skilled employees who have a strong desire for a rural mountain residential location.

9. The only possible exceptions are Clear Creek and Gilpin Counties just outside of Denver, Eldorado and Placer Counties near Sacramento, and Madera County near Fresno.

10. U.S. Department of Commerce, Bureau of Economic Analysis, *Regional Economic Information System, 1969–97*, CD–ROM (Washington, D.C., 1997).

11. One could argue that disclosure removes those counties from the sample for which lumber is a significant industry. This, however, is apparently not the case. In sample counties for which data is available, the mean share for lumber income is a relatively high 3.1%, the standard deviation is 5.1%, and the maximum lumber income share is 22.4%. In short, a good number of relatively timber dependent counties remain in the sample. A similar story can be told for mining in 1997, with a mean income share of 4.0%, a standard deviation of 8.7%, and a maximum lumber income share of 49.6%.

12. The statistical analysis in the appendix indicates that the effect of the lumber industry on the population density gradient is negative but statistically insignificant. This means that the presence of the lumber industry causes a downward shift in population density.

13. As noted in the appendix, the effect of the mining income share on population density is negative but not statistically significant in both 1985 and 1997. The presence of mining shifts population density down by an amount that is just slightly more in 1997 than 1985.

14. Thomas M. Power, *Lost Landscapes and Failed Economies: The Search for Value of Place* (Washington, D.C.: Island Press, 1996), 214–215.

15. One other form of location dependent economic activity could be fueling population density growth. Some counties in the sample are on the edge of the commuting boundary for fairly large urban areas such as Sacramento or Fresno. Employment growth in these areas could be fueling population density growth in adjacent counties. As explained in the appendix, however, commuter income shares are not a statistically significant determinant of population density.

16. Vacation home development could also be driving local economic and population growth. This issue, however, is best addressed after we have a better handle on factors affecting population density.

17. The numbers of interstates, ski areas, and colleges and universities were taken from Rand McNally's *1995 Road Atlas* and *1986 Road Atlas*. The sources for county land area in national parks and national forest wilderness areas were respectively U.S. Bureau of Land Management, "Payments in Lieu of Taxes," and a data request from the USDA Forest Service.

18. An alternative available measure is highway density. This measure was not chosen because of the likelihood that it is, at least partly, determined by local population density. This is less likely the case for the interstate system since the planning for it occurred at the national level. The interstate system is also more important in providing accessibility outside the local area than are local highways. Another access measure available is interstate miles. Because interstate mileage is dependent on county land area, this measure in itself wouldn't divulge much about access. Having two interstates instead of one could make a big difference in access. Consequently, the number of interstates is used as an access measure.

19. Paul Larmer, "Can a Colorado Ski County Say Enough Is Enough?" *High Country News* 28–3 (February 19, 1996): 1, 8–11.

20. Ray Rasker and Dennis Glick, "Footloose Entrepreneurs: Pioneers of the New West?" *Illahee* 10 (1994): 34–43; and Gundars Rudzitis and Harley E. Johansen, "Migration into Western Wilderness Counties: Causes and Consequences," *Western Wildlands* 15 (1989): 19–23.

21. U.S. Department of Commerce, Bureau of the Census, *Census of Housing. Detailed Housing Characteristics* (Washington, D.C.: U.S. Government Printing Office, 1993).

22. The correlation coefficient between per capita income and the share of transfer income for 1997 is -.73, as noted in chapter 2. Across counties, as the transfer income share rises, per capita income falls.

23. Thomas M. Power, "Ecosystem Preservation and the Economy in the Greater Yellowstone Area," *Conservation Biology* 5 (1991): 395–404; and Joan Kendall and Bruce W. Pigozzi, "Nonemployment Income and the Economic Base of Michigan Counties: 1959–1986," *Growth and Change* 25 (1994): 51–74.

24. Sam B. Warner Jr., *Streetcar Suburbs: The Process of Growth in Boston, 1870–1900* (New York: Atheneum, 1974); and Jackson, *Crabgrass Frontier*.

25. A regression equation with the log of per capita income as the dependent variable and the change in population density between 1985 and 1997 as the dependent variable indicates that population growth and relatively high per capita incomes correspond. The regression equation shows that a change in density by one person per thousand acres increases the per capita income by .63 percent. For counties at the mean increase of 6.1 in population per thousand acres, the regression equation predicts that per capita income increased by 3.6 percent. For the county with the largest growth in population density equal to 76.7 persons per acre, per capita income is predicted by the equation to increase by 46 percent. Population growth and income in the rural mountain West are occurring together. The regression equation for the log of income per capita (PCPI) for 1997 is as follows:

log PCPI = 9.827 + .00634Dchange,

where Dchange is the increase of population density from 1985 to 1997. The t-statistic for Dchange is 3.51.

26. Land trusts are voluntary conservation organizations concerned with environmental and ecological problems caused by human settlement.

27. An important issue worthy of mention is the disconnection between place of employment and residential location in some mountain counties. Because of a high concentrations of relatively wealthy homeowners in some high mountain communities, property prices and rents have been pushed out of reach of relatively low paid services and retail sector employees. As a consequence, many have to commute long distances to get work. See Lisa Jones, "El Nuevo West: The Region's New Pioneers Buoy the Economy and Live on the Edge," *High Country News* 28–24 (December 23, 1996): 1, 6–11; and Larmer, "Can a Colorado Ski County Say Enough Is Enough?" for discussions of this issue.

28. Edwin S. Mills and Bruce W. Hamilton, *Urban Economics*, 5th ed. (New York: Harper Collins, 1994), 135.

29. The relationship between two variables is assumed to be linear. The variance of the dependent variable on the vertical axis is the same for all values of the independent variable on the horizontal axis. And the values of the variable on the horizontal axis are independent of one another.

30. Distance is highway miles from the most populated urban place in a county to the nearest regional urban center. See note 5.

31. The mean, standard deviation, and maximum are respectively 2.8 percent, 3.9 percent, and 21.4 percent in a sample of 70, suggesting a fair amount of variation in the data. The rest of the data is not available because of disclosure problems. Due to excessive disclosure problems in the 1985 sample, a regression for that year is not reported.

32. These figures are simply the size of the coefficients in percentage terms on the number of interstates in the regression equations.

33. Again, these figures are the size of the regression coefficients in percentage terms on the number of colleges and universities.

34. Rudzitis and Johansen, "Migration into Western Wilderness Counties;" and Kevin T. Duffy-Deno, "Economic Effect of Endangered Species Preservation in the Non-Metropolitan West," *Growth and Change* 28 (1997): 263–288.

35. These figures are the size of the regression coefficients in percentage terms for ski areas in table 3A.5.

36. Duffy-Deno, "Economic Effect of Endangered Species Preservation."

37. These figures are based on the regression coefficients in table 3A.5. In 1990 the share of vacation homes in the housing stock ranged as high as 71.4 percent, and in 1997 the share of commuting income ranged as high as 57.0 percent.

4

~

The Cumulative Ecological
Consequences of Mountain West
Economic Development

The message of the previous chapters is conceptually simple. New kinds of technology and rising affluence appear to be driving population growth and residential development in the rural mountain West. As with most human endeavors, the spreading of population to mountain West counties and the sprawling of development over the landscape are likely to have environmental consequences. Because the effects are often long lasting or even permanent, human-induced environmental change is frequently a cumulative process. In the new mountain West economy, we are not starting with a clean slate. Grizzly bear habitat, for instance, has been reduced by clear-cut logging because of the old economy, and to further reduce or fragment such habitat through housing development will guarantee grizzly bear extinction in key areas of the northern Rocky Mountains. If we faced a pristine, untouched environment to begin with, then the ecological effects of such development would be much less. Consequently, new forms of disturbance will add to the effects of the old.

Given the cumulative nature of environmental disturbance, the starting point for a new source of environmental stress is not a pristine natural environment, but one that has already been modified by the human hand. We therefore need to have a clear picture of the starting point to be able to judge the significance of the latest type of environmental disturbance. The goals of this chapter are consequently twofold: First, the environmental history of the mountain West will be briefly reviewed to establish the degree of cumulative and permanent environmental change that has occurred historically under the regime of traditional economic arrangements. This will constitute the point of departure for any further disturbances that could result as a consequence of rural development. Second, the potential environmental effects of population spreading and sprawl will be addressed in preparation for considering the specific effects of residential and related development on rare and imperiled species in the next chapter. The final goal is to arrive at a preliminary judgement about the effects of new forms of economic development on the flora and fauna of the mountain West.

This will set the stage for the final topics of the book. In chapter 6 we will consider the impact of mountain West growth on Sierra Nevada voter attitudes toward the loss of open space and natural habitats and the willingness of local voters to institute measures that control and restrict growth and development. In chapter 7 we will consider whether the land trust movement in the mountain West is in fact a response to environmental decline induced by new forms of economic development and resulting local concerns about losses in natural habitats and biotic diversity. In chapter 8 we will use concepts from environmental ethics to explore the kinds of values that would lead society to be concerned about the effects of development on biological diversity. Presuming an ethical obligation to preserve native plant and animal species, concepts from conservation biology will be used as the basis for determining and justifying new patterns in human settlement consistent with the goal of preserving biodiversity in rural areas generally and the rural mountain West specifically. In the last chapter of the book, specific strategies for controlling rural sprawl will be laid out and evaluated.

THE MOUNTAIN WEST NATURAL ENVIRONMENT

The Sierra Nevada

The Sierra Nevada Mountains stretch from northern California near Mt. Lassen in a southeasterly direction for about 360 miles into southern California. The mountain range is for all intents and purposes a massive granite block tilted so that its eastern slope rises abruptly from the Great Basin and its western slope rises gently from the Sacramento and San Joaquin Valleys. This tilting and uplifting are the result of larger tectonic processes created by the collision of the Pacific and North American crustal plates. The initial uplifting began some 70 million years ago and was completed with the greatest amount of uplifting taking place between 1 and 11 million years ago. The mountains north of Lake Tahoe form a rolling upland with elevations seldom exceeding 9,000 feet, while to the south the alpine High Sierra (8,000+ feet in elevation) occurs with the highest peak, Mount Whitney, reaching 14,495 feet. The Sierra Nevada Mountains have been shaped over a geologic time scale by uplifting, erosion, volcanism, and glaciation. Glaciers in the Ice Age did much to shape the Sierras as we know them today with their high mountain tarns and cirques, U-shaped river valleys, and waterfalls created by hanging valleys where large glaciers have carved out valley floors well below tributary stream elevations.[1]

The Sierra Nevada climate features relatively warm, wet winters and comparatively cool, dry summers. The climate at particular localities can vary extensively because of the wide range of elevations and latitudes in the Sierra. In the summer the upper altitudes provide a respite from the hot lowlands on either side of the Sierras. The westerly flow of storms from the Pacific brings moisture to the western slopes of the Sierras and provides the mountains with an ample snowpack in winter. In general, as elevation rises, moisture increases. The eastern slope, however, is relatively arid, lying in a rain shadow created by the mountain crests. Little moisture falls in the Sierras during the summer except at high elevations where upslope air movements cause cooling and the condensing of moisture to form rain.[2]

Water flows divide the Sierra Nevada into twenty-four separate watersheds. Water moves either to the east into the Great Basin where it evaporates, or to the west into the Sacramento and San Joaquin Valleys and ultimately the Pacific Ocean. Stream flows are highest in the spring, when streams are fed by a melting snowpack, and reach their lows in the summer, once the snowpack has melted, and again in the winter, because of higher elevation freezing. The lakes of the High Sierra formed in cirques and tarns and are often naturally "fishless" because they have a short ice-free season and lack sufficient minerals needed for the growth of algae and other organisms at the bottom of the fish food chain.[3]

Plants occupy the base of the Sierra Nevada food web and provide not only sustenance for other organisms, but also habitat niches. A tree, for example, is not only a food source for birds but can also be a perch and a nesting site. The distribution of wildlife in a locality closely parallels the distribution of vegetation. For this reason, ecologists focus on plant communities when describing landscapes and generally refer to specific plants that dominate in naming those communities. The distribution of vegetation and plants follows elevation-determined gradients in the Sierra Nevada, as it does in any mountainous region. On the west side of the Sierras, moisture tends to increase and temperature tends to decrease with elevation, resulting in vegetation belts that parallel the northwest-southeast orientation of the mountain range. Beginning at the edge of the Central Valley (Sacramento and San Joaquin river valleys) and moving west, the foothill landscape is dominated by a mixture of oaks, pines, and dense shrublands called chaparral. Extensive natural grasslands supported large populations of Tule elk in the foothills region at the time of Euro-American settlement. The foothill landscape extends up to approximately 3,000 feet elevation in the north and 5,000 feet in the south. Above the foothill zone extends a transitional mixed conifer zone with varying combinations of Douglas fir, ponderosa pine, white fir, sugar pine, and incense cedar. Beginning about 5,500 feet above sea level in the north and 8,000 feet in the south, the mixed conifer zone gives way to a fir belt, dominated at lower elevations by white fir and at higher elevations by red fir. The High Sierras are capped by a subalpine zone, with such species as lodgepole pine, whitebark pine, and mountain hemlock, and finally an alpine zone mostly composed of low shrubs and cushion plants. On the more arid and steeper east side, a sagebrush belt extends up to 4,200 feet in the north and 7,000 feet in the south, and above that is found a mixed conifer zone where Jeffrey pine is often prevalent. The fir zone tends to be less extensive on the eastside in comparison to the westside. Many animal species depend on the presence of large, old trees, snags, and logs that characterize late successional or old-growth forest habitats. The foothill woodlands also support a diverse array of animal species and provide a critical seasonal habitat for breeding by birds. The forested landscape is broken up by grasslands and mountain meadows that serve as important wildlife habitats on both the east and west slopes.[4]

These broad vegetation bands are dissected by streams and rivers that not only shape the landscape but also provide habitat for a variety of plant and animal species in both the water and adjoining riparian areas. Although there are 40 species of fish native to the Sierra Nevada, fish were largely absent from waters above 6,000 feet elevation prior to introductions of exotic species that began as early as the nineteenth century. Before these introductions, high country streams and lakes were dominated by frogs and invertebrates. Of Sierra Nevada plant species, around 17 percent are associated with or dependent on riparian or wet areas; the same is the case for around 21 percent of vertebrate species. Riparian woodlands are especially important as habitat for birds and mammals.[5]

Disturbance and succession are critical processes causing substantial variation in the composition and character of vegetation distribution over the landscape in the Sierra Nevada. While wind storms and diseases are key agents of disturbance, fire is probably the dominant form of disturbance because of long dry periods in the summer and the presence of lightening as an ignition source. Prior to Euro-American settlement, fire was a common occurrence in the Sierras, a phenomenon to which many species have adapted. Fire is a particularly important phenomenon in chaparral where some plants produce new shoots from root crowns and some seeds germinate only after fires. Fire-return intervals are not available for chaparral, but it is believed that fire was very common in this type of plant community. Presettlement average fire-return intervals for different forest types have been estimated from fire-scar records in tree rings. Low elevation blue oak forests have a pre-1900 fire-return interval of only eight years while the interval for somewhat higher elevation ponderosa pine forests is around 11 years. The thick bark of the ponderosa pine protects it from low-intensity surface layer fires. These fires in turn limit the buildup of brush and small trees that can serve as fuel for more catastrophic stand-replacing fires. The end result of this fire pattern is an open park-like structure for these forests with well-spaced large, old ponderosa pines. High-intensity stand-replacing fires no doubt occurred in pine forests prior to settlement, but they were less common than they are today. The somewhat higher elevation white fir forests were also characterized by frequent low-intensity burns with occasional high-severity fires. As the presettlement fire-return interval lengthened with elevation, the presence of white fir in the over-

story increased. Because white fir seedlings are less tolerant of fire than ponderosa pine, the fir does better in cooler locations with longer fire-return intervals. While fire was historically important in the higher elevation red fir zone, its
occurrence was less frequent than at lower elevations.[6]

The Colorado and Montana Rockies

The Sierra Nevada Mountains are relatively simple in form and self-contained,
at least in comparison to the Rockies. The Rocky Mountains are composed of
a sprawling complex of uplifts created by powerful tectonic forces unleashed by
the confluence of the Pacific and North American crustal plates. Stretching
from Montana in the north to New Mexico in the south, by the time they
reach Colorado, the Rockies have been displaced several hundred miles to the
east. From north to south in Colorado, the Rockies widen and are bordered to
the east by the high plains and to the west by the Colorado plateau. The mountains themselves form a hodgepodge of ranges and valleys including several
large high mountain parks. Much of the mountain-building in this area began
about 70 million years ago with a period of uplifting that caused structural
arching and doming of the landscape along with surface faulting and volcanic
activity. After a period of erosion lasting some 30 million years, a second period of uplifting brought the Rockies to their present height. In the meantime,
rivers have cut narrow undulating canyons through the uplifted landscape, and
glacial activity has shaped the mountains at the higher elevations.[7] The Montana Rockies are drained ultimately by the Snake and Columbia Rivers heading west, and the Yellowstone and Missouri Rivers heading east. The Colorado
Rockies are drained to the east by the South Platte and the Arkansas Rivers,
to the west by the Colorado River and its various tributaries, and to the south
by the Rio Grande.

For most of the interior West, aridity is a dominant feature of the landscape.
Much of the eastern two-thirds of Montana and the eastern half of Colorado gets
less than eight inches of rain a year. The mountains in these states, however, are
"islands of moisture."[8] As one moves up in elevation or up in latitude, temperature drops. As air temperature declines, the ability of air masses to hold moisture
diminishes and, as a result, precipitation increases. This precipitation is greater
in the high mountains and higher latitudes (i.e., Montana) than it is in the lower
mountains and latitudes (i.e., Colorado). As the prevailing westerlies of the Pacific collide with the Rockies, air is forced upward and cools, causing a reduction
in its moisture holding capacity and an increase in precipitation. Much of this
precipitation falls in winter, creating an all-important moisture reservoir in the
form of a snowpack. As any hiker knows, not all precipitation falls in winter;
summer afternoon thunderstorms are common events in the Rocky Mountain
high country. The mountains form a rain shadow causing precipitation to be especially scarce on the eastern slopes and in the Great Plains.

Vegetation and plant community patterns in the Rockies follow the usual mountainous moisture and temperature gradients oriented to elevation. In Colorado the mountains are bordered to the west by the desert of the Great Basin and to the east by the shortgrass prairie of the Great Plains. With elevation increases, grassland or desert quickly give way to shrubby vegetation often dominated by pinon and juniper. Sagebrush, mountain mahogany, and oak are also common components of the foothills vegetation. Beginning at about 6,000 feet elevation, a transition zone of ponderosa pine begins and continues up to about 9,000 feet in Colorado. This zone shades into forests of aspen and lodgepole pine which dominate to about 10,000 feet where the subalpine zone begins with its forests of Engelmann spruce and subalpine fir. At higher elevations and on cooler north facing slopes, Douglas fir replaces ponderosa pine and in some cases white fir occurs instead of Douglas fir. On the drier slopes at high elevations lodgepole pine replaces aspen and bristlecone and limber pine replace spruce and fir. In Montana on the west side of the continental divide, the foothills shrub zone is absent and the montane forest zone is dominated by Douglas fir with ponderosa pine being more prevalent on the drier sites. Western larch is an aggressive fire pioneer, but is eventually overtopped by the successional dominant, Douglas fir. On the east side of the continental divide, Douglas fir is relatively uncommon and lodgepole pine is more prevalent. Where disturbances have occurred at high elevations, dense stands of lodgepole pine usually dominate, crowding out other varieties. Species found in the subalpine zone in Montana include subalpine fir, Engelmann spruce, lodgepole pine, whitebark pine, and subalpine larch.[9] Grand fir often occurs at elevations just above Douglas fir. At the lower elevations, along the many streams and rivers that dissect the Rockies, riparian forests occur with their characteristic cottonwoods and willows. Riparian wetlands are also common and constitute important wildlife habitats.[10]

As in the Sierra Nevadas, fire is generally the dominant form of disturbance to forests in the Rocky Mountains. Ponderosa pine forests, in the absence of fire exclusion prior to settlement, had an open, park-like quality created by frequent low-intensity burns that removed understory vegetation but did little harm to the fire-resistant ponderosa pine. The same was probably true for Douglas fir forests, although in such forests stand-replacing, high-intensity fires were somewhat more common. In the absence of fire exclusion, Douglas fir forests tend to contain more ponderosa pine, and with fire exclusion, the more shade tolerant Douglas fir fills in the understory, eventually becoming the dominant species. The resulting fuel buildup increases the probability of high-intensity fires that result in stand replacement and the restarting of forest succession. In these forests, lodgepole pine often gets established first after stand-replacing fires because the fire itself opens the serotinous cone and allows the seeds within the cone to spread. Eventually, in the forest succession process, lodgepole pine is overtopped by Douglas fir, although in some areas lodgepole pine appears to replace itself as a consequence of periodic high-intensity fire.[11]

POST-SETTLEMENT HUMAN IMPACTS
ON THE MOUNTAIN WEST ENVIRONMENT

The Sierra Nevada Mountains

The mountain landscape in the Sierra Nevada has been profoundly altered since the Euro-American settlement beginning at the midpoint of the nineteenth century. These alterations have occurred primarily as a consequence of the activities of those industries that traditionally operate in mountain landscapes—mining, timber harvesting, grazing, and water diversion for irrigation and hydroelectric generation. More recently, recreational activities and residential and related development have contributed to environmental change. The presence of human activities in mountain landscapes has resulted in still another practice that leads to major changes in the landscape—the suppression of wildfire.

Mining

The California Gold Rush, initiated with the discovery of gold in 1848, marked not only the beginning significant settlement in the state, but also a major transformation of the Sierra Nevada landscape. Early mining involved simple panning in streams and the use of sluice boxes resulting in fairly minor modifications to streambeds. The yield from this type of mining quickly diminished and larger scale, more capital intensive forms of mining soon began. Gold is found in two forms: placer and lode deposits. Gold in lodes is still embedded in the rock, while gold in placers has been freed from rocks through weathering and usually occurs in gravels after being moved and deposited through the forces of mechanical and hydraulic erosion. Once the placers in streams were exhausted, California miners turned to gravels buried in the hills above streambeds, using powerful hydraulic nozzles to dislodge gold-bearing materials. Needless to say, this form of mining permanently altered the landscape. Stream channels were plugged by sand and debris, hills were permanently scarred, and stream systems were permanently modified with the construction of flumes and reservoirs to redirect water to mining operations. Winter and spring flooding carried tons of debris downstream to foothill and valley communities causing devastating flood damage. Many streams became devoid of fish life as a consequence of mining operations. Although streambanks have recovered their vegetation, floodplain forests have been permanently transformed into expanses of dredger tailings lacking plant life. Erosion of fine sediments from hydraulic mine sites continues, and a permanent increase has occurred in the amount of sand and gravel deposited in stream valley bottoms. Each of these phenomena degrades habitat for native aquatic species.[12] The most enduring problem created by mining is the acidification of surface and groundwater. The exposure of sulfide rock to water results in the creation of sulfuric acid and the formation of bacteria that speeds up the acidification process.

As rainwater percolates through old mines, waste rock, and tailings, it acidifies and finds its way to local lakes and streams where it can be tolerated by only a few species adapted to acidic conditions. Moreover, acidified water is highly efficient at liberating toxic heavy metals, such as cadmium, copper, lead, mercury, and zinc, as it leaches through mining wastes and tailings piles. The Iron Mountain mine in Shasta County, abandoned 30 years ago, emits one-fourth of the entire national discharge of copper and zinc for industrial and municipal sources into the Sacramento River annually.[13]

Timber Harvesting and Fire Suppression

The presence of mining led to the creation of the logging and lumber industries in the Sierra Nevada. Hydraulic mining required lumber for the construction of flumes, and lode mining needed considerable timber for railroad ties and for supports in miles of tunnels, and shafts. In addition, lumber was needed for construction of mining buildings and the mining towns themselves. Wood was the primary fuel used to fire boilers to run mining machinery. As a consequence, the landscape around mines and mining towns in the Sierra Nevada foothills was frequently denuded of any standing timber. The early timber industry also supplied ties and other wood needed for railroad construction in the Sierra Nevada and elsewhere. The era of railroad logging began in the 1880s with railroads not only hauling lumber to distant markets, but also transporting logs from previously inaccessible sites to mills, thus opening up new areas to timber exploitation. After World War II, timber harvesting shifted from predominantly lower elevation sites on private lands to higher elevation sites on public lands. Old-growth timber on private lands was fast disappearing at the same time the demand for lumber was rapidly expanding as a consequence of the postwar housing boom. This brought considerable pressure on the U.S. Forest Service to increase its allowable cut not only in the Sierra Nevada, but throughout the western United States.[14]

Timber harvesting has resulted in enduring changes in Sierra Nevada habitats. It has contributed to the reduction in the extent of foothill woodlands and forests, a habitat type that is poorly represented in protected areas such as parks and wilderness. While old-growth forests occur mainly on public lands, the amount and quality have been diminished over the years as a consequence of timber harvesting practices. Although clearcutting is not as commonly used in the Sierra Nevada as elsewhere, the removal of large older trees has reduced the amount of forest that can be classified as old-growth and has also reduced the number of trees that potentially serve as the source for the development of old-growth forest characteristics, such as large snags and large, downed logs. These are the habitat characteristics that old-growth dependent species utilize (i.e., cavity nesting birds). The westside, mid-elevation mixed conifer forests and the eastside pine forests have suffered the greatest losses in old growth, and old growth has a relatively low representation in protected areas such as state and national parks and designated wilderness. The continuing presence of logging roads, used originally to move timber out of the woods, creates erosion problems and increases sediment loads to local streams that reduce habitat quality for fishes and other organisms.[15] The absence of large, old trees as a source of stream shading and woody debris also reduces aquatic habitat quality, particularly for salmonids. Salmon and trout require a pool and riffle stream structure that is often created by the presence of large downed logs in streams.

Closely connected to the issue of logging, as a force behind environmental change, is fire suppression. Fire is an integral component of ecological processes in the Sierra Nevada, as already noted. While there is considerable disagreement over the details of pre-settlement fire cycles, there is little disagreement that fires were important. Some researchers argue that fires in forested areas were generally of low intensity and burned ground layer grasses, shrubs, and small trees while creating open, park-like forests. Other researchers suggest that high-intensity stand-replacing fires and thick, impenetrable forests were more likely the rule. Sierran forests were probably a mix of the two with varying degrees of openness. As a general rule, fire frequency was probably greater in the foothills and lower elevation montane forests than at higher elevations. When fire did occur at higher elevations, it was more likely to be intense enough to be stand replacing.

The policy of fire suppression was adopted in the early 1900s and resulted in a significant reduction in the area burned. As a consequence of the elimination of most low- to moderate-intensity fires, the composition and structure of most Sierra Nevada vegetation have changed, particularly at lower and middle elevations. Coniferous forests have become denser, with increased younger and relatively small trees, and have shifted in composition toward fire sensitive and shade tolerant species. In other words, low-intensity fires are no longer serving the function of clearing the understory periodically of woody fuels and leaving behind the larger, fire-resistant trees.

While the annual acres burned remains stable in the Sierra Nevada, the intensity of fires has been on the increase. With a thick understory and a "fire ladder" of small trees, fire is able to move readily into the crown of large, old trees, resulting in high-intensity, stand-replacing fires. Fire suppression has been more effective in heavily developed areas because of the priority given to protecting property, and fire fighters have had more success dealing with low- to medium-intensity fires than with high-intensity fast moving fires associated with extremely dry weather.[16]

Fire suppression has probably had its most profound ecological effects in foothills chaparral, lower elevation ponderosa pine forests, and mid-elevation mixed conifer forests. Chaparral shrubs are highly flammable, but they are also adapted to fire by either sprouting massively from root bases or producing a large crop of fire-resistant and fire-stimulated seeds that germinate following a fire. Species diversity is highest in chaparral after a fire, suggesting that fire is needed to maintain a high level of diversity. Ponderosa pine is a shade-intolerant, fire-adapted species that does best under a regime of frequent, low-intensity fires. Mature trees are able to survive most fires by virtue of their thick bark, deep roots, and low-flammability crown structure. Ponderosa pine seeds do best in open mineral soils prepared by fire, and well-spaced seedlings and saplings are often able to survive low-intensity fires. Fire suppression in ponderosa pine forests has increased the density of unthinned seedlings, shrubs, and hardwoods. Forest composition is shifting in the direction of hardwoods because of their ability to sprout vigorously after stand-replacing fires. In mixed conifer forests at somewhat higher elevations, the fire-sensitive, shade-tolerant white firs are becoming more prevalent as a consequence of fire suppression relative to the fire tolerant ponderosa pine and Douglas fir. These forests are also somewhat more dense than otherwise as a consequence of fire suppression and have a less diverse ground and shrub layer as a result.[17]

Grazing

Just as timber harvesting received its initial stimulus from mining, so did grazing. The Sierra Nevada meadows were extensively utilized by the sheep industry prior to 1900. Initially, sheep were driven from New Mexico and southern California to foothill mining towns to be sold for consumption. After 1860, low elevation meadows were used as winter pastures and sheep were driven to high elevation meadows for summer grazing. Complaints of overgrazing in the high meadows were common, but grazing was brought under regulation only after the U.S. Forest Service was formed to oversee the newly created forest reserves in the Sierras. The Forest Service favored granting grazing permits to local ranchers as opposed to "gypsy" sheep bands. Gradually sheep were replaced by cattle, resulting in increased damage to riparian zones.[18] Poor grazing practices have contributed to the conversion of Sierra foothills from perennial to exotic annual grasslands. Overgrazing has also resulted in soil compaction, increased erosion, and damage to riparian areas from the destruction of riparian vegetation and reductions in water tables caused by bank erosion and stream downcutting. Damage to riparian areas, however, can be reversed by limiting grazing and undertaking streambank restoration projects.[19]

Dams and Irrigation

Not as easily reversible is the reshaping of the Sierra Nevada system of streams and rivers that began in the mining era. The mining industry constructed some 6,000 miles of ditches and flumes to direct water from higher elevations to hydraulic mining operations in the Sierra foothills. After debris flows from mining buried thousands of acres of farmland in the Central Valley, an 1884 court injunction against the deposit of mining debris in streams brought hydraulic mining to an end for all practical purposes. The legacy of ditches and flumes left by the mining industry was well suited for two other uses, agricultural irrigation and hydroelectric power generation. There are currently 490 medium-to-large dams in the Sierra Nevada with slightly more than half their reservoir capacity devoted to irrigation and the remainder to urban water supply and hydroelectric power. Despite the protests of John Muir and the newly formed Sierra Club, the City of San Francisco was able to get permission from the federal government to build the Hetch Hetchy Dam for the purpose of supplying water and electric power to itself.[20] The result was the inundation of the beautiful Hetch Hetchy Valley.

Dams have a variety of ecological impacts, including a loss of stream and riparian habitats from inundation by reservoirs, altered downstream flow regimes and sediment loads, and a loss of spawning habitat for salmon. Flood control, as a consequence of water storage in reservoirs, reduces the extent of the downstream floodplain and riparian habitat. Because sediment drops out of reservoir waters, downstream flows are sediment starved and thus have a greater capacity to erode streambanks and cause a downward cutting of the stream channel and a lowering of the downstream water table. Dams have largely severed salmon populations from their upstream spawning habitats for several species that now appear on state and federal endangered species lists.[21]

These are not all the consequences of the traditional forms of economic activity in the Sierra Nevada Mountains, but they are the most important ones. Some of the ecological consequences of mining, timber harvesting, fire suppression, grazing, and dams are reversible, and some recovery of disturbed landscapes has occurred, but much change to the natural environment in the last 150 years appears to be irreversible. Consequently, further changes to the natural landscape resulting from a spreading of population into the Sierras will be added to those that have already occurred, and the process of environmental change will be cumulative.

The Colorado and Montana Rockies

Mining

The patterns and effects of settlement and development in the Sierra Nevada and the Rocky Mountains have much in common, although settlement began later in the Rockies. At the midpoint of the nineteenth century, California was more accessible than the Rockies, and the California Gold Rush drew settlers who might have gone elsewhere. The mountain-building process created the resources that ultimately attracted settlement and stimulated the creation of the traditional extractive industries. Heat generated by the collision of tectonic plates caused subsurface rock to melt and convert to magma that pushed into the cracks and fissures of the rocks above. Water in the magma was expelled upward carrying minerals with it and depositing them as veins along the edges of surrounding rocks. This created lode deposits of gold, silver, copper, lead, and other valuable minerals and provided the source for placer deposits created through the forces of erosion and deposition.[22] The upthrusted mountains created "islands of moisture" by forcing the prevailing winds to move upslope and release the precipitation necessary for the development of a rich forested habitat and the snowpack needed to provide year-round stream flows to the arid landscape below.[23]

Mining in the Colorado Rockies began in 1858 with the discovery of a placer deposit near the current city of Denver. While this deposit played out quickly, it set off the rush to find gold in Colorado. With placer deposits in any given location being rapidly exploited and short-lived, the boom and bust in placers moved in a wavelike fashion through the mountains of Colorado. Lode gold mining proved to be more enduring, although it was inhibited by heavy winter snows that often lasted into late spring at the high elevations, frequent rock slides, and gold that was bound up in difficult-to-process, sulfur-rich rock. Railroad construction in the key mining regions set off a second boom in mining by easing the task of shipping out processed minerals and bringing in needed supplies.[24] Roughly two decades after the discovery of gold in Colorado, the silver boom began and was centered in Leadville. Silver mining caused Colorado to become the leading mining state in the country in 1880.[25]

The environmental effects of mining in Colorado were perhaps not as extensive as those in California, but they were substantial nonetheless. Early placer mining left hummocks of discarded cobble, but little more. Temporary dams constructed to dig out downstream creek bottoms with a rush of water were more destructive. Hydraulic mining in Colorado was as damaging as it was in California, but it was less utilized. Dredging of stream bottoms with large floating dredges often divided a single channel into several and caused flat valleys to be dissected by parallel ridges. The most obvious legacy left behind from lode mining is the large tailing piles, although some have eroded and more or less blended with the landscape. A modern problem from old lode mining operations is the leaching of toxic heavy metals from tailing piles and closed mines. The mining towns themselves reshaped the local environment. Often they were located in narrow valleys along creeks that either were filled in or became ditches that drained away the town's wastes. The countryside around the towns would often be depleted of wildlife by hunters.

Many of the landscape's scars created by mining are less apparent today as a consequence of recovery. In some cases, streams have recovered their original form, cleaning out accumulated sediments and redistributing piles of gravel through hydraulic action. Again, the one serious problem that remains is the toxic leachate from mining operations that continues to enter groundwater and streams and rivers.[26] Leadville, Colorado, to this day continues to be threatened by an old tailing pond at California Gulch that, until a recent cleanup effort by the Environmental Protection Agency, leaked cadmium, copper, lead, and other toxic metals into groundwater, local streams, and a drainage tunnel leading to the Arkansas River where toxins entered the river at a rate of 210 tons per year.[27]

The placer mining boom and bust cycle operated in Montana much in the same way as it did in California and Colorado, although in didn't get started until 1862–1863 when major strikes occurred near Bannack and Virginia City. While placer mining lasted somewhat longer in Montana than Colorado with a longer string of more enduring discoveries, it was eventually replaced by the more capital-intensive lode mining. Although silver mining rose to importance in Montana much as it had in Colorado, copper was to be the mineral behind Montana's early economic development. Copper smelting proved to be a difficult and costly undertaking, requiring large amounts of capital and, consequently, dominance by large business organizations. By the mid-1880s, Butte, Montana had surged ahead of Leadville, Colorado, as the center of western mining. Butte's copper mines and the Anaconda Copper Company dominated Montana politics beginning in the first decade of the twentieth century and for several decades to come.[28] In 1910 copper mining employed 60 percent of Montana's wage earners.[29]

The effects of placer mining on the natural environment in Montana were similar to those in Colorado. Streams were dredged in both Montana and Colorado to unearth gold in streambeds that simpler methods used earlier bypassed.[30] The big difference between the two states is found in the environmental impact of copper mining on the Montana landscape. Copper mining required large smelting facilities that created smoke heavily laden with sulfur, arsenic, and toxic heavy metals. Partly to alleviate the smoke problem, the world's largest copper smelter was located in a separate town, Anaconda, some distance away from the mines at Butte.[31] Smelter smoke created acids that damaged vegetation and agricultural crops downwind.[32] While the effects of smelter smoke in the mountain West have declined with increased regulation and smelter shutdowns, the problems of toxic and acidic leachate from tailing piles remain. In Montana, 20,000 to 26,000 hard rock mining sites pollute some 1,300 miles of streams and rivers.[33] The legacy of mining in the state is symbolized by Butte's massive Berkeley Pit, an open pit mine that has proved highly efficient but also highly visible.[34] The priority of mineral rights over surface property rights is clear in Butte where open pits crept up to Butte's business district prior to the closure of mining operations in 1980. The Clark Fork River between Butte and Missoula, a 125-mile stretch, includes four contiguous Superfund sites where a variety of toxic chemicals migrate into surface waters from millions of tons of smelter and mining wastes.[35]

Timber Harvest and Fire Suppression

To this day the forests of the Colorado Rockies reflect the consequences of mining and grazing, the two most important of the traditional extractive industries in Colorado's history. Early mining in Colorado, as in California, was a lumber-intensive industry. Timber was even more important in the Colorado Rockies because of the greater emphasis on mining lodes instead of placers. An abundance of timber was needed for supports in the many tunnels and shafts found in the typical mine; timber was a major source of fuel for mineral processing plants in the early days; and the mining towns absorbed considerable timber in both construction and heating. Old pictures of mining towns typically show a landscape denuded of trees. Douglas fir forests are much less extensive today than historically because of cutting for use in mining and railroad construction and also because of fires started purposely and accidentally by miners. Although reforestation has occurred in old mining areas, lodgepole pine or aspen instead of Douglas fir tend to dominate. While subalpine spruce fir forests are relatively pristine today, they did suffer historically in some areas from fires started by miners to clear mining sites.[36]

Ponderosa pine forests also suffered at the hands of early settlers in the mountains who cut timber for mining or other uses and cleared homestead sites. Many of these sites were abandoned and later the cattle industry moved into these areas to graze the understory of the relatively open ponderosa stands. Because ponderosa seedlings are trampled by cattle, grazing can have the long-term effect of converting a forest into a meadow as the large, old trees succumb to age without a new generation to replace them. Fire suppression in recent years has also altered the character of ponderosa forests. As in the Sierra Nevada, these forests historically were maintained in an open, park-like status by frequent low-intensity fires that burned the ground layer and kept the understory relatively free of shrubs and small trees. Today, with fire suppression, the understories of ponderosa pine forests are denser than in the past and face increased susceptibility to crown fires as a consequence of the greater availability of fuel.[37] Grazing contributed to the effects of fire suppression by removing grasses that served as the principal fuel for the spreading of low-intensity fires. The similar history of extractive industry development in the Sierra Nevada and Rocky mountains has left behind similar problems.

Two forest types that have benefited in Colorado from human activity are aspen and lodgepole pine. Both occur roughly from 8,000 to 10,000 feet elevation, and both are successional forests, ultimately being replaced by longer-lived and more shade tolerant species such as Douglas fir, Engelmann spruce, or subalpine fir. Both aspen and lodgepole pine invade after major disturbances and establish themselves quickly. Fire causes seeds to break free of long dormant serotinous cones for the lodgepole pine, and aspen has the capacity to expand quickly after a fire from root suckers. As a consequence of both logging and fire in climax forest types, both aspen and lodgepole pine are now more extensive than they were prior to Euro-American settlement.[38]

The forests of the Montana Rockies were subjected to exploitation in support of mining operations just as in Colorado, but they also supplied a relatively substantial lumber industry serving a larger market. Apart from timber depredations on public lands, prior to World War II the Montana timber harvest came largely from privately owned lands, a relatively large proportion of which was owned by mining companies.[39] Just as in the Sierra Nevada, timber harvesting on the public lands in Montana accelerated dramatically after World War II to feed the postwar housing boom. With exhaustion of timber on private lands and expanding demand for lumber, the pressure was intense enough to increase the harvest from the public lands. Harvesting peaked at 1.5 billion board feet in 1970 and has declined since then to less than 500 million board feet. Although the harvest levels selected by the U.S. Forest Service were justified using the rhetoric of sustained yield, in practice the peak levels of timber harvest were unsustainable. In addition to dramatically increasing the harvest, the Forest Service also shifted the harvesting system from selective cutting to large-scale clearcutting. The result was serious erosion problems and the clogging of streams causing stress to rare bull trout populations in the northern Rockies. Clearcuts also reduced critical grizzly bear habitat and eliminated large blocks of old-growth forests that are habitat for such species as the Northern Goshawk, Townsend's Warbler, Pileated Woodpecker, Black-backed Woodpecker, Vaux's Swift, northern flying squirrel, and Townsend's big-eared bat.[40]

Grazing

As it did in the Sierra Nevada, cattle grazing and ranching have reshaped the natural environmental in Colorado. The large, open high mountain parks of the Colorado Rockies have been ecologically altered as a result of human use. Settlers cut ponderosa pine to expand park meadows and increase the amount of land available for grazing. The ecology of these meadows has in turn been changed, however, with the introduction of exotic grasses and weeds. Human use of high mountain meadows has also resulted in the degradation of species-rich riparian ecosystems. Settlers often removed willow thickets and converted them to hay meadows accelerating streambank erosion; cattle have frequently trampled the vegetation and tree seedlings preventing restoration of riparian forests that stabilize streambanks; grazing has increased the presence of weedy species; and transportation routes have been established along streams, fragmenting and reducing riparian habitat.[41]

Just as in California, high mountain meadows historically supported cattle and sheep grazing in Montana, although Montana sheep grazing has diminished since the 1930s. In the Madison Valley located in southwestern Montana, ranchers settled on private lands in the valley bottom and in the summer grazed their livestock in the upland meadows on national forest lands. This pattern resulted partly as a consequence of overgrazing in the valley bottom and on the surrounding bench lands. Mountain meadows and valleys both suffered degraded riparian habitats that reduced downstream fish populations. Competitive grazers such as elk and antelope also suffered. Since the 1930s, a combination of changing market conditions and stricter grazing management by the U.S. Forest Service has resulted in improved range conditions. Because of poor market prices, sheep populations have declined substantially. The number of grazing cattle in the valley more than doubled between 1930 and 1960, but since then a number of ranchers have gone out of business and the Forest Service has reduced the number of grazing allotments. Elk and antelope populations have increased as a consequence of reduced competition from cattle, and mule deer have benefited from the invasion of meadows by shrubs and trees in the wake of less cattle grazing. Small ranchettes of 40 acres or less have appeared on some 20 percent of the valley's open lands.[42]

One of the most profound ecological changes in the species composition of the mountain West landscape is the loss of the gray wolf in Montana and elsewhere. This loss can be at least partly attributed to the trapping and shooting of wolves in order to reduce predation on cattle and sheep. Ranching thus played a role in the local extinction of the gray wolf. Experimental efforts to reintroduce the wolf to its former habitat in the northern Rockies are currently underway.[43]

Dams and Irrigation

Much like the Sierra Nevada, the Rocky Mountain's drainage system has been extensively reworked through the construction of hydroelectric dams and irrigation projects. While dams on the lower Colorado River have garnered much of the public's attention over the years, perhaps because of the high visibility of natural habitat losses from dam construction,[44] the upper reaches of the Colorado have been extensively reshaped by dams and irrigation as well. Both have contributed to the decline of four native fish species now considered to be threatened—the Colorado squawfish, the razorback sucker, the humpback chub, and the bonytail chub. These species are endemic to the upper Colorado River and were once abundant. Dam construction fragmented their habitat and altered the stream flow and temperature regimes they confront. In some cases, dams have prevented young and adult fish from returning upstream after downstream migrations. Large dams releasing cold water from their reservoirs render downstream areas uninhabitable for squawfish and razorback suckers. Before dams, the Colorado River water was relatively silty and ran high in the Spring. After dam construction, flows were evened out, reducing the suitability of river habitat for native species. High flows in the Spring, for instance, are necessary to maintain the backwaters, pools, and side channels that serve as nursery habitats for juvenile squawfish. Moreover, after dam construction, native fishes were sometimes poisoned to clear the way for the introduction of cold-water nonnative trout and other exotics, including the channel catfish, the northern pike, the red shiner, and the fathead minnow.[45] Fish trapped in irrigation ditches fed by reservoirs behind dams were often simply dumped in hayfields or orchards. All of these human-induced changes have contributed to the decline of native fish species in the Colorado River.

In Montana, fish also suffer from the effects of irrigation projects. Irrigation agriculture occurs in both the Bitterroot and Gallatin River Valleys, and the Gallatin alone contains 984 miles of irrigation canals.[46] Fish losses to irrigation canals in both valleys have been documented and include adult and juvenile salmonids. Species found in Montana irrigation canals include mountain white-fish and rainbow, bull, brown, cutthroat, and brook trout.[47] A recent study found that approximately 15 percent of the West Gallatin River trout population was lost to irrigation canals in 1994, although this loss did not appear to threaten trout populations in the river at the time. This situation could change, however, if the intensities of other stresses to trout populations increase, such as whirling disease. Trout losses to irrigation ditches can be mitigated through such measures as screen installations at diversion intakes and staged drawdowns at the end of the irrigation season to entice trout to swim back upstream into the river.[48]

The presence of an extensive system of dams in the Columbia River watershed has created an interesting management dilemma for dam operations in Montana. The threatened Snake River chinook salmon require high flows in the Columbia River system in the late summer to facilitate their downstream migration. This in turn requires Montana dams in the Columbia River watershed to draw down their reservoirs in order to augment stream flows. Ironically, reservoir de-pletions and stream flow augmentations in the late summer pose a threat to res-ident species that are already endangered. The Hungry Horse Dam, located on the south fork of the Flathead River upstream from Flathead Lake, is one of the dams supplying late summer flow augmentation. The Hungry Horse reservoir contains significant populations of endangered west slope cutthroat and bull trout. A summer reservoir drawdown appears to reduce the availability of forage species for these fishes. Moreover, the augmentation of summer flows down-stream from the Hungry Horse Dam alters the natural flow regime and disturbs the food web of the river, stressing resident fishes including the endangered Flat-head Lake bull trout.[49]

THE ECOLOGICAL EFFECTS OF
POPULATION SPREADING AND RURAL SPRAWL

The traditional economy in the mountain West has thus permanently altered the presettlement landscape, caused some species to go extinct and others to become endangered, and substantially reduced and degraded the habitat of still others. While a decline in the traditional economy will allow a partial recovery in some stressed ecosystems, some changes to the natural environment resulting from tra-ditional forms of economic activity appear to be irreversible. The traditional economy is indeed declining as a major economic force in the mountain coun-ties, as described in chapters 2 and 3, and is being replaced by the phenomenon of population spreading and associated rural residential development. The econ-omy of the rural mountain West appears to be converging in structure toward ur-ban economies. The rural landscape in the foothills and valley bottoms is taking on suburban-like features that many rural mountain West migrants had hoped to escape. At least one observer of this movement has described it as "exurban" sprawl.[50]

Will population spreading and exurban development cause added pressures on already stressed natural systems? Because the phenomenon is comparatively recent, responses to this question are necessarily speculative. However, enough is known about the effects of human activity on ecosystems and species to explore the possibilities. For the remainder of this chapter, what is known about the impact of population spreading and exurban development on the natural landscape will be summarized. In the next chapter, a more detailed analysis of the effects of development on rare and threatened species will be presented using the results of an experts' survey.

Before digging into the apparent effects of population spreading and exurban development, we need to be clear on the nature of the phenomenon. The term *exurban* is new and is being used to describe residential, commercial, and highway development that is being induced by population spreading beyond existing metropolitan boundaries.[51] Another expression used to describe this phenomenon is *rural sprawl*. These terms apply to development that is taking place in rural counties just beyond the edge of metropolitan areas as well as in more remote localities where daily commuting to even the boundary of an existing metropolitan area is out of the question. The type of development occurring in such areas includes so-called ranchettes of 5 to 40 acres that often include relatively large and expensive new houses. In some cases, development is in the form of large luxury subdivisions associated with a golf course, or in the form of condominiums linked to ski areas where the supply of land that can be developed is limited. Since high elevation landscapes are largely in public ownership, development and associated threats to critical habitats are primarily confined to the valley bottoms and foothills of the Sierra Nevada and Rocky Mountains. Any threats to higher elevation habitats associated with development are consequently indirect.

Valley bottoms and connected foothills are subject to development not only because they are mostly in private ownership, but also because the task of development in these landscapes is comparatively easier and less costly than in the rugged high mountains. Valley bottoms universally are the first to attract human settlement. In the mountain West, valley bottoms were homesteaded originally because of their agricultural potential and are utilized for agriculture to this day, primarily for cattle grazing and hay production to feed cattle in the winter. Some lowland areas in arid landscapes remain virtually in their presettlement condition, such as those dominated by sagebrush, pinyon, and juniper, for example. The foothills are usually shrublands or forested with lower montane species. So the question is: How do residential development and the attendant commercial and roadway construction alter the ecology of these landscapes?

One way of looking at a landscape is through the perspective of ecology. A specific ecosystem occurs in an abiotic physical environment that is defined by such elements as the local climate, the bedrock from which soils are derived, and the presence and movement of water. In addition to its abiotic components, a local ecosystem is also defined by the array of organisms that occupy it. Ecosystems can be looked at in terms of their functions, structure, and composition. Ecosystem functions includes productivity in the form of energy fixation through photosynthesis, the cycling of the resulting carbon-based energy from producers to consumers, the cycling of such nutrients as nitrogen or phosphorus from the physical environment through organisms and back again, and the cycling of water by organisms through uptake and transpiration. Ecosystem structure has to do with the physical shape of dominant species, such as large, old trees at one extreme or shrubs and grasses at the other. A large, old tree provides habitat niches for a variety of species, as do shrubs and grasses. Ecosystem composition is defined by the species present and their relative population levels, and it is related to, although not entirely determined by, structure and function. The presence of large, old trees offers habitats to a number of species ranging from arthropods to raptores. A highly productive ecosystem may support a larger number of species. Abiotic characteristics, such as climate and the presence of water, also play a role in determining composition. Certain ecosystem processes effect composition over different time and spatial scales. Periodic disturbances, such as fire, favor fire-adapted species and opportunists able to quickly colonize burned-over areas. On a larger spatial scale, periodic disturbances will result in a patchy landscape with some areas recently burned and some not. As time passes in forested landscapes, shade-intolerant invasive opportunist and fire-adapted species will often be replaced by shade-tolerant species whose seedlings can flourish in the sheltered understory. Consequently, more species will be present at a larger spatial scale.[52]

Human activity can affect any or all of these ecosystem features. Residential development in rural localities, for example, can alter the hydrology of an area and the abiotic environment by drawing down the water table as a consequence of the residential use of wells as a water source. This shift in utilization can reduce the availability of water to plants and animals by decreasing stream levels and by drying up wetlands dependent on groundwater. Runoff from lawns, parking areas, and roads can affect ecosystem functioning by increasing the amount of silt, nutrients, and toxins in local streams and lakes as well as by increasing peak flows. The greater presence of impervious surfaces is one of the critical features of urban development that inevitably expands nonpoint water pollution. Septic systems can also fail, leading to groundwater contamination. While these circumstances are all possibilities, little is known about their actual importance, although there have been cases of septic system failure in the Sierra Nevadas.[53] If aquatic ecosystems were not already under stress from mining runoff and silt loads originating from logging roads, the effects of rural sprawl on toxin and sediment loads in local streams might not be such a problem. The ecological starting point matters in assessing the environmental effects of new forms of development and economic activity.

Possibly the most significant effect of rural residential development is habitat loss and habitat fragmentation. Habitat fragmentation involves the carving up of a habitat into smaller pieces that by themselves may fail to meet the minimum habitat area requirements of certain species or may prevent gene flows among subpopulations of particular species. The latter would eventually cause a reduction of genetic diversity in subpopulations that could ultimately cause a reduction in fitness, increasing the risk of extinction.

Valley bottom residential development can cause habitat loss through the simple removal of a habitat from use by particular species. While valley bottoms constitute a relatively small proportion of the total land in many mountain counties, for some species they are critically important habitats at certain times of the year. Ungulates, such as elk and mule deer, spend the summers foraging in the high mountain meadows, but migrate to lower-elevation valley bottoms in the winter. In addition, elk calving grounds critical for successful reproduction are also frequently found in valley bottoms. Suburban-style development can reduce the amount of valley bottom available for winter forage and for calving. Moreover, human presence and disturbance can increase energy requirements at a critical time of low food availability by stimulating flight responses. In the winter, ungulates survive on summer fat stores and whatever food is available. Energy conservation is a key element of their winter survival strategy. While snowmobiles are apparently a major source of disturbance in wintering areas, surprisingly cross-country skiers cause even greater energy expenditures among ungulates in some situations because skiers are unanticipated by animals. In some cases, ungulates become habituated to urban environments, causing landscape damage that residents may be unwilling to tolerate and attracting mountain lions that pose an intolerable threat to residents and their pets.

The loss of ungulate winter range is not the only problem. Development at higher elevations around ski areas combined with increased summer recreation activity can effectively reduce summer range for elk and deer as well.[54] On the other hand, to the extent that valley bottom subdivision development on ranch lands reduces ranching activity and summer cattle grazing in mountain meadows, summer range conditions for ungulates may actually improve as they have in the Madison Valley. This improvement, however, is partly due to a change in Forest Service policy that restricts grazing activity.[55]

Carnivores also make seasonal use of valley bottom and foothill habitats and therefore are potentially threatened by development. Grizzly bears move to lower elevations in the spring to take advantage of the availability of green vegetation. Grizzlies that are not habituated to human presence avoid the use of private lands and areas where development is concentrated, suggesting that increased development diminishes grizzly habitat. Residential development offers food opportunities (in the form of garbage and livestock) for bears that become habituated to human presence, increasing the likelihood of human-bear encounters where bears are usually killed. Human-caused bear mortality is the primary reason for grizzly population decline, and mortality of this type is highest on private lands and in areas where residential development is present.[56] Migration routes for grizzlies between large, core habitat areas may also be lost because of valley bottom development.[57]

Valley bottom residential development in some areas is built on stream and lake edges, causing reductions in a riparian habitat. The shores of the comparatively pristine Yellowstone River in Montana have become a popular place to put up a new house. Periodic flooding, however, reshapes the river and threatens new residences with erosion and inundation. Landowners have reacted by armoring streambanks with a layer of large boulders. Another term for this procedure is *riprap*. Riprap results in the removal of riverside trees and other vegetation, eliminates the meandering quality of the river, and increases the velocity of the river eliminating slow-flowing resting and feeding habitat for trout. Approximately 25 percent of the streambank in Park County has been covered with riprap, and trout population in a recent survey was down 60 percent from a previous study. Riprap displaces stream energy and the forces of streambank erosion downstream, begetting still more riprap by landowners.[58] Trout losses from this kind of development can be especially important if trout populations are already stressed by silt loading from logging roads upstream or by irrigation agriculture downstream.

In addition to the human disturbance of streamside riparian areas, residential development can reduce habitat along lake shores. For the Common Loon, loss of shoreline habitat and nesting sites to development in Montana is a serious threat. Breeding waterfowl is especially sensitive to human disturbance and may vacate nests either temporarily or permanently as a consequence. Boating activity is a critical source of disturbance on lakes, especially for Loons, and the volume of such activity is likely to be associated with the extent of shoreline development.[59]

Habitat fragmentation is harmful to native species not only because it carves habitat into pieces that may well be too small for use by some species, but also because it increases the amount of habitat edge which can reduce useful habitat and cause stress for interior species. Residential development and roads go together. Roads provide the essential human link between patches of residential activity. The resulting matrix of roads and development not only reduces the amount of habitat available to native species, but it also chops it into smaller pieces. While the effects of roads in areas subject to rural residential development have not been studied, the impact of roads in general on ecosystem processes and native flora and fauna has been considered. Studies of several different, small mammal populations and herpetiles found that animals rarely venture onto road surfaces or cross roads. Such behavior subdivides populations into separate genetically isolated demographic groups that, as a consequence, become more vulnerable to extinction. Isolated subpopulations can suffer extinctions from inbreeding depression, gender imbalances, and habitat disturbances that a larger connected population would avoid. For example, genetic differences across roads have been found for frogs in Germany suggesting that genetic isolation is more than just a theoretical possibility. Larger animals may experience habitat reduction and fragmentation because of behavior modifications in the presence of roads. Black bears, grizzlies, wolves, mountain lions, elk, and mule deer all appear to avoid suitable habitats near roads. Unfortunately, not all species avoid roads, and as a result their populations are reduced as a consequence of collision mortality. Roadkill is not confined just to large, visible mammals such as moose or deer. Avian victims of vehicle collisions include Kestrels, Barn Owls, and Northern Saw-whet Owls. Amphibians migrating between wetland and upland habitats may be especially vulnerable to roadkill. The local abundance of toads and frogs is inversely related to the traffic volume on area roads in one study, and according to another, roadkill may be contributing to the endangerment of the prairie garter snake. In addition to fragmenting the landscape, roads, in effect, are mortality black holes for many species.[60]

For interior bird species, forest edges created by residential development can also act as a reproductive black hole. Birds attracted to nest sites on forest edges are subject to nest predation and brood parasitism by edge-dwelling species. Crows, jays, opossums, squirrels, and raccoons all prey on nests near forests edges, and parasitic Brown-headed Cowbirds add their eggs to the nests of songbirds who choose forest edges for reproduction. The presence of residential dwellings can intensify negative edge effects by creating feeding opportunities from garbage, especially for such edge species as raccoons and crows. Edges created by roads or residences in forested landscapes alter environmental conditions and the kinds of plants present for some distance into the forest interior. Edges tend to be drier and less shady than forest interiors, more affected by blowdowns, and more likely to contain opportunistic weedy plant species and exotics.[61] Local residents may inadvertently or purposely introduce exotic species that compete with native species such as Scotch broom, a highly invasive aggressive plant present in the Sierra Nevadas and elsewhere.[62]

Edge effects and disturbances unique to residential development include the presence of pets, noise, and light. Cats are known to suppress bird populations in suburban areas through predation, extending the environmental effect of development well beyond the immediate location of dwellings.[63] Predation by cats on songbirds will be especially significant where they are already under stress from habitat fragmentation caused by agriculture or logging. The effect of dogs on wildlife is a matter of increasing concern among wildlife biologists. Dogs frequently hunt, chase, and possibly injure or even kill wildlife within a three to five mile radius around a rural dwelling. Because ungulates in the Rockies are adapted to harsh winter conditions through energy conservation, any disturbance that causes ungulate movement consumes energy and reduces survival ability. Dogs are an unpredictable source of disturbance, and, unlike humans, are instinctively programmed to engage in chasing wild ungulates.[64] Dogs investigating wolf habitats can cause wolf den abandonment, can be killed by wolves, and can cause the introduction of diseases into wolf populations.[65] In the summer months, avian species are especially vulnerable to human pedestrian disturbance that is significantly intensified in the presence of dogs. Dogs by themselves can cause disturbance responses and injure and kill birds. Shorebirds, such as Piping and Golden Plovers, have been observed to respond to human and dog disturbances by flushing. This upsets nesting and feeding activity and exhausts energy resources. In one study, grouse interrupted their display activity and departed from their lek as a result of human and dog disturbance.[66] Dogs clearly have the potential to harass, disturb, and injure wildlife within a comparatively large radius of residential dwellings. Thus the presence of residences, their human occupants, and uncontrolled pets can stress wildlife populations in the surrounding landscape. Even seemingly innocuous actions such as the installation of residential floodlights can have ecological consequences. A number of amphibians and reptiles breed and forage at night, raising the possibility that lighting from residential dwellings could disrupt such activities.[67]

In sum, there are numerous paths by which increased residential development in a locality can disrupt its ecology and cause stress to various plant and animal species, although at this point the relative importance of each potential source of disturbance or stress is unknown. In the next chapter, the effects of probable sources of stress for rare and imperiled species will be explored more fully using an expert's survey. A key point to reiterate is that ecological stresses from rural sprawl are especially significant because the populations of many species are already critically low as a consequence of the continuing environmental effects of the old-economy industries—mining, agriculture, and logging. This is most likely the case for such large mammals as grizzly bears and wolves, aquatic species such as trout, and various species of songbirds. If rural development were occurring in the context of a pristine environment, its ecological effects would likely be less significant.

A final indirect source of ecosystem disruption and stress to species is fire-suppression activities. Of course fire suppression predates significant population concentrations in much of the mountain West and was started largely to protect timber resources. A destructive fire in northern Idaho and northwest Montana in 1910 signaled the modern era of fire suppression. While some foresters advocated light underburning in the pine forests of the Sierra Nevada, by the 1920s the opponents prevailed, and the official policy became the suppression of all fires, even the low-intensity ground fires that maintained open understories in the dry ponderosa pine forests of the mountain West. The result of this policy was a buildup of fuel in the understory and an increased frequency of high-intensity stand-replacing fires as opposed to low-intensity burns that left large, old trees standing. Not until the 1970s was the practice of underburning reintroduced, particularly in national parks. In the 1980s natural fire policies were also adopted in some Forest Service wilderness areas as well where any fires caused by lightening were allowed to burn. After the Yellowstone fires of 1988, natural fire policies and underburning were suspended until management practices improved. In the 1990s natural fire policies were reintroduced on a limited scale in national parks and wilderness areas.[68]

Although fire suppression has deep historical roots preceding extensive residential development in rural areas, such development alters both the nature of fire-suppression efforts and the motivations behind it. The presence of residences in forested landscapes results in a reallocation of fire fighting resources to the protection of residential property. Fire crews and vehicles defending residential property are no longer available for fighting the fire itself, and the mere presence of residential dwellings in an area rules out the use of backfires. The existence of dwellings thus increases the cost and difficulty of fighting fires. Human activities associated with such residences also constitute potential additional ignition sources—i.e., sparks from a wood stove or the failure to extinguish a cigarette butt—although the effect of these added ignition sources may be offset by increased local resources for fighting fires.[69]

The motivation for fighting fires in the presence of residential development has thus expanded from simple forest protection to the protection of property as well as human life. As a consequence of rural residential development, the use of underburning and natural wildfire as a strategy for preventing understory fuel buildup and restoring a more natural fire regime is threatened politically because of the possibility of such fires getting out of hand. The recent Cerro Grande fire in New Mexico that destroyed more than 230 homes in the Los Alamos area was started by a prescribed burn in the Bandalier National Monument that grew out of control. This fire illustrates the ironies of fire suppression on the urban-rural boundary. Los Alamos is surrounded on three sides by thick ponderosa pine forests that are popular locations for residential dwellings. These same forests suffer from understory fuel buildups because of fire suppression and a history of grazing. Grasses outcompete shrubby vegetation and provide the medium for spreading of low-intensity fires. Grazing removes the grasses, limiting the extent of low-intensity fire that prevents major fuel buildup. Without the competition of grasses, shrubby vegetation gains a foothold and increases the forest understory fuel load. By eliminating low-intensity burns that would otherwise keep shrubby vegetation to a minimum, fire suppression increases understory fuel loads. The inevitable result of fire suppression and fuel buildup is a stand-replacing fire. It was simply bad luck that the ignition source for the Cerro Grande fire was a controlled burn intended to eliminate the conditions that lead to stand-replacing fires. What is even worse is that this accident could hinder federal efforts to use prescribed burns in western forests for the purpose of limiting excessive fuel buildup and preventing high intensity fires of the sort that hit Los Alamos.[70] Without low-intensity fire, fire-adapted species, such as the ponderosa pine, will eventually experience declining numbers. Some oak woodlands of the type found in the Sierra Nevada, particularly blue and black oak, may also depend on fire for their long-term perpetuation. Chaparral is a fire-adapted plant type too and experiences compositional shifts in the absence of fire.[71] Fire suppression not only alters the ecology of a landscape, but in the presence of rural residential development it actually increases the long-term danger of threats to property and human life from highly destructive fires fed by years of fuel buildup. The presence of rural sprawl in forested landscapes thus increases the difficulty of reintroducing the natural fire regimes needed by many species for long-run survival as well as the avoidance of catastrophic fires. The original desire to suppress fire in order to save forests is now augmented by the desire to save human property. In the absence of rural residential development, returning to a natural fire regime would be much easier.

OUTDOOR RECREATION AND THE ENVIRONMENT

A discussion of human impacts on the natural environment in the mountain West would be incomplete without a consideration of outdoor recreation. Because the environmental effects of outdoor recreation is a topic deserving of extensive treatment in its own right, and is in fact discussed in considerable detail elsewhere,[72] only a brief introduction to it will be offered here. Outdoor recreation at a given locality is partly related to the density of local population. Consequently, the growth of recreation activity in a locality depends in part on population growth and thus the spreading of population to the rural counties of the mountain West. Indeed, one of the reasons people move to remote mountainous areas is to take advantage of close access to outdoor recreation opportunities.[73] However, the majority of recreation activity, particularly on public lands in the West, is attributable to individuals whose residence is outside the immediate local area.[74] The rapid historical growth of recreational activity since World War II, nonetheless, is substantially attributable to the same forces that underlay population spreading to the mountain West, namely increased affluence and technologies that make remote locations more accessible. Rising affluence results in more affordable outdoor recreation for a larger portion of the population, and automobile and highway mobility increases the accessibility of remote mountain landscapes. In addition, the development of lightweight outdoor gear and various kinds of off-road vehicles has undoubtedly contributed to the growing popularity of outdoor recreation in mountain landscapes.[75] Prior to World War II, the backcountry was largely a playground of the wealthy. National park resorts, for example, were only accessible by rail at great expense and featured relatively luxurious accommodations.[76]

Trends in current and projected outdoor recreation participation are presented in table 4.1 for key recreation activities that have the potential to disturb wildlife in mountain environments. Fishing is the most popular form of outdoor activity and is projected to grow in the Rocky Mountain and Pacific regions of the country, although participation for the United States as a whole has declined some in recent years. Hunting participation, on the other hand, is expected to continue its downward trend nationally and in the Pacific region, but it is expected to expand somewhat in the Rockies. Three important winter recreation activities—cross-country skiing, downhill skiing, and snowmobiling—have all grown in popularity in recent years in both the Pacific and Rocky Mountain regions and are expected to continue to do so. This is also true for backpacking and off-road driving. With the exceptions of fishing and hunting, outdoor recreation participation is growing strongly in those regions of the country that include the mountain West.[77]

Table 4.1. Trends in Current and Projected Outdoor Recreation Participation

Recreation Activity	United States Percent Change: 1982–1983 to 1994–1995	Baseline Participation: (millions) 1995	Projection Index		
			2000	2010	2020
Cross-country Skiing					
United States	22.6	6.5	1.04	1.18	1.26
Rockies		0.7	1.07	1.31	1.41
Pacific		1.1	1.06	1.23	1.33
Downhill Skiing					
United States	58.5	16.8	1.03	1.13	1.22
Rockies		1.7	1.04	1.14	1.15
Pacific		3.6	1.06	1.21	1.31
Snowmobiling					
United States	34.0	7.1	1.00	1.04	1.09
Rockies		0.8	1.02	1.06	1.10
Pacific		0.7	1.09	1.42	1.54
Fishing					
United States	−3.8	57.9	1.03	1.09	1.17
Rockies		4.6	1.05	1.16	1.26
Pacific		7.5	1.05	1.12	1.20
Hunting					
United States	−12.3	18.6	0.97	0.93	0.91
Rockies		2.0	1.01	1.05	1.12
Pacific		1.7	0.94	0.85	0.79
Hiking					
United States	93.5	47.8	1.03	1.13	1.23
Rockies		5.0	1.05	1.15	1.24
Pacific		10.9	1.08	1.23	1.34
Backpacking					
United States	72.7	15.2	1.00	1.04	1.11
Rockies		1.8	1.03	1.11	1.18
Pacific		3.8	1.05	1.12	1.23
Off-road Driving					
United States	43.8	27.9	1.00	1.02	1.05
Rockies		3.0	1.04	1.09	1.17
Pacific		4.7	1.04	1.10	1.20

Source: Data from H. Ken Cordell and Susan M. McKinney, *Outdoor Recreation in American Life: A National Assessment of Demand and Supply Trends* (Champaign, Ill.: Sagamore Publishing, 1999), 239 and 326–340.

The kinds of disturbances to wildlife and plants caused by recreation are similar in many respects to those resulting from residential development in mountain areas. Essentially, both are forms of human population spreading into mountain areas. Recreation can affect wildlife populations through disturbance, exploitation, habitat modification, and pollution.[78] All of these are possible effects of one or more of the kinds of recreational activities listed in table 4.1.

Winter sports have the potential, for example, to disturb wildlife and alter wildlife habitat. As noted in the above discussion of residential development, human disturbance to wintering ungulates can be critical to their fitness because disturbance usually leads to movement, and movement uses up scarce energy resources. Also, disturbance can cause ungulates to move off of favored grazing habitats, reducing critical caloric inputs. Oddly, snowmobilers appear to be less disturbing to ungulates than cross-country skiers as noted above, possibly because skiers are more likely to surprise wildlife than the noisier snowmobiles.[79] Moreover, skiers and snowmobilers alter winter habitat through snow compaction, increasing interspecific competition for the Canada lynx. The lynx relies on the snowshoe hare for prey almost exclusively in winter. In its mid- to upper-elevation mountain habitats, competition from other predators, such as coyotes, is largely excluded by deep, low-density snow. The broad paws of the lynx have a much greater support capacity on such snow than its competitors who tend to sink deeper into the snow and for this reason are much less effective in catching snowshoe hares. Snow compaction in the high country by skiers and snowmobilers opens up this habitat to coyotes, bobcats, and mountain lions, reducing the prey base for lynx.[80]

Both hunting and fishing have the potential to disturb wildlife and reduce wildlife populations directly through harvesting. Apart from direct impacts on fish populations, fishing is also a potential source of disturbance to breeding waterfowl or birds of prey. Disturbance to nest sites can reduce hatching success and increase hen and egg predation, and, in extreme cases, disturbance can lead to nest abandonment. Fishing and hunting outside the breeding season can cause waterfowl to take flight, using up energy resources and potentially reducing fitness.[81] Pet dogs accompanying hunters extend the range and intensity of disturbance to wildlife generally and can result in increased wildlife mortality. While hunting is an important management tool, it also results in exhausting ungulate fat reserves and disrupting reproduction cycles. Hunting appears to negatively affect populations of mature bulls in elk populations, reducing the productivity of healthy calves.[82] During hunting season, wolves are often killed illegally, and during black bear hunts, grizzlies are frequently misidentified and killed even though hunting grizzlies is illegal. Grizzly bears are also sometimes killed in attempted appropriation of carcasses from hunters.[83] Fishing is indirectly implicated in amphibian decline through the introduction of nonindigenous recreational species that prey on amphibians to lakes that were originally fishless and the use of chemicals to manage unwanted fish species.[84]

Although hiking and backpacking are popularly thought to be relatively benign forms of outdoor recreation, this may not be the case. Hikers are as likely as other recreationists to disturb nesting or roosting birds.[85] In alpine areas, human presence can have a negative effect on foraging activity by marmots.[86] Grizzlies tend to avoid using areas near popular hiking trails and campsites, thus reducing effective grizzly habitat. Backcountry human encounters with grizzlies in national parks and wilderness areas has resulted in increased bear mortality.[87] Hikers who bring their dogs with them and let them range off-trail extend human disturbance to local wildlife species and increase the chance of wildlife mortality, especially for small mammals and birds.[88]

Off-road vehicle (ORV) use is a popular activity and one that is increasingly controversial because of its effects on wildlife and local ecosystems. ORV use has its most profound effect on vegetation and soils and has left very few kinds of ecosystems untouched in the United States. Vegetation suffers directly from the destructive force of ORV passage and indirectly from soil compaction and erosion. Compaction and erosion negatively affect the capacity for plants to intake carbon dioxide and nutrients, to grow roots, and even to grow in an upward direction.[89] Erosion from ORV use can also result in the increased sedimentation of nearby streams and lakes. Damage to vegetation and soils reduces habitat quality for herpetiles and small mammals. Studies have shown that amphibian, reptile, and small mammal populations are smaller in areas of heavy ORV use in comparison to unused but similar control areas. This is apparently due to vegetation and soil changes as well as changes in microclimates and in some cases direct mortalities.[90] An obvious problem created by ORVs is noise. Leopard frogs exposed to high noise levels, for example, remain immobilized for a longer period of time than a similar unexposed control group. Lizards were found to suffer from reduced noise sensitivity through exposure to ORVs. Noise is an important cue in discovering prey and avoiding predators for lizards.[91] Motorized vehicles operating at night may keep certain bat species from using echolocation and thus communicating, navigating, and seeking prey.[92] Large mammals, such as bighorn sheep, can also be negatively affected by ORVs as well as by other recreational activities such as camping and hiking.[93]

Recreational activity, like residential development, thus appears to have impacts on local flora and fauna that are just beginning to be studied and evaluated. On the surface, the modern amenity-based economy may appear to be environmentally benign, but a deeper look suggests that it too will contribute to the cumulative effects of prior human impacts on local ecosystems from the traditional extractive economy.

CONCLUSION

Changes to the mountain West natural landscape caused by resource-dependent industries, such as mining, have been blunted by time and the resiliency of nature, although the residents of Butte, Montana, are reminded daily by the legacy of mining. Presumably over the course of decades, the forests of the northern Rockies will recover from the effects of clearcuts, if given the opportunity to do so. The damming and redirecting of western mountain streams and rivers appear to be more permanent phenomena. While riparian damage caused by grazing can be repaired in many instances, the introduction of exotic vegetation as a consequence of grazing appears to be a comparatively permanent change. The effect of the traditional extractive industries on the mountain West natural environment has elements of permanence. The effects of population spreading into the rural mountain West and exurban residential development on the natural environment have yet to be investigated by ecologists, botanists, and zoologists in any detail. Nonetheless, the research that exists suggests a clear potential for additional significant environmental threats. These threats would in most instances constitute a net addition to environmental changes that have already occurred. If we were starting with a clean ecological slate today, the consequences of rural development in the mountain West would be more benign. To gain more insight into the nature of the ecological threats from rural sprawl, we will summarize and interpret the results of an experts' survey on the consequences of residential development for rare and imperiled species in the next chapter.

NOTES

1. Tracy I. Storer and Robert L. Usinger, *Sierra Nevada Natural History* (Berkeley: University of California Press, 1963); and Sierra Nevada Ecosystem Project, Final Report to Congress, *Status of the Sierra Nevada, Volume I: Assessment Summaries and Management Strategies* (Davis, Calif.: Centers for Water and Wildland Resources, University of California, Davis, 1996).

2. Storer and Usinger, *Sierra Nevada Natural History*; and Sierra Nevada Ecosystem Project, *Status of the Sierra Nevada, Volume I*.

3. Storer and Usinger, *Sierra Nevada Natural History*; Sierra Nevada Ecosystem Project, *Status of the Sierra Nevada, Volume I*; and Peter B. Moyle, Ronald M. Yoshiyama, and Roland A. Knapp, "Status of Fish and Fisheries," in *Status of the Sierra Nevada, Volume II: Assessment and Scientific Basis for Management Options*, Sierra Nevada Ecosystem Project, Final Report to Congress (Davis, Calif.: Centers for Water and Wildland Resources, University of California, Davis, 1996), 953–973.

4. Storer and Usinger, *Sierra Nevada Natural History*; Sierra Nevada Ecosystem Project, *Status of the Sierra Nevada, Volume I*; and William C. Kinney, "Conditions of Rangelands before 1905," in *Status of the Sierra Nevada, Volume II*, 31–45.

5. Storer and Usinger, *Sierra Nevada Natural History*; Sierra Nevada Ecosystem Project, *Status of the Sierra Nevada, Volume I*; and Kinney, "Conditions of Rangelands before 1905."

6. Storer and Usinger, *Sierra Nevada Natural History*; Sierra Nevada Ecosystem Project, *Status of the Sierra Nevada, Volume I*; Kinney, "Conditions of Rangelands before 1905"; James. K. Agee, *Fire Ecology of Pacific Northwest Forests* (Washington, D.C.: Island Press,

1993); and Carl N. Skinner and Chi-ru Chang, "Fire Regimes, Past and Present," in *Status of the Sierra Nevada, Volume II*, 1041–1069.

7. William Wyckoff, *Creating Colorado: The Making of a Western American Landscape: 1860–1940* (New Haven: Yale University Press, 1999); and William Wyckoff and Larry M. Dilsaver, "Defining the Mountainous West," in *The Mountainous West: Explorations in Historical Geography*, ed.William Wyckoff and Lary M. Dilsaver (Lincoln: University of Nebraska Press, 1995), 1–59.

8. This expression is taken from Wyckoff and Dilsaver, "Defining the Mountainous West;" and Thomas R. Vale, "Mountains and Moisture in the West," in *The Mountainous West: Explorations in Historical Geography*, 141–165.

9. Ruth A. Nelson, *Handbook of Rocky Mountain Plants* (Niwot, Colo.: Roberts Rinehart Publishers, 1992); and Agee, *Fire Ecology of Pacific Northwest Forests*.

10. Nelson, *Handbook of Rocky Mountain Plants*; Agee, *Fire Ecology of Pacific Northwest Forests*; and Stephen Whitney, *Western Forests* (New York: Alfred A. Knopf, 1985).

11. Agee, *Fire Ecology of Pacific Northwest Forests*.

12. David Beesley, "Reconstructing the Landscape: An Environmental History," in *Status of the Sierra Nevada, Volume II*, 3–24; G. Mathias Kondolf, Richard Kattelmann, Michael Embury, and Don C. Erman, "Status of Riparian Habitat," in *Status of the Sierra Nevada, Volume II*, 1009–1030; and Randall Rohe, "Environment and Mining in the Mountainous West," in *The Mountainous West: Explorations in Historical Geography*, ed. William Wyckoff and Lary M. Dilsaver (Lincoln: University of Nebraska Press, 1995), 169–193.

13. James S. Lyon, Thomas J. Hilliard, and Thomas N. Bethell, *Burden of Gilt: The Legacy of Environmental Damage from Abandoned Mines, and What America Should Do about It* (Washington, D.C.: Mineral Policy Center, 1993).

14. Beesley, "Reconstructing the Landscape."

15. Sierra Nevada Ecosystem Project, *Status of the Sierra Nevada, Volume I*; Jerry F. Franklin and Jo Ann Fites-Kaufmann, "Assessment of Late-Successional Forests of the Sierra Nevada," in *Status of the Sierra Nevada, Volume II*, 627–661; and Kondolf, Kattelmann, Embury, and Erman, "Status of Riparian Habitat."

16. Sierra Nevada Ecosystem Project, *Status of the Sierra Nevada, Volume I*; Skinner and Chang, "Fire Regimes, Past and Present."

17. Chi-ru Chang, "Ecosystem Responses to Fire and Variations in Fire Regimes," in *Status of the Sierra Nevada, Volume II*, 1071–1099.

18. Beesley, "Reconstructing the Landscape."

19. Sierra Nevada Ecosystem Project, *Status of the Sierra Nevada, Volume I*.

20. Sierra Nevada Ecosystem Project, *Status of the Sierra Nevada, Volume I*; and David J. Larson, "Historical Water-Use Priorities and Public Policies," in *Status of the Sierra Nevada, Volume II*, 163–185.

21. Kondolf, Kattelmann, Embury, and Erman, "Status of Riparian Habitat;" and Moyle, Yoshiyama, and Knapp, "Status of Fish and Fisheries."

22. Wyckoff and Dilsaver, "Defining the Mountainous West."

23. Vale, "Mountains and Moisture in the West."

24. Rohe, "Environment and Mining in the Mountainous West"; and Wyckoff, *Creating Colorado*, 45–60.

25. Duane A. Smith, *Rocky Mountain West: Colorado, Wyoming, and Montana, 1859–1915* (Albuquerque: University of New Mexico Press, 1992), 84.

26. Rohe, "Environment and Mining in the Mountainous West"; and Wyckoff, *Creating Colorado*, 68–78.

27. Lyon, Hilliard, and Bethell, *Burden of Gilt.*

28. Smith, *Rocky Mountain West*, 23–42, 82–97, and 162–173; and K. Ross Toole, *Twentieth-century Montana: A State of Extremes* (Norman: University of Oklahoma Press, 1972), 99–122.

29. Toole, *Twentieth-century Montana*, 4.

30. Smith, *Rocky Mountain West*, 165.

31. Smith, *Rocky Mountain West*, 93.

32. Katherine Aiken, "Western Smelters and the Problem of Smelter Smoke," in *Northwest Lands, Northwest Peoples: Readings in Environmental History*, ed. Dale D. Goble and Paul W. Hirt (Seattle: University of Washington Press, 1999), 502–522.

33. David Stiller, *Wounding the West: Montana, Mining, and the Environment* (Lincoln: University of Nebraska Press, 2000), 15.

34. Smith, *Rocky Mountain West*, 76.

35. The Environmental Protection Agency runs the Superfund program designed to clean up the country's most contaminated hazardous waste sites. See Lyon, Hilliard, and Bethell, *Burden of Gilt.*

36. Cornelia F. Mutel and John C. Emerick, *From Grassland to Glacier: The Natural History of Colorado* (Boulder: Johnson Books, 1984).

37. Mutel and Emerick, *From Grassland to Glacier.*

38. Mutel and Emerick, *From Grassland to Glacier.*

39. Toole, *Twentieth-century Montana*, 5.

40. Paul W. Hirt, "Getting Out the Cut: A History of National Forest Management in the Northern Rockies," in *Northwest Lands, Northwest Peoples: Readings in Environmental History*, ed. Dale D. Goble and Paul W. Hirt (Seattle: University of Washington Press, 1999), 437–461; and Bruce G. Marcot, Michael J. Wisdom, Hiram W. Li, and Gonzalo C. Castillo, "Managing for Featured, Threatened, Endangered, and Sensitive Species and Unique Habitats for Ecosystem Sustainability," in *Eastside Forest Ecosystem Health Assessment, Volume III*, ed. R. L. Everett (Portland, Oreg.: USDA Forest Service, Pacific Northwest Research Station, 1994). The latter reference refers specifically to forests in the Blue Mountains of Oregon, but the type of forests mentioned are similar to those found in the Rocky Mountains. See pages 281 and 321 of Agee, *Fire Ecology of Pacific Northwest Forests*, for confirmation of this point.

41. Agee, *Fire Ecology of Pacific Northwest Forests.*

42. William Wyckoff and Katherine Hansen, "Environmental Change in the Northern Rockies: Settlement and Livestock Grazing in Southwestern Montana, 1860–1995," in *Northwest Lands, Northwest Peoples: Readings in Environmental History*, ed. Dale D. Goble and Paul W. Hirt (Seattle: University of Washington Press, 1999), 336–361.

43. James J. Claar, Neil Anderson, Diane Boyd, Ben Conard, Gene Hickman, Robin Hompesch, Gary Olson, Helga Ihsle Pac, Tom Wittinger, and Heidi Youmans, "Carnivores," in *The Effects of Recreation on Rocky Mountain Wildlife: A Review for Montana*, co-ord. G. Joslin and H. Youmans (Montana: Committee on Effects of Recreation on Wildlife, Montana Chapter of the Wildlife Society, 1999), 7.1–7.63.

44. Marc Reisner, *Cadillac Desert: The American West and Its Disappearing Water* (New York: Penguin Books, 1986).

45. Douglas B. Osmundson and Lynn Kaeding, "Relationships between Flow and Rare Fish Habitat in the 15-Mile Reach of the Upper Colorado River: Final Report" (Denver: U.S. Fish and Wildlife Service, 1995); Fred Quartarone and Connie Young, "Historical Accounts of Upper Colorado River Basin Endangered Fish: Final Report" (Denver: Colorado Division

of Wildlife, 1993); and Jerry J. Vaske, Maureen P. Donnelly, and Michelle Lyon, "Project Report: Knowledge, Beliefs, and Attitudes toward Endangered Fish of the Upper Colorado River Basin" (Fort Collins, Colo.: Human Dimensions in Natural Resources Unit, College of Natural Resources, Colorado State University, 1995).

46. Eric W. Reiland, "Fish Loss to Irrigation Canals and Methods to Reduce These Losses on the West Gallatin River, Montana" (Master's thesis, Bozeman, Mont., Montana State University, 1997), 1–3.

47. Reiland, "Fish Loss to Irrigation Canals," 5–7, 127.

48. Reiland, "Fish Loss to Irrigation Canals," 1–10, 80–96.

49. Independent Scientific Advisory Board, "Ecological Impacts of the Flow Provisions of the Biological Opinion for Endangered Snake River Salmon on Resident Fishes in Hungry Horse, and Libby Systems in Montana, Idaho, and British Columbia" (Portland, Oreg.: Northwest Power Planning Council, National Marine Fisheries Service, 1997).

50. Timothy P. Duane, *Shaping the Sierra: Nature, Culture, and Conflict in the Changing West* (Berkeley: University of California Press, 1999), 37–54.

51. Duane, *Shaping the Sierra*, 37–54, uses this term in describing development patterns in the Sierra Nevada Mountains.

52. Gary K. Meffe and C. Ronald Carroll, *Principles of Conservation Biology* (Sunderland, Mass.: Sinauer Associates, 1994), 78–109; Reed F. Noss and Allen Y. Cooperrider, *Saving Nature's Legacy: Protecting and Restoring Biodiveristy* (Washington, D.C.: Island Press, 1994), 30–66.

53. Timothy P. Duane, "Human settlement: 1850–2040," in *Status of the Sierra Nevada, Volume II*, 235–360.

54. Jodie E. Canfield, L. Jack Lyon, J. Michael Hillis, and Michael J. Thompson, "Ungulates," in *The Effects of Recreation on Rocky Mountain Wildlife: A Review for Montana*, coord. Gayle Joslin and Heidi Youmans (Committee on Effects of Recreation on Wildlife, Montana Chapter of the Wildlife Society, 1999), 6.1–6.25.

55. Wyckoff and Hansen, "Environmental Change in the Northern Rockies."

56. Claar et al., "Carnivores"; and Richard D. Mace, John S. Waller, Timothy L. Manley, L. Jack Lyon, and H. Zuuring, "Relationships among Grizzly Bears, Roads and Habitat in the Swan Mountains, Montana," *Journal of Applied Ecology* 33 (1996): 1395–1404.

57. Richard D. Mace, John S. Waller, Timothy L. Manley, Katherine Ake, and William T. Wittinger, "Landscape Evaluation of Grizzly Bear Habitat in Western Montana," *Conservation Biology* 13 (1999): 367–377. Grizzly habitat issues are discussed more fully in chapter 6.

58. Hal Herring, "Strangling the Last Best River," *High Country News* 31-7 (April 12, 1999): 6; and American Rivers, "Yellowstone River Named One of Nation's Most Endangered Rivers," http://www.amrivers.org/pressrelease/pressmeryellowstone1999.htm, 1999 [accessed 12 January 2002].

59. Betsy Hamann, Heather Johnston, John Gobielle, Mike Hillis, Sara Johnson, Lynn Kelly, and Pat McClelland, "Birds," in *The Effects of Recreation on Rocky Mountain Wildlife: A Review for Montana*, 3.1–3.34; and Lynn M. Kelly, "The Effects of Human Disturbance on Common Loon Productivity in Northwestern Montana" (Master's thesis, Bozeman, Mont., Montana State University, 1992).

60. Noss and Cooperrider, *Saving Nature's Legacy*, 50–57; Meffe and Carroll, *Principles of Conservation Biology*, 246–258; and Stephen C. Trombulak and Christopher A. Frissell, "Review of Ecological Effects of Roads on Terrestrial and Aquatic Communities," *Conservation Biology* 14 (2000): 18–30.

61. Meffe and Carroll, *Principles of Conservation Biology*, 254–256.

62. Duane, "Human Settlement: 1850–2040."

63. Michael E. Soulé ("Land Use Plannning and Mildlife Maintenance–Guidelines for Conserving Wildlife in an Urban Landscape," *Journal of the American Planning Association* 57 [1991]: 313–323) and Eric A. Odell and Richard L. Knight ("Songbird and Medium-Sized Mammal Communities Associated with Exurban Development," *Conservation Biology* 15 [2001]: 1143–1150) find that populations of domestic dogs, cats, and other human-tolerant species diminish with distance from rural residential dwellings in Pitkin County, Colorado, while human-sensitive species of birds (i.e., the Green-tailed Towhee, the Dusky Flycatcher, and the Plumbeous Vireo) and mammals (i.e., the red fox and the coyote) increase in numbers with distance from dwellings. This is one of the few studies that focuses on the consequences of exurban sprawl for biodiversity.

64. Carolyn A. Sime, "Domestic Dogs in Wildlife Habitats," in *The Effects of Recreation on Rocky Mountain Wildlife*, 8.1–8.17.

65. Claar et al., "Carnivores."

66. Sime, "Domestic Dogs in Wildlife Habitats."

67. Bryce A. Maxell and Grant Hokit, "Amphibians and Reptiles," in *The Effects of Recreation on Rocky Mountain Wildlife*, 2.1–2.29.

68. Agee, *Fire Ecology of Pacific Northwest Forests*, 58–74.

69. Duane, *Shaping the Sierra*, 243–249.

70. Tony Davis, "The West's Hottest Question: In the Wake of Cerro Grande Fire, Everyone Ponders Prescribed Burning," *High Country News* 32–11 (June 5, 2000): 4–5.

71. Chang, "Ecosystem Responses to Fire."

72. Gayle Joslin and Heidi Youmans, coords., *The Effects of Recreation on Rocky Mountain Wildlife*; and Richard L. Knight and Kevin J. Gutzwiller, *Wildlife and Recreationists: Coexistence through Management and Research* (Washington, D.C.: Island Press, 1995).

73. See the survey results in chapter 6.

74. According to Duane ("Recreation in the Sierra"), in the mid-1990s the Sierra Nevada region alone received 50–60 million visitor days per year for various kinds of recreational activities on public lands. Given the size of this number, many of these recreationists must be nonlocal. In "Human Settlement: 1850–2040," Duane contends that the population of Sierra Nevada counties in 1990 was approximately 2.4 million. Among typical outdoor recreation participation rates, the local population in the Sierra Nevada would account for only a portion of the total recreation visitor days. For participation rates in outdoor recreation activities, see H. Ken Cordell and Susan M. McKinney, *Outdoor Recreation in American Life: A National Assessment of Demand and Supply Trends* (Champaign, Ill.: Sagamore Publishing, 1999), 221–234.

75. Cordell and McKinney, *Outdoor Recreation in American Life*, 15–24.

76. Alfred Runte, *National Parks: The American Experience*, 2d ed. (Lincoln: University of Nebraska Press, 1987).

77. See Cordell and McKinney, *Outdoor Recreation in American Life*, for a more complete analysis of outdoor recreation trends.

78. Richard L. Knight and David N. Cole, "Wildlife Responses to Recreationists," in *Wildlife and Recreationists*, 51–69.

79. Canfield et al., "Ungulates."

80. Claar et al., "Carnivores."

81. Hamann et al., "Birds."

82. Canfield et al., "Ungulates."

83. Claar et al., "Carnivores."

84. Maxell and Hokit, "Amphibians and Reptiles."

85. Hamann et al., "Birds."

86. Gene Hickman, Beverly G. Dixon, and Janelle Corn, "Small Mammals," in *The Effects of Recreation on Rocky Mountain Wildlife*, 4.1–4.16.

87. Claar et al., "Carnivores."

88. Sime, "Domestic Dogs in Wildlife Habitats."

89. Betsy Hamann and Gayle Joslin, "Vegetation, Soil, and Water," in *The Effects of Recreation on Rocky Mountain Wildlife*, 9.1–9.11.

90. Hickman et al., "Small Mammals"; and Maxell and Hokit, "Amphibians and Reptiles."

91. Maxell and Hokit, "Amphibians and Reptiles."

92. Hickman et al., "Small Mammals."

93. Canfield et al., "Ungulates."

5

Rural Sprawl and Rare and Threatened Species in the Mountain West

The predominant threats to plant and animal species in the rural mountain West continue to be those related to the aging extractive and agricultural sectors of the traditional economy. Even though mining, timber production, and farming and ranching are declining in economic importance, many of their ecological effects endure. Acidic leachate from mining tailing piles continue even though mines may no longer be operational. The restoration of an old-growth forest after timber harvesting may take as long as 200 years. The recovery of riparian habitat from degradation by cattle grazing does not occur overnight.

New economic development trends rooted in expanded human mobility and new communications technology manifest themselves in the mountain West in population growth and housing construction, increased local road construction and use, and expansion of commercial facilities. The predominant effect of these trends appears to be relatively low-density housing development well beyond the boundaries of existing urban concentrations. A term we have already suggested that can be used to describe this form of development is *exurban sprawl*—that is, development that is extra-urban and is occurring at low densities. This new form of development has environmental effects of its own that add to the cumulative impacts of the traditional economy. The ecological impacts of low-density housing, road, and commercial development at first glance appear to be substantially less than, say, that of a large copper mine or clear-cut timber harvesting. While this could turn out to be true, the research to establish the point has yet to be undertaken on a large scale. Even if this conclusion is warranted, it is important to remember that the ecological effects of the new economy are being added to the cumulative impacts of the traditional economy. Replacing the traditional with the new economy will not wipe out the ecological history of the old. The effects of the new, whatever they may be, will be added to the old. If the new economy were facing a clean ecological slate and a pristine environment to begin with, then the consequences of new development would be less stressful. But the slate is not clean and new development has the potential to push species and ecosystems already stressed by the old economy over key thresholds into precipitous decline.

Because the ecological effects of the new economy have yet to be studied extensively, a simple literature review is an insufficient vehicle for summarizing new economy environmental impacts. An alternative approach is to ask experts who spend time in the field whether new economy style development appears to be causing stress on the species they study and what the specific sources of such stress might be. After offering a justification for focusing on rare and imperiled species in judging the effects of human population expansion on biodiversity, the experts' survey results will be summarized by broad species categories and by sources of stress. The extent to which stressed species occur in high-growth counties will then be established, and for the state of Colorado a more detailed study of the effect of actual and projected rural housing development on stressed species will be undertaken. The chapter will conclude with a survey of what is known about the effects of development on species suggested by experts to be suffering from stress related to exurban sprawl.

THE FOCUS ON RARE AND IMPERILED SPECIES

Since common species that are not endangered are unlikely to face immediate threats from development, to focus on rare and imperiled species makes some sense. Rare species are more likely to face local extinctions from development than common species. Moreover, most ecosystems contain relatively few species with large populations and many species with small populations. Because of this, ecosystem stresses more likely threaten rare species. Of course, human-induced stresses of sufficient magnitude can ultimately cause common species to become rare and to face extinction. This certainly was the case for the passenger pigeon.[1] Common species, such as elk and mule deer, appear to be abundant today, but the habitat they occupy is much smaller than it was prior to Euro-American settlement. Even though they appear abundant today, further shrinkage of their habitat range could be catastrophic. For this reason, the effects of development on both rare and common species should be studied.[2] Nonetheless, the focus is on rare and imperiled species here because they are likely to be the first to be faced with local extinction from development.

Species can be locally rare or imperiled for any number of reasons, including natural or human-induced habitat restrictions, a naturally restricted range, naturally low population densities, local human-induced stresses, or various combinations of these factors.[3] Local rarity can also occur if a particular species is at the edge of its range. In such cases, local rarity may or may not be an important issue. If ranges are shifting because of climate changes, then local conservation of suitable habitats currently occupied by rare species at their range periphery may be important on a bioregional scale.[4] Species populations on the periphery of their range today could be located in a new core in the future as a consequence of climate change. Normally, peripheral populations have trouble reproducing sufficiently and must be augmented by core populations from time-to-time.[5] If, however, a species is imperiled because of intensive development in the central core of its range, then peripheral populations may be of importance to conserve the species. This reverses the usual source-sink view of core and periphery, but there are cases where peripheral populations have been important for species survival.[6] Local threats to rare species are of special importance if they are endemics and thus located in the core of their range, if they are rare and imperiled throughout their range, and if local populations are genetically isolated.[7] In the latter case, local populations may have genetic characteristics adapted to local conditions. A local population may diverge genetically from populations elsewhere and thus contribute to biodiversity. The preserving of local populations in these cases will be important for preserving biodiversity generally.

In addition to contributing to biodiversity, local populations of species that are present elsewhere may be important for ecological reasons. A particular species may serve different ecological roles in different locations. A wading bird, for example, could be a keystone predator locally, one that has a controlling effect on prey populations.[8] A particular plant that is drought resistant and normally present in low numbers could contribute to ecosystem resilience by expanding its role as a primary producer when less resistant dominants succumb for lack of moisture.[9]

This discussion of course implicitly assumes that conserving biodiversity is a desirable end. A variety of arguments have been offered to support this position.[10] Perhaps the most common one is that certain features of biotic organisms, such as their chemical composition, may well be of material value to human beings. An often cited case is the cancer fighting ability of taxol, a chemical found in the Pacific yew, an old-growth forest understory tree.[11] Another reason to preserve biodiversity is the simple desire to live in a varied and interesting world. A diverse local flora and fauna containing the full spectrum of locally native species may well be more aesthetically pleasing than one that doesn't.[12] A more sophisticated, controversial, and complex argument for conserving species is that local species diversity is essential to maintain the functioning and resilience of local ecosystem. Local ecosystems will simply work better the more diverse they are. A loss of species can lead to threats to valued local ecosystems.[13] The classic example noted by Aldo Leopold is a deer eruption caused by the loss of a key predator on deer—the wolf.[14] Finally, humans may feel like they have a moral obligation to preserve species. After all, each species is a product of the same evolutionary processes that created us.[15]

THE EXPERTS' SURVEY

A rare and imperiled species list was developed using the Natural Heritage database in California, Colorado, and Montana for occurrences in the 86 sample counties.[16] Species with rank S1, S2, and S3 were included on the list for herpetiles, mammals, birds, and vascular plants.[17] The state ranks were used under the assumption that potential losses of local biodiversity is an important issues. A species with an S1 rank is defined as critically imperiled in a state because of extreme rarity (5 or fewer occurrences) or because of some biological characteristic making it especially vulnerable to extirpation. A species having an S2 rank is considered to be imperiled because of rarity (6 to 20 occurrences) or, again, because of some biological characteristic rendering it vulnerable to extirpation. And an S3 rank is applied to a species that is rare in a state (21 to 100 occurrences).

Lists of experts were requested from Natural Heritage Programs for the three states, and university and state Web sites were searched for additional names. Respondents were also asked to provide names of experts as well. All participating experts were sent the full list of S1–S3 ranked species in their area of expertise for the counties in their state. The number of experts participating in the survey by organism category for each state are listed in table 5.1. Also listed are the number of species with rank S1–S3, species respondents believe to be stressed by development.[18] In all, 41 experts provided information on sources of stress.[19]

A survey instrument was formulated for the purpose of asking local experts to evaluate species in their area of research expertise. A list of possible sources of stress to plants and animals from exurban sprawl was provided and experts were asked to indicate whether a particular source of stress is affecting a given species. The sources of stress experts were asked to evaluate appear in table

Table 5.1.   Number of Experts and Species by Category for Each State

	Herpetiles	Birds	Mammals	Vascular plants
Number of experts:				
California	3	5	4	4
Colorado	4	3	3	5
Montana	3	3	5	4
Number of rare and imperiled species:				
California	13	36	10	260
Colorado	14	45	24	255
Montana	11	33	21	189
Number of species stressed by development:				
California	12	34	10	60
Colorado	12	38	14	49
Montana	8	17	13	57

Note: The list of species stressed by development will be provided by the author on request.

5.2.[20] The selection of these sources of stress is based on the discussion of the ecological effects of development in chapter 4. Each respondent was sent a list of species in their area of expertise and were asked to indicate whether a particular source of stress applies for each species. Respondents were also asked to indicate other development-related sources of stress, other affected species not on the survey, and to provide any available literature references documenting development-related stress.

As can be seen from table 5.1, the species lists were comparatively short for herpetiles, birds, and mammals, but fairly lengthy for vascular plants. The length of the list for botanists did not appear to be a deterrent to participation given the relatively high number willing to contribute. The primary problem encountered in finding participants was to locate experts familiar with both the species and the stress sources faced by species in the sample counties.[21] The codes listed in

Table 5.2.   Development-Related Sources of Stress Code Sheet

Code	Significant Direct or Indirect* Source of Stress on Species
NOT	Species is *not* stressed by any human activities.
HABT	Terrestrial habitat area reduction or habitat degradation from subdivision/commercial development and associated roads.
FRAG	Terrestrial habitat fragmentation and creation of migration barriers from subdivision/commercial development and associated roads; creation of edges and the expansion of edge species populations in and around subdivisions.
HABA	Aquatic habitat area reduction, degradation, or fragmentation from subdivision/commercial development and associated roads on or near rivers or streams, lakes, or wetlands, including stream channel modification.
EXOT	Introduction of exotic plants and/or animals in subdivisions and spreading to surrounding habitats
SEPT	Surface water contamination from subdivision septic systems.
SFLO	Reduction in surface water flows from subdivision groundwater drawdowns.
RUNF	Runoff from impervious surfaces and lawns in subdivisions; runoff from commercial development; runoff from associated roads and highways, and subdivision, commercial, and associated road construction sites.
PETS	Cats, dogs, and other pets residing in subdivisions.
NOIS	Noise and artificial light from subdivisions and surrounding areas used by subdivision residents including local roads.
RDKL	Roadkill from traffic associated with subdivisions and commercial development.
FIRE	Disruption of natural fire regimes due to fire suppression to protect residential/commercial development.
PRED	Killing of large predators (i.e., bears) who are perceived to be a danger to local residents.
RECR	Outdoor recreation by local subdivision residents (including motorized, nonmotorized, hunting, fishing, hiking, off-road vehicle use).
OTHR	The species is stressed by other human activities not listed above.

Note: An indirect source of stress is more than one step removed from the affected species, as when one species affects another.

table 5.2 were placed opposite each species name in a table, and respondents were asked to mark any codes that apply to a specific species. A zoologist and a botanist at the Colorado Natural Heritage Program were asked to review the survey instrument, and modifications were made at their suggestion.

The proportion of rare and imperiled species respondents believe to be stressed by rural residential and related development are comparatively high for herpetiles, birds, and mammals in all three states and lower for plants, although the absolute number of plant species is high in comparison to other species, as can be seen in figure 5.1. This follows from the presence of many more species of plants in any given geographic area than vertebrate animals. A lot of the rare

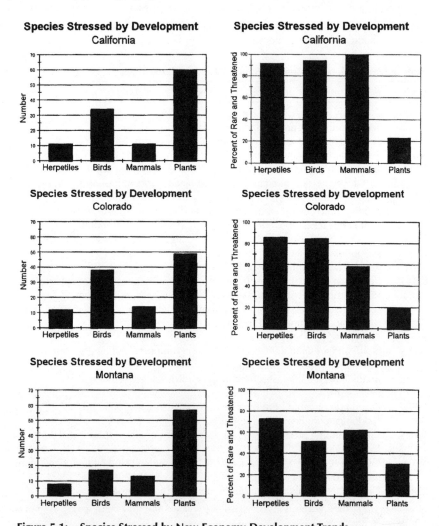

Figure 5.1:   Species Stressed by New Economy Development Trends

plants are found exclusively on public lands at relatively high elevations and are thus less likely to be directly affected by development taking place in valley bottoms on private lands. Moreover, plant surveys on public lands are likely to be more complete than on private lands, causing the rare and threatened plant list for public lands to be longer than for private lands subject to potential development pressures. The proportion of stressed species is generally lower for Montana than California or Colorado, possibly because human population densities and development pressures are somewhat less there.

The relative importance of different sources of stress can be gauged by considering the number of species affected by each source (figures 5.2–5.4). Terrestrial habitat loss, terrestrial habitat fragmentation, aquatic habitat loss, and recreation appear to be the most important sources of stress overall. In addition to these sources of stress, herpetiles are also imperiled by exotics and septic system pollution in California, by pets and roadkill in Colorado, and by the introduction of exotic species in Montana. For birds, habitat loss, habitat fragmentation, and recreation are the dominant sources of stress in all three states. In California and Colorado, pets are a stress source for a relatively large number of mammal species, and in all three states habitat loss and fragmentation are a problem for a fair number of mammal species. Finally, plants suffer primarily from habitat loss in all three states. In sum, new economic development trends in the form of exurban sprawl appear to be causing stress to rare and imperiled species. The primary negative effect of development appears to be habitat loss and fragmentation. While the survey results

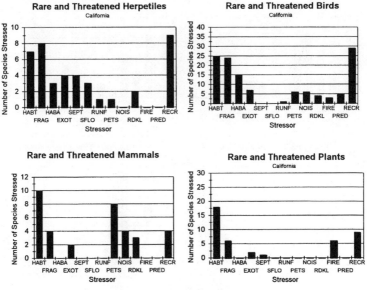

Figure 5.2:   Stresses to Species in California*
*See table 5.2 for definitions of stressors.

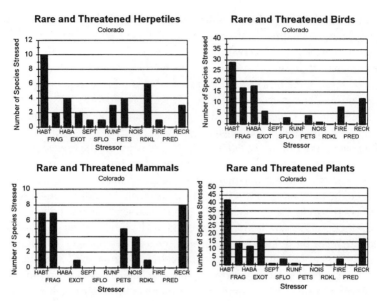

Figure 5.3: Stresses to Species in Colorado*
*See table 5.2 for definitions of stressors.

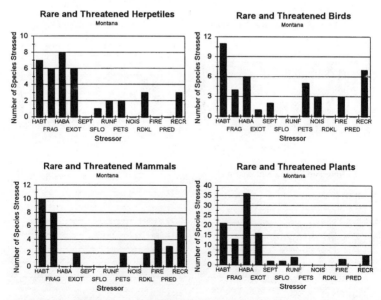

Figure 5.4: Stresses to Species in Montana*
*See table 5.2 for definitions of stressors.

don't address the intensity of such stresses, they do indicate that, in the opinion of experts, such stresses exist. The degree to which these stresses threaten the con-

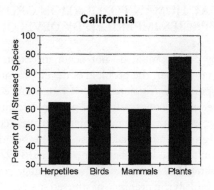

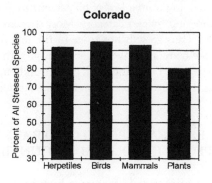

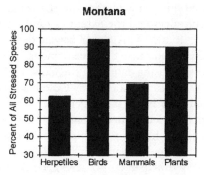

Figure 5.5: Stressed Species in High-Growth Counties

tinued existence of rare species in the mountain counties of the three states can only be established through extensive field research that has yet to be done.

LOCAL HUMAN POPULATION GROWTH
AND SPECIES IMPERILED BY DEVELOPMENT

If species stressed by development do not occur in counties where population growth is relatively rapid, then the problem of development-related stress would not be of much importance. To determine if mountain counties in the three states that were experiencing relatively rapid growth contained species indicated by experts to be affected by development-related stresses, counties were divided into high- and low-growth groups according to whether their growth rate for population density on private lands between 1985 and 1997 was above or below the median for the sample as a whole.[22] Natural Heritage county-level data were then consulted to establish the presence of stressed species. As can be seen in figure 5.5, the proportion of stressed species present in high-growth counties is comparatively high, ranging from a low of 60 percent to as much as 95 percent, depending on the state and species category. Most stressed species are found in high-growth counties. Thus growth hot spots in the mountain West appear to contain species that are being negatively affected by growth. New economy style development thus appears to be taking a toll on rare and imperiled species and is adding to the stresses that already exist from the old extractive economy.

EXURBAN SPRAWL AND RARE
SPECIES IN COLORADO COUNTIES

Establishing the presence of stressed species in high-growth counties is a rather crude approach to determining the impact of growth on rare and imperiled species. A more refined method is to compare the actual location of rare and imperiled species occurrences and the extent of rural residential development where occurrences are found. This would reveal the extent to which such species are potentially threatened by development. For Colorado counties, such an analysis is possible using data from the Colorado Natural Diversity Information Source, a Web site maintained by Colorado State University in cooperation with a number of other state agencies.[23] This data source provides mappings of both species occurrences from the Colorado Natural Heritage database and the density of housing development. Housing density is divided into five categories: urban (more than 1 unit per 2 acres), suburban (1 unit per 2–10 acres), exurban (1 unit per 10–40 acres), ranchette (1 unit per 40–80 acres), and rural (less than 1 unit per 80 acres). These housing density categories are mapped by county for 1960 and 1990 using actual data and for 2020 using projections.

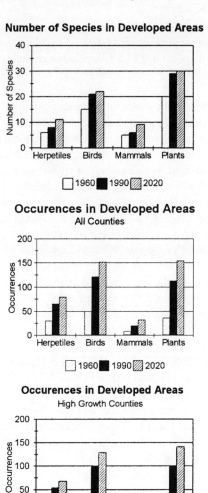

Figure 5.6: Development-Stressed Colorado Species: Ranchette or Greater Density

To determine the extent to which housing development is spreading into habitats of rare and imperiled species suffering from development-related stress, species occurrences were recorded for areas with ranchette or greater housing density in 1960, 1990, and 2020 for each of the 36 sample counties in Colorado. As can be seen in figure 5.6, the number of species, as well as the total occurrences of species within the matrix of development, increased substantially from 1960 to 1990 and will increase even more if the 2020 projections for development hold up. By 2020, 11 of 12 stressed herpetile species, 22 of 38 stressed bird species, 9 of 14 stressed mammal species, and 30 of 49 stressed plant species will be encompassed in ranchette or higher housing density levels.

As noted above, mountain counties experiencing high levels of population density growth also contain most of the species experiencing stress from development. Is this result consistent with the more refined approach of comparing maps of occurrences and development? If it is, high-growth counties should contain most occurrences of stressed species within ranchette or greater density areas. As can be seen in figure 5.6, a large proportion of the occurrences in the sample counties for stressed species are found in high-growth counties. By 2020, the high-growth counties contain 68 of 79 occurrences for herpetiles, 129 of 151 occurrences for birds, 29 of 32 occurrences for mammals, and 141 of 154 occurrences for plants. Clearly, counties subject to rapid growth in Colorado are the same counties where occurrences of rare and imperiled species potentially stressed by development are increasingly being overtaken by housing construction. Rural sprawl is invading the habitats of rare and imperiled species believed by experts to be under stress from development.

RESEARCH ON SPECIES STRESSED
BY EXURBAN RESIDENTIAL DEVELOPMENT

Expert opinion on whether particular species are stressed from development could be wrong. To determine if there is further evidence that exurban development is causing stress to species, several local sources of information on potentially imperiled species were reviewed as were comments and references offered by survey experts to back up their opinions. The results of this review are summarized below.

Herpetiles

Concern has been expressed in all three states about sharp declines in some amphibian and reptile populations. Receiving widespread attention recently are discoveries of deformities in frogs and toads and the disappearance of some species of these animals from habitats where they were previously abundant. Speculation on the cause of stress to frog and toad populations includes increased exposure to ultraviolet radiation, pesticide poisoning, introduced predators, habitat decline, and pathogens. While exurban sprawl is by no means the apparent predominant threat to amphibians and reptiles, in some cases it appears to be a contributing factor.

In his survey of the status of amphibians in the Sierra Nevada, Jennings includes both road building and urbanization in his list of potential threats to amphibians.[24] He notes that the "disappearance of all of the middle- to low-elevation species is due largely to habitat alteration from agriculture, urbanization, water development, placer mining, livestock grazing, drought, and the introduction of a wide variety of non-native predatory fishes, crayfish, and bullfrogs."[25] In specific comments about lungless salamanders, including the Kern Canyon slender and limestone salamanders, Jennings notes that they are "vulnerable to activities that disrupt the hydrology of riparian canyons, the forest floor, and other mesic habitats" including "road building, mining, dam construction, and logging."[26] Another imperiled amphibian, the Del Norte salamander (*Plethodon elongatus*), is found primarily in old-growth forests and is likely to suffer stress from logging and conversion of old-growth to even-aged younger stands, although experts indicated that residential development is also a stressor for this species.[27]

The true frogs in the Sierra Nevada are among the amphibians suffering from serious population declines. The black toad (*Bufo exsul*) is a narrowly distributed endemic found in the Deep Springs Valley in Inyo County and is being affected by development-related activity according to survey respondents.[28] By contrast, the California toad (*Bufo boreas halophilus*) is widely distributed throughout the Sierra Nevada. This species is not a part of the Natural Heritage database and was not considered in the experts' survey. Jennings notes that its populations seem to have been reduced by urbanization and changing farming practices, although it still seems to be comparatively abundant. The highly threatened Yosemite toad (*B. Canorus*) is a high-elevation species and is thus not subject to threat by development. The same is the case for the mountain yellow-legged frog (*Rana muscosa*).[29] Although the northern leopard frog (*R. pipiens*) is threatened in California, survey respondents disagree on whether it is affected by residential development. The foothill yellow-legged frog (*R. boylii*) is found in habitats subject to strong development pressures, although it wasn't listed in the Natural Heritage database for the sample counties at the time the species list for the experts' survey was assembled (Spring 1998).[30] Degradation of riparian habitat from road building and other human activities is a critical problem for the foothill yellow-legged frog as well as stress from introduced bull frogs.[31] Another species, the western spadefoot (*Scaphiopus hammondii*), is found on the edge of the Sierra Nevada foothills and is apparently negatively affected by urbanization according to Jennings, although introduced predators may be a more important source of stress.[32] The more northerly cascade frog (*Rana cascadae*) is declining significantly at the southern end of its range in California near Mt. Lassen, primarily because of (1) the presence of non-native, predatory fish which have restricted habitat and limited dispersal of frogs, (2) loss of breeding habitat due to a five-year drought, and (3) the gradual loss of open meadows and associated aquatic habitats.[33] This species may also be threatened by increased ultraviolet radiation.[34] In sum, exurban development is apparently not the predominant threat to California amphibians, although for some species it appears to be contributing to population declines fostered in large part by extractive activities. In other words, exurban development is adding to the already existing threat as a consequence of the traditional forms of rural economic activity.

Certain California reptile species appear to be more significantly affected by development than amphibians. In his review of the status of terrestrial vertebrates, Graber suggests that the blunt-nosed leopard lizard (*Zambelia silus*) is experiencing habitat loss as a consequence of urbanization in the Sierra foothills.[35] The same is the case for the California horned lizard (*Phryonosoma coronatum frontale*), a species that has experienced significant declines in population and appears to be negatively affected by domestic cats.[36] Stresses on the western pond turtle (*Clemmys marmorata*) in the Sierra Nevada appear to be primarily from predation on young turtles by introduced bull frogs and from riparian habitat modification such as dam construction.[37] However, Brattstrom has documented significant population declines in the pond turtle in southern California because of urban development.[38] The desert tortoise (*Xerobates agassizi*) occupies desert habitat at the very southern end of the Sierra Nevada where experts indicate that exurban residential development is a stressor, although other kinds of disturbances are the primary source of population declines, including habitat decline, ravens, vehicle kills, and vandalism.[39] Again, rural sprawl is not the predominant problem facing reptile species but is contributing to stresses created by the traditional rural economy.

As in California, amphibians in the Rocky Mountains have also undergone disquieting declines in populations. In both Colorado and Montana, the boreal toad (*Bufo boreas boreas*) has disappeared from many of its historically recorded sites and cannot be found in suitable habitats.[40] The northern leopard frog (*Rana pipiens*) has also suffered from significant declines in both states.[41] Survey experts agree that rural development is a source of stress for both species. In Colorado, the immediate cause of decline for the boreal toad appears to be disease in at least one case, but the ultimate cause could well be environmental toxins. The boreal toad occurs at elevations above 7,000 feet in Colorado, so only the lower part of its range is likely to be significantly affected by development pressures. The leopard frog, on the other hand, is found at lower elevations and is potentially subject to somewhat greater development pressure. Nonetheless, 26 occurrences for the boreal toad in Colorado were located in areas subject to ranchette or higher densities in 1990, while the comparable number for the northern leopard frog was 16. Also, according to Livo, boreal toads are subject to predation from raccoons able to survive at high elevations in part because of the foraging opportunities associated with residential dwellings.[42] The same may be true for an observed predation on a toad by a red fox. Livo reports predation on a toad by a dog that could be associated with local residential development. Moreover, water quality problems from road runoff and other sources may be a significant source of boreal toad egg mortality. Only four occurrences of the wood frog (*Rana sylvatica*) are located within areas of ranchette or greater housing density, and this species has been recently delisted from its imperiled status in Colorado.[43] The decline of the leopard frog can be attributed in part to the presence of bullfrogs, although not entirely.[44] In Montana, the Great Plains toad (*Bufo cognatus*) occurs predominantly on private lands and is thus potentially subject to development pressure.[45]

Reptiles in Colorado and Montana are also facing population declines and development may be a contributing factor in some cases. In Colorado, residential development is occurring at the margins of protected habitat for the longnose leopard lizard (*Gambelia wislizenii*) according to Livo.[46] For this species, 2 occurrences in the mountain counties (out of 26 occurrences for the state) are expected to be overtaken by ranchette or greater density of development by the year 2020. Although habitat for this species is fairly common (sagebrush and greasewood stands on deep, sandy soils), its suitability is being reduced by the invasion of cheatgrass.[47] The southern plateau lizard (*Scleoporus undulatus tristichus*) is at the northern margin of its range and has a relatively small number of occurrences. While not currently threatened, human population growth is taking place in localities where the species is found.[48] One occurrence currently is within an area of ranchette plus housing density. The western yellowbelly racer (*Coluber constrictor mormon*) and the Utah milk snake (*Lampropeltis trangulum taylori*), like most snakes, are vulnerable to mortality from road traffic. Extensive residential development has occurred in the Grand Valley of Colorado (Mesa County) where both snake species are found.[49] The western yellowbelly racer at present has eight occurrences within areas with ranchette or greater residential density, while the Utah milk snake has five occurrences. The only other reptile with a significant number of occurrences (four in two counties) within areas having ranchette or greater residential density is the southwestern blackhead snake (*Tantilla hobartsmithi*). Threats to this snake are apparently minimal, although human encroachment is a problem in some localities.[50] The ringneck snake (*Diadophis punctatus*) is facing stress from development-related habitat loss in Colorado according to two survey respondents. A subspecies of this species (*Diadophis punctatus edwarsii* Merrem) is apparently sensitive to habitat fragmentation in central Canada.[51] The blackneck garter snake (*Thamnophis cyrtopsis*) is at the northern edge of its range in Colorado and consequently occurs in relatively low numbers. Currently there is one occurrence of the species within areas having ranchette or higher housing density and it suffers mortality from road traffic.[52]

In the view of experts, the four Montana reptiles affected by development are all found predominantly on private land, are poorly surveyed, and have few known occurrences.[53] The snapping turtle (*Chelydra serpentina*) is a long-lived species having a relatively low rate of reproduction. It is a species that is highly co-evolved with its environment and for this reason does not respond well to chronic disturbances.[54] Both the snapping turtle and the spiny softshell (*Apalona spinifer*) are human consumption targets in part because of the large body size of some adults.[55] Little is known about threats to the western hognose snake (*Heterodon nasicus*) or the milk snake (*Lampropeltis triangulum*) in Montana, although certainly roadkill is a potential problem in areas of relatively dense residential development and resulting high levels of road use.

For many amphibians and reptiles, the specific causes of population decline are not known with certainty. However, in a number of cases, rural residential development appears to be adding to other stresses on rare and imperiled herpetiles. The critical problems caused by development appear to be habitat loss, altered riparian habitats, and increased populations of predators associated with human presence (including pets).

Birds

Of the vertebrates, the sheer number of rare and imperiled birds in the mountain counties of the three states is substantially greater than for reptiles and mammals combined. This holds true for bird species experts believe to be affected by exurban development as well. In California, 34 of 36 rare and imperiled bird species are considered by experts to be suffering some form of stress from development-related human effects. The figures are respectively 38 of 45 for Colorado and 17 of 33 for Montana.

In the Sierra Nevada, stresses to bird species from development appear to include the loss of foothill riparian communities and oak woodlands, threats from Cowbird parasitism, and increased populations of house cats. Rare and imperiled species, mentioned by experts as stressed by development, that require foothill habitats include the Burrowing Owl (*Athene cunicularia*), the Long-Eared Owl (*Asio otus*), Yellow Breasted Chat (*Icteria verens*), and the Tricolored Blackbird (*Agelaius tricolor*). Moreover, rare and imperiled species, mentioned by experts as stressed by development, that use, but don't require, foothill habitats include the California Condor (*Gymnogyps californianus*),[56] Osprey (*Pandion haliaetus*), Bald Eagle (*Haliaeetus leucocephalus*), Cooper's Hawk (*Accipiter cooperii*), Golden Eagle (*Aquila chrysaetos*), Prairie Falcon (*Falco mexicanus*), Great Gray Owl (*Strix nebulosa*),[57] Horned Lark (*Eremophila alpestris actia*), and Yellow Warbler (*Dendroica petechia brewsteri*). Large areas of mowed grass attract Brown-headed Cowbirds (*Molothrus ater*) that cause brood parasitism problems for such species as the Least Bell's Vireo (*Vireo bellii pusillus*) and Yellow Warbler. The Least Bell's Vireo is extinct in the Sierra Nevada and remains only in a few locations in southern California and the central coast. House cats prey on a variety of bird species as well reptiles and small mammals that serve as food sources for many birds. In general, landbirds of the Sierran oak woodland and lower foothill grasslands, whether rare and imperiled or not, appear to be experiencing population declines.[58] While the many stresses on bird species that use the Sierran foothills predate significant exurban development, such human encroachment is apparently now adding to problems faced by bird species of the Sierra Nevada. On the eastern side of the Sierras, development pressure is less extensive, but there is one instance where development around the Mammoth Lakes Airport could eliminate habitat for the Sage Grouse (*Centrocercus urophasianus*).[59]

As in California, rare and imperiled bird species affected by exurban development in Colorado are comparatively large in number. In 1990, 21 bird species indicated by experts to be stressed by development had occurrences within ranchette or higher housing density. Since these species are most likely to be threatened by development, the Natural Heritage database comments were reviewed for indications of development-related stresses.

Birds dependent on aquatic habitat are affected by development pressures that lead to aquatic habitat alteration or occur on or near wetlands, streams, or lakes. While the Great Blue Heron is widespread and adaptable, like many bird species it is threatened by human disturbance to nest sites and by wetland destruction and contamination. Although there is no specific evidence for Colorado, these threats can be the result of housing development and new roads. Eleven occurrences for the Great Blue Heron (*Ardea herodias*) were found within ranchette or higher density development for 1990. The Snowy Egret (*Egretta thula*) is relatively uncommon in Colorado and occurs at 11 breeding sites. One occurrence is within ranchette or higher density. While the population appears stable in Colorado, it is subject to stress from human disturbances to nesting colonies and habitat loss. Suffering similar threats (although less common than Snowy Egrets) are Green Herons (*Butorides virescens*) with two to four breeding occurrences in Colorado. One occurrence is within the sphere of ranchette or higher housing density, and the species is especially threatened by human disturbance along the Front Range. The Black-crowned Night Heron (*Nycticorax nycticorax*) is somewhat more prevalent in the state with at least 17 breeding sites. Threats include wetland loss, pollution and draining of reservoirs, river and marsh pollution, and human disturbance to nests during the breeding season. Two of these occurrences are within ranchette or higher housing density. The White-faced Ibis (*Plegadis chihi*) has eight confirmed breeding locations in the state and one occurrence within ranchette or higher housing density. It also suffers from threats to habitat and human encroachment, although breeding success appears to have improved nationally.

Birds of prey are also subject to development pressures that decrease habitat or disturb nesting sites. The Osprey (*Pandion haliaetus*) is near the southern end of its range in Colorado with 11 breeding sites. Five occurrences of the species are found within ranchette plus housing density. The species is considered vulnerable in Colorado because of low numbers, although it has expanded its range in the state somewhat. Both the Bald Eagle (*Haliaeetus Leucocephalus*) and the Northern Goshawk (*Accipter gentilis*) are comparatively abundant in the state, although 25 and 28 occurrences respectively for the two species are within ranchette or greater housing density. The Bald Eagle is threatened by loss of habitat from waterfront development along the state's waterways, lakes, and reservoirs, while the Northern

Goshawk suffers threats from forest fragmentation and development. Although the American Peregrine Falcon (*Falco peregrines anatum*) may have 70 pairs breeding in the state, its numbers are still considered to be critically low, and 19 occurrences are found within ranchette or higher density.

A variety of landbirds potentially suffer from the effects of residential and related development. The Gunnison Sage Grouse (*Centrocercus minimus gunnisonii*) is an endemic sub-species with a population of about 5,000 individuals and three occurrences with ranchette plus housing density. The population appears to have been reduced by habitat fragmentation and degradation. This is in part the result of the application of fire and herbicides to sagebrush habitat and the encroachment of pinyon-juniper forests upon sagebrush parks as a consequence of long-term fire suppression in forests. The Columbia Sharp-tailed Grouse (*Tympanuchus phasianellus columbianus*) also has 3 occurrences within ranchette or higher housing density and at least 15 total occurrences in the northwest part of the state. It suffers from habitat loss and fragmentation due to rangeland conversion, herbicide treatment, mineral exploration, and urban development. The Greater Sandhill Crane (*Grus canadensis tabida*) is a spring and fall migrant species with a population in the San Luis Valley that may be as high as 17,000, although records of breeding occurrences are fairly low. With just two occurrences within ranchette or higher residential density, exurban encroachment does not appear to be a major problem yet. The Mountain Plover (*Charadrius montanus*) migrates to summer breeding grounds on shortgrass prairies and prairie dog towns and occurs within the Arkansas valley and southern Park County where two occurrences are within ranchette or higher residential density. The current population of 3,000 plover in Colorado is below historical levels because of habitat decline. The Long-billed Curlew (*Numenius americanus*) also migrates to summer breeding grounds on shortgrass prairies and has approximately 86 breeding occurrences in the state with 2 occurrences within ranchette or higher residential density. The species has probably experienced population reductions because of disturbance to breeding areas. The Mexican Spotted Owl (*Strix occidentalis lucida*) inhabits forested canyons and old-growth, mixed conifer forests with most occurrences found in the southern part of the state. Of approximately 18 occurrences, 4 are found within areas having ranchette or higher residential densities. The Short-eared Owl (*Asio flammeus*) is a year-round resident of Colorado, occupying open fields, marshes, dunes, and grasslands. There are 20 documented breeding sites with 1 occurrence within ranchette or higher residential density. While the population appears to be stable, it is relatively low and breeding is apparently infrequent. The Marsh Wren (*Cistothorus palustris*) occupies cattail marshes year-round in Colorado and features 11 breeding sites in the state and 1 occurrence within an area with ranchette or higher residential density. This species has relatively low population levels in the state primarily because of a scarcity of its preferred habitat and the effects of water management practices. With 1 occurrence in an area of ranchette or higher residential density, the American Redstart (*Setophaga ruticilla*) is at the periphery of its range in Colorado, and it occurs at relatively low numbers but faces no known threats. The Sage Sparrow (*Amphispiza belli*) has more than 60 occurrences in the state, but is facing a loss of sagebrush shrubland habitat. Four occurrences of the sparrow are within the sphere of ranchette or greater housing density. The Bobolink (*Dolichonyx oryzivorus*), a neotropical migrant, is comparatively rare in Colorado with breeding occurring in moist tallgrass meadows and hayfields. Three occurrences of this species are found in areas with ranchette or higher residential densities, and it is threatened by conversion of meadows and hayfields to other uses. Finally, Scott's Oriole (*Icterus parisorum*) is a minimal breeder in the state with less than 10 known records. This species breeds in isolated pinyon-juniper or juniper groves in the arid shrublands of western Colorado and has two occurrences within areas of ranchette or higher residential density.[60]

The research on the consequences of exurban development for Colorado bird species is clearly limited in scope. The information that is available does, however, suggest that development-related stresses could well have a negative impact on bird species. Clearly, more work is needed to establish the extent of stresses to birds from rural residential development in Colorado.[61]

Of the three states, Montana rare and imperiled bird species are probably the least affected by development pressures (given the relatively low number of birds judged by experts as affected by development pressures). While some counties are experiencing development pressure, as noted in chapter 3, population density levels and growth are rather less in Montana than California or Colorado.

Of the birds dependent on aquatic habitat in Montana, loons are perhaps the most threatened. The only significant populations west of the Mississippi for the Common Loon (*Gavia immer*) are found in Montana where threats from recreation and development are significant. Approximately 200 loons are found in Montana with about 65 breeding pairs.[62] Loons are flushed from their nest sites by boats approaching within 70 to 140 meters during incubation.[63] In addition to stresses from recreation, habitat loss from shoreline development is also a threat to continued reproduction success because of the loss of nesting sites. Successful hatching decreases as the number of cottages within 150 meters of the nesting site increases, and loons avoid lakes under 20 hectares unless at least half of the shoreline is undisturbed by houses and roads.[64] Like loons, the Clark's Grebe (*Aechmophorus clarkii*) also seems to be highly sensitive to development pressures on lakes and is prone to nest abandonment when approached by humans. One other aquatic species, the Trumpeter Swan (*Cygnus buccinator*), has experienced increasing numbers in recent years because of recovery efforts and appears to suffer moderate disturbance from nearby road traffic when it occurs near swan habitat.[65]

A critical problem for all birds of prey is human trespass on nesting territory. Disturbance to nesting sites can cause a variety of problems including parental abandonment of eggs, increased predation on eggs, trampling of young by parent birds, and premature departure of nestlings. Bald Eagles, with breeding territories associated with rivers, lakes, and reservoirs in Montana, appear to be sensitive to a variety of human disturbances including urban development activities. Northern Goshawks, who occupy coniferous forests in Montana, are known to have abandoned nests because of human disturbance, although the relationship of such disturbance to residential development is unknown. The Ferruginous Hawk (*Buteo regalis*) in Montana finds optimum habitat in sagebrush and grassland areas and suffers from unpredictable disturbances during breeding season that cause nest abandonment or reduce parental attentiveness to nestlings. Disturbance to foraging habitats can increase mortality to young birds by disrupting hunting or causing collisions with vehicles.[66] The Burrowing Owl (*Athene cuicularia*) suffers mortality as a by-product of prairie dog and gopher hunting, while owls in general, including the Flammulated Owl (*Otus flammeolus*) are attracted to roadsides for perching and hunting and as a consequence suffer from increased mortality from vehicle collisions.[67]

Threats to Montana landbirds include predation on the Piping Plover (*Charadrius melodus*) by pets. This species is also negatively affected by human disturbance on river shorelines, popular for both recreation and development. The Mountain Plover (*Charadrius montanus*) appears to be suffering from the loss of prairie dog towns where it finds optimum habitat. The Columbian Sharp-tailed Grouse (*tympanuchus phasianellus columbianus*) is losing rangeland habitat to a variety of land uses, including urbanization. Cavity nesters, such as the Black-backed Woodpecker (*Picoides arcticus*), appear to be sensitive primarily to habitat loss from logging.[68]

As in the case of Colorado, research on the effects of residential development on bird species in Montana is very limited. The one instance where work has been done on the effects of development suggests that shoreline residential activity has a negative effect on Loon reproduction.

Mammals

Judging by the relatively low number of rare and imperiled species listed in the Natural Heritage database and the limited numbers of species experts believe to be stressed by exurban residential development, mammals are less threatened than other vertebrate species. The one exception perhaps is the grizzly bear (*Ursus arctos horribilis*) in Montana.

In California, according to experts mammals affected by residential development include one species of bat, several small mammals, two medium-sized predators, and bighorn sheep. Experts suggest that the pallid bat (*Antrozous pallidus*) is stressed by the presence of pets and is suffering habitat loss as a result of development. This bat requires Sierran foothills habitat, an area subject to strong development pressures. Generally speaking, feral and pet cats prey on small mammals adjacent to residential development and are in competition with small carnivores. Experts agree that the Fresno (*Dipodomys nitratoides exilis*), Tipton (*Dipodomys nitratiodes nitratiodes*), and Panamint (*Dipodomys panamintinus panamintinus*) kangaroo rats experience stress from the presence of pets. Medium-sized carnivores potentially affected by development—the Sierra Nevada red fox (*vulpes vulpes necator*) and the California wolverine (*gulo gulo luteus*)—are seldom observed and not extensively studied. The historical decline of the California bighorn sheep (*Ovis canadensis californiana*) occurred for a variety of reasons, including disease transferred from domestic sheep to bighorns, hunting, and overgrazing by domestic animals. Experts suggest that habitat loss from residential development, pets, noise, roadkill, and recreation are all currently additional sources of stress for bighorn sheep.[69]

In Colorado the effects of residential development on mammals have yet to be studied, so very little definitive information is available.[70] Nonetheless, there are currently 20 occurrences of rare and imperiled mammal species within ranchette or higher residential density, and the number of such occurrences is projected to grow to 33 by 2020.

In Colorado the desert, pygmy, and dwarf shrews (*Notiosorex crawfordi*, *Sorex hoyi montanus*, and *Sorex nanus*) are all projected to have occurrences within the sphere of ranchette or greater residential density by 2020, although only the pygmy shrew has an occurrence in such an area currently. The desert shrew is projected to have three occurrences by 2020, the dwarf shrew four, and the pygmy shrew just one. The desert shrew is at the northern edge of its range in Colorado and occurs in arid and semi-arid habitats. Little is known about its relative abundance. The pygmy shrew, in contrast, occupies certain relatively high-elevation forest meadow (9,600 feet), bog, and parkland habitats and may be a relict population remaining from glacial times. While data to determine abundance is unavailable, it is believed to be quite rare in the state. The dwarf shrew, on the other hand, is fairly widespread in suitable habitats of the state, although its numbers are somewhat limited by a relative scarcity of such habitats.[71] Experts suggest that pets are a source of stress for all three shrews.

Of the bats that experts indicate are affected by residential development, the spotted bat (*Euderma maculatum*) and the Yuma myotis (*Myotis yumanensis*) lack occurrences in areas having ranchette or higher residential density levels, while Townsend's big-eared bat (*Plecotus townsendii*) and the Brazilian free-tailed bat (*Plecotus townsendii pallescens*) have respectively five and two occurrences in such areas. The limiting factor for the Townsend's big-eared bat appears to be undisturbed abandoned mines and caves for day roosts and winter hibernacula. Human disturbances to mines and caves are apparently key sources of stress to wintering and roosting bats, and such disturbances are likely to be greater in areas where residential development occurs. Townsend's big-eared bat occurs in shrublands, pinyon-juniper woodlands, and open montane forests near appropriate cave habitats.[72] The Brazilian free-tailed bat is at the northern edge of its range in Colorado and occurs seasonally in lower-elevation, pinyon-juniper woodlands, semidesert shrublands, and arid grasslands. In Colorado the species is known from a single, large colony at the Orient Mine protected by an agreement with a landowner and several other non-breeding occurrences. Although no concrete population estimates are available, this species is thought to be declining both locally and globally.[73]

Amongst the small- to medium-sized predators, the kit fox (*Vulpes macrotis*) is at the eastern edge of its range in Colorado. This species is secretive and difficult to detect and is known from a restricted range in the Colorado River Basin and southwest corner of the state. Urban encroachment into low-elevation native habitat is one of several sources of stress for this rare species, as well as mortality from motor vehicles.[74] By 2020, two occurrences of this species are predicted to be encompassed in areas of ranchette or higher residential density. Both the wolverine (*Gulo gulo*) and the lynx (*Lynx canadensis*) are known in the state primarily from historical occurrences. The wolverine is at the southern edge of its range in the Colorado mountain habitat and probably no longer occurs in the state. The lynx, however, has recent documented occurrences in Eagle County. A total of five historical occurrences for the lynx are found in areas of ranchette or higher residential density, while six historical occurrences are found in such areas for the wolverine.[75]

For the remaining mammals, the badger (*Taxidea taxus berlandieri*), the plains pocket gopher (*Thomomys talpoides agrestis*), and Ord's kangaroo rat (*Dipodomys ordii sanrafaeli*) lack any occurrences within areas having ranchette or higher residential density while Botta's pocket gopher (*Thomomys bottae pervagus*) has two currently. Colorado is on the northeastern edge of the range for the latter species, and it appears not to be threatened by human activity in the state.[76] Apart from the opinion of experts and the existence of occurrences within ranchette or greater residential density, there is no indication in the comments for Natural Heritage occurrences that residential development is a source of stress for mammals, except possibly the kit fox.

Small mammals in Montana that are apparently affected by residential development include Preble's shrew (*Sorex preblei*), Merriam's shrew (*Sorex merriami*), fringed myotis (*Myotis thysanodes*), Townsend's big-eared bat (*Corynorhinus townsendii*), black-tailed jack rabbit (*Lepus californicus*), pygmy rabbit (*Brachylagus idahoensis*), and the black-tailed prairie dog (*Cynomys ludovicianus*). As noted for Colorado, bats suffer primarily from human disturbance to their roost sites in caves and mines. Two other problems occur for bats that may be related to exurban residential development. As human settlement and use expands into areas where abandoned mines are found, mines are being closed and buildings and culverts are being demolished, reducing bat roosting habitat. In addition, noise at night from local roads and subdivisions can interfere with the ability of bats to use echolocation for communication, navigation, and prey location. Local road traffic is also a source of mortality for other small mammal species. Preble's shrew, the dwarf shrew, and the pygmy and black-tailed jack rabbit occur at lower elevations in low shrub and sagebrush habitat where private ownership of land and development is somewhat more likely to occur. Recreational shooting is a serious source of stress for increasingly rare populations of prairie dogs.[77]

Among the mammals in Montana, the carnivores appear to be affected the most by human activity. By the 1930s, the gray wolf (*Canus lupus*) suffered virtual extirpation from the western United States as a consequence of shooting and trapping. However, wolves have recolonized northwestern Montana and are being reintroduced in the Yellowstone area. Experts indicate that wolves suffer habitat loss, habitat fragmentation, and increased mortality from human interactions as a consequence of exurban development. Studies in the northern Great Lakes area show that wolves tend to avoid regions with high road densities, suggesting that subdivisions and related roads reduce the amount of habitat for wolves. In the more rugged Rocky Mountains, wolves tend to be found closer to roads because wolves prefer environments in valley bottoms where roads are typically located. Valley bottoms feature lower snow levels in winter, ungulates as a food source, and rendezvous and den sites. Because residential subdivisions are also attracted to valley bottoms, wolf mortality from human-wolf interaction is likely to rise as subdivision development increases. Humans are responsible for a significant proportion of wolf mortalities through vehicle collisions, abandonment of dens, and increased energy costs from human-induced disturbances, as well as from illegal shooting and trapping. Pet dogs create problems for wolf populations by causing the abandonment of den or rendezvous sites. Dogs also have the potential to introduce diseases into wolf populations. While wolves are a highly adaptable species, they require landscapes where human influence is minimized.[78]

The swift fox (*Vulpes velox*) is more of a habitat specialist than the wolf, occurring in prairie locales in mountain counties along the Rocky Mountain front. Historically the swift fox suffered population declines because of predator-control, hunting and trapping, and loss of prairie habitat. In 1969 swift fox were declared extinct in Montana, but have been observed in the state since then and may be reestablishing themselves. The primary effects of subdivision and related development on the swift fox include increased vehicular collisions and the presence of domestic dogs and the diseases they can potentially transmit to swift fox populations.

The mammal species most associated with Montana—the grizzly bear (*Ursus arctos horribilis*)—is possibly the one most threatened by exurban development. Historically, grizzly bears were viewed as a threat and were eliminated from all but a few mountainous locations in the lower 48 states. Grizzly bears continue to occur in the northern Rockies in Montana as well as in the Yellowstone area. The biggest threats to the grizzly are human-caused mortality that occurs as a result of back country human-bear confrontations, conflicts with bears attracted to livestock food and human garbage, efforts to protect livestock, encroachment of human settlement on bear habitat, and legal and illegal hunting.[79] Residential development is accelerating in grizzly bear habitat, increasing the likelihood of human-grizzly conflicts.[80] Habitat-space limitations, along with human-related food sources, are apparently causing some grizzlies to utilize private lands and suffer greater mortality levels as a result.[81] In these areas, mortalities occur from both malicious killing and the legal removal of bears conditioned to human-related sources of food such as garbage. In one case, a new Whitefish, Montana area subdivision development is apparently funneling grizzlies into a relatively high-density residential area that has an abundance of food sources.[82] In addition to serving as death traps for bears, residential development and associated road construction are constraining grizzly bear habitat. Residential development and high road densities in the Swan Valley may be preventing grizzlies from using an area with high spring habitat potential for females and closing off a linkage for bears between the Bob Marshall and Mission Mountain wilderness areas. Eventually this may limit use of the Mission Mountains by grizzlies.[83] Grizzlies also tend to avoid utilizing their natural food resources, such as whitebark pine nut middens constructed by squirrels, near roads and town sites.[84]

The three remaining carnivores that experts suggest are stressed by exurban development in Montana, are the fisher (*Martes pennanti*), the North American wolverine (*Gulo gulo*), and the lynx (*Felis lynx*). The fisher is generally found in a variety of conifer-dominated habitat, while the wolverine tends to prefer higher-elevation subalpine areas. The lynx prefers mid- to upper-elevation cool, moist forest types. All three species have suffered historical population declines because of trapping. Also, all three potentially suffer from vehicle collision mortality because they are wide-ranging species, and the lynx is vulnerable to habitat loss from resort and a ski area development.[85]

Although the total acres of land subjected to exurban development is comparatively small relative to the total acres of land in the sample counties for Montana, much development is occurring along lake and river shorelines and in valley bottoms. These types of landscape are limited in area and are critical habitats for rare and imperiled species such as the loon, the gray wolf, and the grizzly bear. Consequently, although exurban development in Montana has yet to reach the kinds of densities that occur in California or Colorado, the location of such development appears to be causing added stress to certain species.

Plants

Because local plant populations often include endemics or are frequently genetically isolated from populations elsewhere, exurban development that reduces or alters local habitat can have a significant effect on the biodiversity of plants. With 36 percent of its native flora being endemic and restricted to a particular locality or habitat within the state, plant diversity in California is especially vulnerable to development pressures. The large number of rare plants in the state can be explained in part by its climate which features dry summers and cool, wet winters. The state's diverse topography and latitudinal diversity also contribute to the presence of a large number of rare plant species.[86] According to the California Native Plant Society, California's rare plants are increasingly threatened by "the spread of urbanization, by our conversion of land to agriculture, by alteration of natural hydrological cycles, by recreational activities and nonnative plants and animals and by pollution."[87] Annual plants suffer the special threat of infrequent (or stochastic) events, such as unusual weather that can inhibit reproduction and cause local extinctions, and are especially endangered because of their relative concentration in lowland habitats where urban and agricultural development predominate. Most plant extinctions in California have occurred among the low-land flora, including plants found in grasslands, wetlands, oak woodlands, and chaparral. Blue oak savannas, a habitat type in the western slope foothills, are suffering habitat losses for rare plants because of the subdivision of large land parcels into ranchettes and other forms of exurban residential development. Alteration of fire frequency, because of development in chaparral habitats, may be reducing populations of fire-dependent species.[88] While high-elevation habitats are frequently protected as parks or designated wilderness, this is seldom the case for the species-rich lowland areas and foothills in the Sierra Nevada region where threats to native plant species from development are greatest.

Among the three states considered in this book, the expansion of residential development into rural mountain areas has been most extensive in California. Moreover, in California evidence of the effects of residential development on plants is relatively substantial. Of the 260 rare and endangered species in the Natural Heritage database for the mountain counties, site information in the database from field survey forms indicates that residential development is a threat to 48 species. For these species, 11.6 percent of the reported occurrences in the database are listed as threatened by development. In addition, residential development is also indicated to be a threat for 30 of these species in the California Native Plant Society's Inventory of Rare and Endangered Vascular Plants of California.[89] Another 12 rare and threatened species in the Natural Heritage database are listed in the Plant Society's inventory as endangered by residential development for a total of 60 species. Of the 60, survey experts commented on 21 of them, indicating that habitat loss was a problem for 19 species. Moreover, because 50 of these species are California endemics, their local extinction would result in a global loss of biodiversity at the species level. Among the California endemics are 15 annuals subject to their own special dangers of extinction because of infrequent (stochastic) but inevitable events. All 60 species have occurrences at elevations below the range of upper montane forests and therefore in landscapes where protection in parks and wilderness areas is fairly rare.[90]

In California mountain counties, plants are clearly suffering stress from the pressures of exurban development, particularly in the foothills and valley bottoms where both plant diversity and development pressures are relatively high. The experts' survey results suggests a similar situation for Colorado. As already noted, experts indicate that a total of 49 plant species are stressed by development in Colorado. Of these 49, by 2020, 30 will have a total of 154 occurrences in areas with ranchette or higher residential density, up from 112 occurrences in 1990, and 50 occurrences in 1960. Residential development is clearly spreading into habitats for rare and imperiled plants in the mountain counties of Colorado. Of the 30 species occurring within areas of ranchette plus residential density, 15 are endemics and don't occur outside the region. Thus their loss would reduce species diversity at both the local and global level. Moreover, 16 of the species have occurrences below 7,000 feet elevation where protection in national parks or designated wilderness is less likely.[91] The species that appears to be most affected by development in the eyes of experts, Harrington beardtongue (*Penstemon harringtonii*), occurs in valleys and is an endemic.[92]

With its lower level of development pressure, threats to plants in Montana from exurban development are likely to be diminished relative to California and Colorado. Because the valley bottom and foothill flora of Montana is not well studied, little is know about the stresses to plants posed by residential development. There may well be only a few plants that are directly threatened by subdivision development currently.[93] Nonetheless, experts did list a total of 57 species that appear to be affected by development. Of these, all but three have occurrences below 5,000 feet elevation where protection in national parks and designated wilderness is less likely than at higher elevations. Of the 57 species, 5 are endemics, 9 are annuals, and 30 have 25 percent or more of their occurrences partly or wholly on private (nonindustrial timber) lands. Four of the five endemics have 25 percent or more of their occurrences partly or wholly on private lands and occur below 5,000 feet elevation. These species are the sapphire rockcress (*Arabis fecunda*), Howell's gumweed (*Grindelia howellii*), Lemhi beardtongue (*Penstemon lemhiensis*), and Missoula phlox (*Phlox kelseyi var missoulensis*).[94]

CONCLUSION

The research needed to establish with reasonable certainty that population spreading and rural residential development is causing stress to rare and imperiled plants and animals in the mountain West has yet to be done. Nonetheless, expert opinion suggests that such development cannot be dismissed as benign, and that further research on the subject ought to be undertaken. In terms of total acres, the impact of exurban development may seem small, but it tends to occur in valley bottom and foothill habitat types that are relatively rare to begin with and that are seldom in a protected status. These habitats often contain endemic plants that don't occur elsewhere. Those species of amphibians, reptiles, birds, and small mammals that use valley bottom and foothill habitat types exclusively appear to be suffering stress from exurban development. Finally, large carnivores, such as the wolf and grizzly bear, make seasonal use of valley bottoms and suffer the consequences of conflicts with human residents. Valley bottoms for such species also serve as corridors connecting large core habitats, the loss of which would serve to isolate populations and ultimately re-duce genetic fitness by inhibiting gene flow between core habitats. Many of these species have suffered reduced populations historically as a consequence of resource extraction and associated economic activity. Consequently, the impact of rural development and sprawl can serve as the straw that breaks the camel's back. The added stress of rural sprawl need not be very substantial in some cases to push species over the edge and into the black hole of extinction.

NOTES

1. Gary K. Meffe and C. Ronald Caroll, *Principles of Conservation Biology* (Sunderland, Mass.: Sinauer Associates, 1994), 127.
2. See the previous chapter for discussion of the effects of exurban sprawl on some species that are not rare or endangered, particularly ungulates. For a general discussion of the range shrinkage problem, see James H. Brown, *Macroecology* (Chicago: University of Chicago Press, 1995), 212–217.
3. Meffe and Caroll, *Principles of Conservation Biology*, 124–130.
4. Reed F. Noss and Allen Y. Cooperrider, *Saving Nature's Legacy: Protecting and Restoring Biodiversity* (Washington, D.C.: Island Press, 1994), 57–59.
5. Meffe and Caroll, *Principles of Conservation Biology*, 186–190.
6. Brown, *Macroecology*, 216.
7. Noss and Cooperrider, *Saving Nature's Legacy*, 101–103; Meffe and Caroll, *Principles of Conservation Biology*, 81.
8. Meffe and Caroll, *Principles of Conservation Biology*, 129–130.
9. David Tilman, "Biodiversity and Ecosystem Functioning," in *Nature's Services: Societal Dependence on Natural Ecosystems*, ed. Gretchen C. Daily (Washington, D.C.: Island Press, 1997), 93–112
10. See the discussion of this issue in chapter 8.
11. Noss and Cooperrider, *Saving Nature's Legacy*, 19.
12. Bryan G. Norton, *Why Preserve Natural Variety?* (Princeton: Princeton University Press, 1987), 98–118.
13. Norton, *Why Preserve Natural Variety?* 73–97.
14. Aldo Leopold, *A Sand County Almanac* (New York: Ballantine Books, 1970), 137–141.
15. See chapter 8 for more on this issue.
16. See table 2.1 for a list of the counties. The data for each county was obtained upon request from the California, Colorado, and Montana Heritage Programs. Contact information for National Heritage Programs is available at http://www.NatureServe.org/nhp/us programs.htm.
17. Fish were originally included in the survey, but because a number of experts in California and Colorado questioned whether new economy forms of development were contributing to stresses on rare and imperiled species, the results on fish are not included here. Dams and other physical modifications of streams and rivers and the introduction of species were suggested by these experts as the primary source of stress for rare and imperiled fish species and that these phenomenon largely preceded new forms of economic development.

As discussed in the last chapter, the Yellowstone River appears to be an exception to the rule. Housing development along rivers creates pressure for channel modifications that limit the local effects of flooding and also degrade local habitat for certain species of fish.

18. Where experts disagreed on whether a species is stressed by development, the species was only included in the analysis if a majority agreed that development sources of stress are present.

19. One expert responded for three different categories and another for one category in two states.

20. The methodology used here is a simplified version of the approach taken in Richter et al. (Brian D. Richter, David P. Braun, Michael A. Mendelson, and Lawrence L. Master, "Threats to Imperiled Freshwater Fauna," *Conservation Biology* 11 [1997]: 1081–1093). In the article, experts were asked about the stress itself and the sources of a given stress separately. Since the ultimate concern here is with sources of stress, to simplify the questionnaire experts were asked about a stress and a source simultaneously, as can be seen in table 5.2.

21. The total number of experts participating in the study is about as large as one can probably expect for a study of this type. A comparable nationwide survey on aquatic species undertaken by The Nature Conservancy queried 89 experts (Richter et al., "Threats to Imperiled Freshwater Fauna"). This compares to the 41 experts queried here covering a much more geographically restricted area.

22. See chapter 3 for a discussion of net population density and its growth in the 86 sample counties.

23. The Web site can be found at http://ndis.nrel.colostate.edu [accessed 12 January 2002].

24. Mark R. Jennings, "Status of Amphibians," in *Status of the Sierra Nevada, Volume II: Assessment and Scientific Basis for Management Options*, Sierra Nevada Ecosystem Project, Final Report to Congress (Davis, Calif.: Centers for Water and Wildland Resources, University of California, Davis, 1996), 921–944.

25. Mark R. Jennings, "Status of Amphibians," 938.

26. Mark R. Jennings, "Status of Amphibians," 928.

27. Hartwell H. Welsh Jr., "Relictual Amphibians and Old-Growth Forests," *Conservation Biology* 4 (1990): 309–319; Lowell V. Diller and Richard L. Wallace, "Distribution and Habitat of *Plethodon Elongatus* on Managed, Young Growth Forests in North Coastal California," *Journal of Herpetology* 28 (1994): 310–318; and Hartwell H. Welsh Jr. and Amy J. Lind, "Habitat Correlates of the Del Norte Salamander *Plethodon elongatus* (*Caudata: Plethodontidae*), in Northwestern California," *Journal of Herpetology* 29 (1995): 198–210.

28. Frederick W. Schuierer, "Remarks Upon the Natural History of *Bufo exsul* Myers the Endemic Toad of Deep Springs Valley, Inyo Country, California," *Herpetologica* 17.4 (1962): 260–266; and B. Brattstrom, "Social Behavior and Habitat Requirements of Desert Reptiles," in *Herpetology of the North American Deserts: Proceedings of a Symposium*, ed. Philip R. Brown and John W. Wright (Special Publication No. 5, Southwestern Herpetologists Society, October 1994), 127–142.

29. Charles A. Drost and Gary M. Fellers, "Collapse of a Regional Frog Fauna in the Yosemite Area of the California Sierra Nevada, USA," *Conservation Biology* 10 (1996): 414–425.

30. The foothill yellow-legged frog is currently listed in the Natural Heritage database for the sample counties. The comments for one occurrence of fifteen records indicates that development is a threat.

31. Jennings, "Status of Amphibians"; and David M. Graber, "Status of Terrestrial Vertebrates," in *Status of the Sierra Nevada, Volume II*, 709–734.

32. Robert N. Fisher and H. Bradley Shaffer, "The Decline of Amphibians in California's Great Central Valley," *Conservation Biology* 10 (1996): 1387–1397. This species also did not appear in the Natural Heritage database at the time the species list for the experts' survey was put together.

33. Gary M. Fellers and Charles A. Drost, "Disappearance of the Cascades Frog *Rana cascadae* at the Southern End of Its Range, California, USA," *Biological-Conservation* 65 (1993): 177–181.

34. Katherine V. Fite, Andrew Blaustein, Lynn Bengston, and Heather E. Hewitt, "Evidence of Retinal Light Damage in *Rana cascadae*: A Declining Amphibian Species," *Copeia* 4 (1998): 906–914.

35. Graber, "Status of Terrestrial Vertebrates."

36. Graber, "Status of Terrestrial Vertebrates." This species did not appear in the Natural Heritage database in 1998 and was not included in the experts' survey, although it is now listed.

37. Graber, "Status of Terrestrial Vertebrates"; and Devin A. Reese and Hartwell H. Welsh Jr., "Habitat Use by Western Pond Turtles in the Trinity River, California," *Journal of Wildlife Management* 62 (1998): 842–853.

38. B. Brattstrom, "Habitat Destruction in California with Special Reference to *Clemmys marmorato*," in *Proceedings of the Conference on California Herpetology*," ed. H. F. De Lisle, P. R. Brown, B. Kaufman, and B. M. McGurty (Southwestern Herpetologists Society, 1988), 13–24.

39. Kristin H. Berry, Laura Stockton, and Tim Shields, "18 Years of Change in Protected and Unprotected Desert Tortoise Populations at the Interpretive Center, Desert Tortoise Research Natural Area, California" (paper presented at the twenty-third annual meeting and symposium of the Desert Tortoise Council, Tucson, Ariz., April 1998).

40. Cynthia Carey, "Hypothesis Concerning the Causes of the Disappearance of Boreal Toads from the Mountains of Colorado," *Conservation Biology* 7 (1993): 355–362; Bryce A. Maxell and Grant Hokit, "Amphibians and Reptiles," in *The Effects of Recreation on Rocky Mountain Wildlife: A Review for Montana*, coord. G. Joslin and H. Youmans (Montana: Committee on Effects of Recreation on Wildlife, Montana Chapter of the Wildlife Society, 1999), 2.1–2.29; and Colorado State University, "Boreal Toad," *Natural Diversity Information Source* (Ft. Collins, Colo.: 1999) http://ndis.nrel.colostate.edu/escop/doc/borealtoa/borealtoad.html [accessed 12 January 2002]. In a recent article, Paul S. Corn ("Effects of Ultraviolet Radiation on Boreal Toads in Colorado," *Ecological Applications* 8 [1998]: 18–26) suggests the UV–B radiation is not the primary cause of decline in western toad populations in Colorado.

41. Maxell and Hokit "Amphibians and Reptiles"; and Colorado State University, "Northern Leopard Frog," *Natural Diversity Information Source* (Ft. Collins, Colo.: 1999) http://ndis.nrel.colostate.edu/escop/ [accessed 12 January 2002].

42. Lauren J. Livo, EPO Biology, University of Colorado, personal communication.

43. Chuck Loeffler, Wildlife Manager, Division of Wildlife, State of Colorado, personal communication.

44. Geoffrey A. Hammerson, "Bullfrog Eliminating Leopard Frogs in Colorado?" *Herpetological Review* 13 (1982): 115–116.

45. Maxell and Hokit, "Amphibians and Reptiles."

46. Lauren J. Livo, personal communication.

47. Colorado State University, *Natural Diversity Information Source* (Ft. Collins, Colo.: 2000) http://ndis.nrel.colostate.edu/escop/ [accessed 12 January 2002].

48. Colorado State University, *Natural Diversity Information Source* (2000).

49. Colorado State University, *Natural Diversity Information Source* (2000).

50. Colorado State University, *Natural Diversity Information Source* (2000).

51. Heather A. Hager, "Area-Sensitivity of Reptiles and Amphibians: Are There Indicator Species for Habitat Fragmentation?" *Ecoscience* 5 (1998): 139–147.

52. Colorado State University, *Natural Diversity Information Source* (2000).

53. Maxell and Hokit, "Amphibians and Reptiles."

54. Justin D. Congdon, Arthur E. Dunham, and R. C. Van-Loben-Sels, "Demographics of Common Snapping Turtles (*Chelydra serpentina*): Implications for Conservation and Management of Long-Lived Organisms," *American Zoologist* 34 (1994): 397–408.

55. Maxell and Hokit, "Amphibians and Reptiles."

56. The California condor is extinct in the wild and is being reintroduced experimentally.

57. This species is naturally rare with scattered local populations that are stable.

58. This paragraph is based on Graber, "Status of Terrestrial Vertebrates."

59. Robert Gibson, Professor of Biological Sciences, University of Nebaska, personal communication.

60. All the above information is found for Natural Heritage database occurrences at Colorado State University, *Natural Diversity Information Source* (2000).

61. In a recent article, Eric A. Odell and Richard L. Knight ("Songbird and Medium-Sized Mammal Communities Associated with Exurban Development," *Conservation Biology* 15 [2001]: 1143–1150) have started this work. In this article they show that populations of several songbird species diminish closer to exurban residential development. None of these species, however, was listed as locally rare or imperiled in Colorado as of 1998.

62. Betsy Hamann, Heather Johnston, John Gobielle, Mike Hillis, Sara Johnson, Lynn Kelly, and Pat McClelland, "Birds," in *The Effects of Recreation on Rocky Mountain Wildlife*, 3.1–3.34.

63. Lynn M. Kelly, "The Effects of Human Disturbance on Common Loon Productivity in Northwestern Montana" (Master's thesis, Bozeman, Mont., Montana State University, 1992).

64. Hamann et al., "Birds"; and Marrianne Heimberger, David Euler, and Jack Barr, "The Impact of Cottage Development on Common Loon Reproductive Success in Central Ontario," *Wilson Bulletin* 95 (1983):431–439.

65. Hamann et al., "Birds."

66. Hamann et al., "Birds"; Clayton M. White and Thomas L. Thurow, "Reproduction of Ferruginous Hawks Exposed to Controlled Disturbance," *The Condor* 87 (1985): 14–22; Ken D. De Smet and Michael P. Conrad, "Status, Habitat Requirements, and Adaptations of Ferruginous Hawks in Manitoba," in *Proceedings of the Second Endangered Species and Prairie Conservation Workshop. Natural History Section Provincial Museum of Alberta, Occasional Paper No. 15*, ed. Geoffrey L. Holroyd, Gordon Burns, and Hugh C. Smith (Edmonton, Alberta, 1991), 219–221; and Josef K. Schmutz and Richard W Fyfe, "Migration and Mortalilty of Alberta Ferruginous Hawks," *The Condor* 89 (1987): 169–174.

67. Hamann et al., "Birds."

68. Hamann et al., "Birds."

69. Graber, "Status of Terrestrial Vertebrates."

70. David M. Armstrong, Professor, University of Colorado, personal communication. The one exception is a recent article, Odell and Knight, "Songbird and Medium-Sized Mammal Communities."

71. James P. Fitzgerald, Carron A. Meaney, and David M. Armstrong, *Mammals of Colorado* (Niwot, Colo.: University Press of Colorado, 1994), 71–91; Colorado State University, *Natural Diversity Information Source* .

72. Fitzgerald et al., *Mammals of Colorado*, 94, 123.

73. Colorado State University, *Natural Diversity Information Source* (2000); and Fitzgerald et al., *Mammals of Colorado*, 126–128.

74. Colorado State University, *Natural Diversity Information Source* (2000); and Fitzgerald et al., *Mammals of Colorado*, 308–310. Odell and Knight ("Songbird and Medium-Sized Mammal Communities") have found that populations of red foxes (*Vulpes vulpes*) diminish with distance from exurban residential development in Pitkin County, Colorado. This species was not listed as locally rare or imperiled in Colorado as of 1998.

75. Colorado State University, *Natural Diversity Information Source* (2000).

76. Colorado State University, *Natural Diversity Information Source* (2000).

77. Gene Hickman, Beverly G. Dixon, and Janelle Corn, "Small Mammals," in *The Effects of Recreation on Rocky Mountain Wildlife*, 4.1–4.16.

78. James J. Claar, Neil Anderson, Diane Boyd, Ben Conard, Gene Hickman, Robin Hompesch, Gary Olson, Helga Ihsle Pac, Tom Wittinger, and Heidi Youmans, "Carnivores," in *The Effects of Recreation on Rocky Mountain Wildlife*, 7.1–7.63.

79. Claar et al., "Carnivores."

80. Vanessa Johnson, "Rural Residential Development Trends in the Greater Yellowstone Ecosystem since the Listing of the Grizzly Bear" (Bozeman, Mont.: Sierra Club Grizzly Bear Ecosystem Project, 2000).

81. Richard. D. Mace and John S. Waller, "Demography and Population Trend of Grizzly Bears in the Swan Mountains, Montana," *Conservation Biology* 12 (1998): 1005–1016.

82. Michael Jamison, "Whitfish-Area Growth May Be Funneling Grizzlies into Town," *Missoulian* (November 23, 1999): A1; A7.

83. Jamison, "Whitfish-Area Growth May Be Funneling Grizzlies into Town."

84. D. J. Mattson and D. P. Reinhart, "Excavation of Red Squirrel Middens by Grizzly Bears in the Whitebark Pine Zone," *Journal of Applied Ecology* 34 (1997): 926–940.

85. Claar et al., "Carnivores"; and Bill Ruediger, "Rare Carnivores and Highways—Moving into the 21st Century," in *Proceedings of the International Conference on Wildlife Ecology and Transportation*, ed. Gary L. Evink, Paul Garrett, David Zeigler, and Jon Berry (Tallahassee, Fla.: Florida Department of Transportation, 1998), 10–16.

86. California Native Plant Society, *California Native Plant Society's Inventory of Rare and Endangered Vascular Plants of California* (Sacramento, Calif.: California Native Plant Society, 1994), 1.

87. California Native Plant Society, *Inventory of Rare and Endangered Vascular Plants*, 1.

88. James R. Shevock, "Status of Rare and Endemic Plants," in *Status of the Sierra Nevada, Volume II: Assessment and Scientific Basis for Management Options*, Sierra Nevada Ecosystem Project, Final Report to Congress (Davis, Calif.: Centers for Water and Wildland Resources, University of California, Davis, 1996), 691–707.

89. California Native Plant Society, *Inventory of Rare and Endangered Vascular Plants*.

90. California Native Plant Society, *Inventory of Rare and Endangered Vascular Plants.*

91. Colorado Natural Heritage Program, *Colorado Rare Plant Field Guide* (Fort Collins, Colo.: Colorado Natural Heritage Program: 2000) http://ndis.nrel.colostate.edu/ndis/rareplants/cover.html [accessed 12 January 2002].

92. Carol S. Spurrier, Botanist, Colorado State Office, U.S. Department of the Interior, Bureau of Land Management, personal communication.

93. Bonnie Heidel, Botanist, Montana Natural Heritage Program, personal communication.

94. Montana Natural Heritage Program, *Montana Rare Plant Field Guide* (Helena, Mont.: 2000) http://nhp.nris.state.mt.us/plants/ [accessed 12 January 2002].

6

~~⌒~~

Local Growth and Support for Preserving the Natural Landscape in the Sierra Nevada Mountains

Mountainous areas of the western United States currently face unprecedented rates of population expansion and housing development. If the previous chapters are right, this spread of population to remote areas of great natural beauty continues the process of urban population spreading that began with the outward movement of population away from high-density central cities. In the modern era, the choice of where to live is much less constrained than it used to be. During the nineteenth-century industrial revolution, most people were forced to live in urban centers where factories were heavily concentrated. In the information age, the production and communication of much information can take place almost anywhere. The earning of income no longer necessarily requires a close proximity to urban centers. Businesses can locate in remote areas without penalty and draw on a local labor force attracted by the amenities of a rural landscape. Individuals who are self-employed increasingly have the freedom to live in remote locations and to continue to earn an income. To put it more bluntly, location is increasingly rooted in consumption as opposed to production. In the era of the modem, the Internet, overnight package delivery, and satellite TV, many consumers can fulfill their dream of living in a naturally beautiful, remote area without sacrificing their connection to the global economy.

Unfortunately, population expansion and development has the potential to forever change the character of the western mountain landscape. This is especially the case in the Sierra Nevada Mountains in the West's most popular state, California. Because of rapid population growth in the Sierra Nevada, as already noted in chapter 1 (figure 1.1), open space and natural areas are being threatened, and, as suggested by the discussion in the last chapter, stresses to native species are increasing. In response, local residents are increasingly interested in measures to preserve the natural character of the landscape, including zoning, conservation easements and land purchases, and restrictions on the development of open space.[1]

Given the depth of support for the free exercise of property rights in American culture, advocacy for land use controls is somewhat surprising. Property ownership is a key element of the Jeffersonian vision of rural life.[2] The Jeffersonian vision presumes an agricultural society in which the small landowner has a special right to appropriate the products and benefits from the land by virtue of the labor invested in it. Through universal and responsible property ownership comes the capacity for a truly democratic society according to the Jeffersonian view. While the belief that ownership rights are related to labor has largely disappeared, the idea of full freedom in the exercise of property rights has not. One of the attractions of rural life is the freedom to do what one wants with one's possessions. Part of the reason suburbanization has been so popular is the opportunity it affords people to participate in property ownership.[3] Ironically, suburban property owners have not been reluctant to place restrictions on property development when their quality of life has been threatened.[4] Rural landowners, however, especially farmers and ranchers, have generally resisted measures to restrict the use of their property.[5] Nonetheless, movements to control and limit growth in rural areas are becoming more commonplace, suggesting that concerns with the consequences of growth are beginning to overpower value commitments to property rights.[6]

This trend indicates a clear need to better understand public attitudes toward land use controls and growth management in rural areas. The critical question that requires answering is whether growth itself generates support for measures on limiting growth. Growth not only can bring people with different values into the community, but the consequences of growth can transform the attitudes and values of existing residents. Literature on the suburban antigrowth revolt indicates that perceptions of rapid growth, not necessarily growth itself, and perceptions of a decline in the quality of life tend to drive antigrowth sentiments and support for measures to limit growth.[7] This same literature finds little support for the hypothesis that the antigrowth movement is associated with affluence and the desire of the wealthy to keep those with lower incomes out of their communities. Finally, there is little evidence in this literature that either political orientation or environmental values affect the extent of antigrowth sentiments. Do these findings extend to expressions of antigrowth sentiments and to support for limitations on growth in rural areas? Who, in terms of demographic characteristics and basic political and environmental attitudes in local Sierra Nevada communities, supports environmental and land use controls and are the relative numbers of supporters changing? More specifically, does the arrival of numerous new residents, with different attitudes from older residents, increase support for growth controls and environmental conservation measures? Moreover, does growth itself lead to increasing support for measures to control growth among the existing population, independent of demographics and basic attitudes? In short, is growth leading to a more favorable political climate for land use measures that could limit growth? Results from the voter survey undertaken for the Sierra Business Council (discussed in chapter 1) shed light on these and other critical questions associated with growth.[8] In particular, the survey results will help us understand whether the population-spreading process has the potential to be politically self-limiting. The survey results will also set the stage for the discussion to take place in the final chapters of various strategies for limiting and guiding population growth in the mountain West.

ANALYSIS OF SURVEY RESULTS

The Survey

Population growth and housing development are clearly altering the Sierra Nevada landscape, more in some localities than others. What is the public's response to such changes? To gauge public attitudes on issues related to growth in the Sierra Nevada, the Sierra Business Council had a survey conducted for them by J. Moore Methods, Inc., in November 1995 of 1,000 randomly selected registered voters living in the Sierra Nevada Mountains.[9] While voters may be unrepresentative of the population as a whole, they do exercise greater political influence than nonvoters and are thus likely to disproportionately affect local political decision making.[10] The sample is unstratified by county and was randomly selected from registered voter lists. The survey was conducted by telephone and took about 15 minutes.[11] Of the 1,000 respondents sampled, 982 responses were complete enough for analysis. Since the goal here is to focus on exurban and rural growth in the Sierra Nevada Mountains, and because Fresno and Kern counties have relatively large urban populations, they will henceforth be excluded from the analysis, further reducing the sample to 880. In the analysis of specific survey questions below, respondents expressing no opinion or not answering are excluded, resulting in additional reductions in the sample size.

The Analytical Framework

The basic goal here is to establish whether economic growth is altering Sierra Nevada rural voter attitudes toward regulatory measures that would in turn limit growth. This could occur in two ways. First, the experience of economic growth in the recent past could be altering the perceptions of voters about threats to open space and the natural environment and the attitudes of voters toward measures to limit such threats. Second, growth could be altering the composition of the voting public by bringing in new voters through immigration that have different perceptions and attitudes than existing voters. The basic hypotheses to be tested using survey results are as follows: first, the demographic characteristics of respondents (age, income, and education), environmental orientation, political orientation, and the actual experience of economic growth in the recent past affect respondent perceptions of threats to the local natural environment; and second, all these variables and threat perceptions in turn affect attitudes toward specific measures to regulate land use and control economic growth. The hypothesized path of effects on environmental threats and attitudes toward regulatory measures are presented schematically in figure 6.1. The experience of growth is hypothesized to affect attitudes toward growth control measures directly and indirectly through perceptions of threats. The same is the true for demographic variables and political and environmental orientation. The first step in the formation of voter attitudes is the perception of a threat. Most likely, a threat has to be present before voters are willing to support policy measures. Moreover, the perceived significance of the threat is likely to have a positive influence on a voter's willingness to support policy measures to alleviate the threat. Again, the key issue to be investigated is whether population growth in a local area affects perceptions of threats by voters and their willingness to support policy measures that control growth.[12]

Once we have established whether demographic characteristics of respondents and their political and environmental orientation affect their perceptions of environmental threats and attitudes toward growth control measures, we can consider whether the composition of the Sierra Nevada voting population has been changing over time by comparing characteristics for longtime residents and recent arrivals. A judgement can then be made about whether the attitudes of the typical voter toward growth controls has been shifting over time as growth and population inmigration have occurred. If new arrivals are more likely to perceive threats to the local environment from growth and are more willing to support

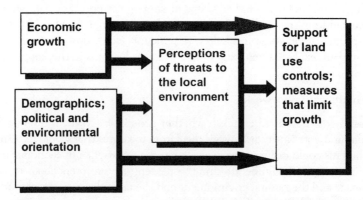

Figure 6.1:   Impact of Demographics, Attitudes, and Growth on Environmental Threats and Support for Land Use Controls and Measures That Limit Growth

policies that limit growth, then the process of growth itself may stimulate opposition to further growth. In other words, the most recent arrivals who have carved out their piece of paradise may want to shut the door on development to protect what they now have. This, of course, is the cynical view. The important point is that growth itself may be self-limiting.

Threats to the Future of Respondent Communities

The survey asked respondents their views on a variety of possible threats to their communities as a consequence of growth. The specific questions asked and the responses are reported in table 6.1. The total response differs slightly for the different questions because of missing data as a consequence of "no opinion" or "don't know" responses. A majority of respondents see poor land use planning, a declining quality of the natural environment, and rapid population growth as either somewhat or very much of a threat to the future of their community. In short, most see manifestations of growth and population spreading as threatening to their local environment.

As in chapter 3, a discussion of descriptive data will be undertaken in the body of this chapter and a parallel discussion of statistical analyses of the data will be carried out in the appendix. The basic hypothesis to be addressed first is that beliefs about threats to respondent communities will depend on environmental orientation, demographics, political orientation, and population density growth. For example, someone who is an environmentalist will probably be more threatened by deterioration in environmental quality than someone who

Table 6.1.   Environmental Threats to the Local Community: Questions and Responses

	Number (Percent) of Responses:		
Question	*Not Too Threatening*	*Somewhat Threatening*	*Very Threatening*
How much of a threat is poor land use planning to the future of your community?	263 (38.2)	151 (21.9)	275 (39.9)
How much of a threat is declining quality of the natural environment to the future of your community?	319 (45.9)	172 (24.7)	204 (29.4)
How much of a threat is loss of open space and scenic views to the future of your community?	354 (51.9)	136 (19.9)	192 (28.2)
How much of a threat is rapid population growth to the future of your community?	294 (42.4)	149 (21.5)	251 (36.2)

is not an environmentalist. Moreover, one's views on threats could well be influenced by age, income, education, and political orientation. A philosophical conservative, for example, may see poor land use planning as less threatening than a philosophical liberal might. Finally, the actual experience of local population growth could influence perceptions of threats. To capture the experience of growth, data on net population density growth as described in chapter 3 are used. Respondents are identified by county, and net population density growth is included as a respondent characteristic and independent variable in the study. In figures 6.2 and 6.3 population density growth for Sierra Nevada nonfederal lands from 1985–94 is presented for 14 rural counties.[13]

To gain insight into the impact of respondent characteristics on beliefs about threats to respondent communities described by the questions in table 6.1, the percentage of respondents having a given characteristic and expressing concerns about threats is presented in figure 6.4. The first bar graph for each possible threat indicates the percentage of all respondents who claim there is either somewhat or very much of a threat. This will provide the benchmark to which groups of respondents with specific characteristics can be compared. For instance, 61 percent of all respondents believe poor land use planning to be a threat, while 65 percent of those claiming to be environmentalists and 69 percent of those with a college degree believe it to be a threat. On the other hand, 58 percent of respondents over the age of fifty and 57 percent of political conservatives indicate poor land use planning to be a threat. So environmentalists and the college educated tend to put upward pressure on the proportion of the respondent population who believe that poor land use planing is a threat, while older residents and

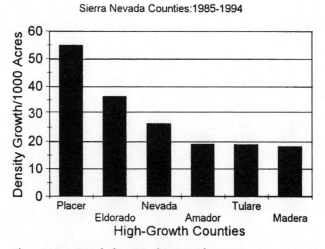

Figure 6.2:   Population Density Growth

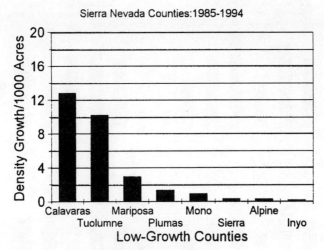

Figure 6.3:   Population Density Growth

conservatives tend to pull it down.[14] The threat-perception response rate is higher than the 61 percent average for environmentalists and college graduates and lower for older respondents and conservatives. As can be seen in figure 6.4, respondents over fifty and political conservatives are less inclined than all respondents to believe that loss of open space, declining environmental quality, and population growth are threats, while environmentalists and the college educated are more inclined to do so.[15] Income differences among respondents don't appear to have much impact on respondent attitudes toward threats to respondent communities. In sum, environmentalists and college graduates are more likely to perceive threats to the environment from growth and its manifestations, while older residents and political conservatives are less likely to perceive such threats.

Does economic growth itself affect respondent attitudes toward threats to communities? As noted above, county population density growth data can be added to the analysis by identifying respondent counties and assigning the appropriate density growth figures. Population density growth indeed affects respondent beliefs as can be seen in figure 6.5. Clearly, average density growth experienced by respondents is greater for those who perceive threats than those who don't. Density growth faced by those who perceive threats ranges from 24 to 25 per thousand acres while the same figure for those who don't perceive threats is around 15 to 16 per thousand acres. The amount of density growth does affect the perception of threats to the local environment. The experience of growth seems to matter in the expression of concerns about threats that are caused by population growth.[16]

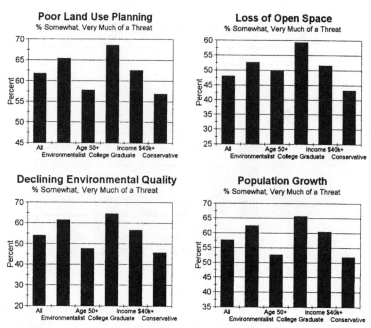

Figure 6.4: Percent of Respondents with Different Characteristics Expressing Somewhat or Very Much of a Threat

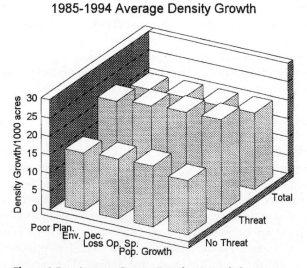

Figure 6.5: Average County Density Growth for Respondents Indicating that Poor Planning (Poor Plan.), Environmental Decline (Env. Dec.), Loss of Open Space (Loss Op. Sp.), and Population Growth (Pop. Growth) Are or Are Not Threats to Their Communities

Attitudes toward Land Use and County Government Policy

Perceived environmental threats presumably foster a desire for governmental action to mitigate those threats. In other words, there should be some correspondence between those who feel threatened and those who desire action. The specific policy measures addressed in the survey that correspond to the threats in table 6.1 are presented in order in tables 6.2 and 6.3. The threat of poor land use planning can be addressed through zoning; the threat of a decline in the quality of the natural environment can be addressed by protecting wildlife habitat and ecosystems; the threat to open space can be addressed through its protection; and the threat of population growth can be addressed by directing the resulting development to existing towns in order to avoid sprawl. The support for policy measures to address threats is fairly high, ranging from around 70 percent of respondents for zoning at the low end, to 87 percent of respondents for preserving open space at the high end. The basic hypotheses to test now are whether the belief that a threat

Table 6.2. Respondent Views on Zoning: Questions and Responses

Question: Which of the following statements more closely reflects your view?	Number of Responses	Percent of Responses
I support zoning because it can be an important way to protect the quality of life and property values in my community.	479	69.5
People should have a right to do whatever they want with their own property, without interference from government.	188	27.2
Neither of the above.	22	3.2

Table 6.3. Respondent Views on Land Use Policies: Questions and Responses

Question: Some people say the following. Do you agree or disagree?	Number of Respondents in Agreement	Percent of Respondents in Agreement
We need to protect wildlife habitat and ecosystems in the Sierra Nevada to maintain the health of our natural environment for people and for wildlife.	600	86.3
We should do more to permanently protect open space around towns in the Sierra Nevada to help agriculture survive and keep our region beautiful.	596	87.4
Sierra Nevada counties should do more to steer new development into existing towns instead of allowing it to spread all over the landscape and destroy our rural quality of life.	525	75.6

exists affects support for the land use policies addressed in the questions in tables 6.2 and 6.3, and whether growth itself directly affects support for such policies along with environmental and political orientation and demographics.

One of the most interesting questions asked in the survey was whether respondents favor zoning as a way to protect the quality of life, or whether they support the idea that people should have a right to do whatever they want with their own property. Most respondents (69.5 percent) support zoning over property rights. As suggested by the data in figure 6.6, those respondents who have an environmental orientation, a college degree, and relatively high income tend to support zoning to a greater extent than all respondents.[17] In addition, respondents who perceive a threat from poor land use planning support zoning to a greater degree than

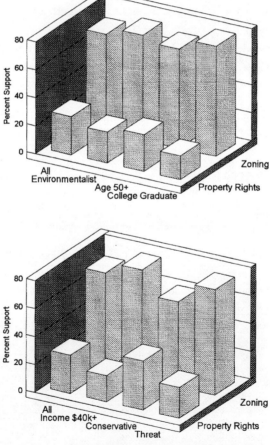

Figure 6.6:   Support for Zoning or Property Rights by Respondents with Different Characteristics

all respondents. On the other hand, conservatives support property rights to a greater extent than all respondents. Moreover, the experience of growth in the form of increased population density appears to influence support for zoning as we can see in figure 6.7. Average density growth in respondent counties is greater for those who support zoning than it is for those who support property rights. Density growth faced by those who support zoning is on average around 22 per thousand acres while growth faced by those who support property rights is around 15 per thousand acres. Supporters of property rights have less population growth to contend with than supporters of zoning. Even though property rights are often thought to be sacred (especially in rural areas), many residents of the Sierra Nevada are willing to give them up for the sake of protecting the local quality of life.[18] Those who perceive threats from poor land use planning and those who are facing high levels of population density growth are especially interested in zoning as a vehicle for controlling land use.

The protection of habitat and ecosystems, the protection of open space, and the steering of development to existing towns are all measures supported to a greater degree by environmentalists and those who perceive threats to their communities, as shown in figure 6.8. As in the case of zoning, political conservatives give less support to these measures than all respondents as a group. Older respondents are more supportive of steering growth to existing towns than all respondents together. Unlike zoning, the experience of growth has no perceptible impact on support for the three measures, although growth has an indirect

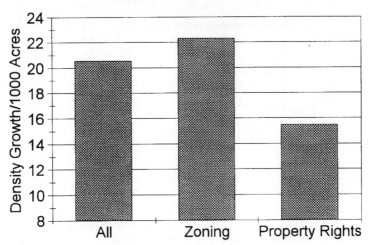

Figure 6.7: **Average County Population Density Growth (1985–1994) for Supporters of Zoning and Property Rights**

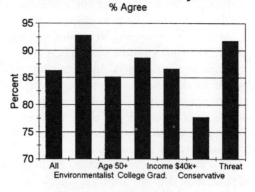

Protect Habitat and Ecosystems
% Agree

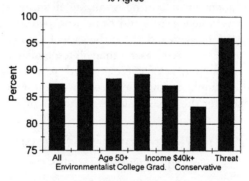

Protect Open Space
% Agree

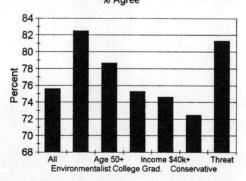

Steer Development to Existing Towns
% Agree

Figure 6.8: Support for Ecosystem and Habitat
Protection, Open Space Protection, and Steering
Development to Existing Towns by Respondents
with Different Characteristics

effect through threat perceptions.[19] Higher rates of density growth experienced by respondents result in greater threat perceptions, and greater threat perceptions in turn result in higher support for policies that limit and mitigate the effects of population growth.

Out of these results, a rough profile emerges. Those who express an environmental orientation favor measures that protect the natural environment and manage growth. Older residents are unlikely to perceive threats to their community, although they do support zoning and steering development to existing towns. The well-educated favor zoning but don't show strong support for other measures protecting the local environment even though they perceive threats to their communities. Those who are politically conservative are less inclined to perceive threats and request that less effort be expended on regulatory measures. The experience of population growth has a positive and relatively substantial impact on perceptions of threats, and it directly affects support for zoning. Support for the conservation of ecosystems and open space and steering development to existing towns is not directly affected by the experience of growth, but it is indirectly affected through threats to communities, although the indirect effect is probably modest.[20] To summarize, there is substantial support for growth limiting measures among respondents, and the experience of growth contributes to this support.

Population Growth, Population Composition, and Support for Growth Control Measures

The respondents to the Sierra Business Council Survey offer overwhelming support for land use policies that mitigate and limit the effects of population growth in rural mountain counties (tables 6.2 and 6.3). Statistical analysis suggests that the historical experience of growth has a positive impact on this support, directly for zoning and indirectly through threats for all measures to control growth. A second path for population growth to affect support for such policies is through the impact of growth on population composition. If, for example, as a result of population migration into Sierra Nevada counties, the proportion of those with an environmental orientation increases, then support for policies among voters is likely to increase, given the above analysis showing that an environmental orientation increases the probability of support for policies that have the potential to limit residential development and population growth.

Because the survey asked respondents how long they have lived in their county, survey results can be used to judge whether those who have moved into their county more recently have a different environmental or political orientation or different demographic characteristics than long-term residents. Since population growth is being largely driven by inmigration, voter support for growth control policies could change if newer residents have different views than older ones.[21] As already noted above, support for growth control policies is dependent in part on a respondent's environmental and political orientation, age, and educational attainment.

Cross tabulations for respondents' length of time in a county of residence and their demographics as well as political and environmental orientations are presented in tables 6.4–6.8. According to statistical tests, age, income, and education are related to duration in a residence, while political and environmental orientation are not related.[22] The data in table 6.4 suggests that respondents who have lived in the Sierra Nevada longer tend to be older. In addition, those respondents who have lived longer in the area tend to have somewhat lower incomes and less education than new residents, according to the data in tables 6.5 and 6.6. Finally, the data in tables 6.7 and 6.8 suggest that time in a residence doesn't much affect political or environmental orientation, except that lifetime residents appear to be more conservative and less likely to see themselves as environmentalists. Given that a slight majority of residents, about 51 percent, philosophically see themselves as conservatives, it is surprising that such a large portion of the respondents claim to be environmentalists—56 percent.

Since those who have arrived recently are likely to be the main contributors to population growth, the proportion of their characteristics should be expanding in the voting population as a whole over time. Because political and environmental orientation are not significantly different for new arrivals and long-term residents,

Table 6.4. Respondent Age and Length of Time Living in Their County of Residence

Length of time respondents have lived in their county. Chi-square=36.52, p=.002	Ages					
	18–29	30–39	40–49	50–64	65+	Total*
Less than 5 years	4.4	27.8	22.2	28.8	16.7	99.9
5–10 years	4.4	15.8	28.7	29.2	21.8	99.9
10–20 years	5.9	13.2	31.8	22.7	26.4	100
More than 20 years	1.9	9.4	22.6	30.8	35.2	99.9
Lifetime	6.9	13.8	22.4	22.4	34.4	99.9
All respondents	4.5	15.0	27.0	27.0	26.5	100

Note: Numbers are percents.
* Some totals are rounded off.

Table 6.5. Respondent Income and Length of Time Living in Their County of Residence

Length of time respondents have lived in their county. Chi-square=24.58, p=.016	Incomes				
	$20,000 or less	$20,000– $40,000	$40,000– $75,000	$75,000 or more	Total*
Less than 5 years	11.1	33.3	35.6	20.0	100
5–10 years	10.9	35.6	39.1	14.4	100
10–20 years	14.5	32.2	40.0	13.2	99.9
More than 20 years	22.2	40.3	27.7	10.1	99.9
Lifetime	25.9	34.5	25.9	13.8	99.9
All respondents	15.6	35.3	35.4	13.7	100

Note: Numbers are percents.
* Some totals are rounded off.

Table 6.6. Respondent Education and Length of Time Living in Their County of Residence

Length of time respondents have lived in their county Chi-square=16.73, p=.033	Education			
	High School	Some College	College Graduate	Total*
Less than 5 years	16.7	43.3	40.0	100
5–10 years	22.8	38.1	39.1	100
10–20 years	17.7	45.0	37.3	100
More than 20 years	24.5	42.7	32.7	99.9
Lifetime	37.9	41.3	20.7	99.9
All respondents	22.1	42.1	35.8	100

Note: Numbers are percents.
* Some totals are rounded off.

Table 6.7. Respondent Political Orientation and Length of Time Living in Their County of Residence

Length of time respondents have lived in their county Chi-square=11.18, p=.191	Political Orientation			
	Liberal	Moderate	Conservative	Total*
Less than 5 years	11.1	43.3	45.5	99.9
5–10 years	13.4	42.1	44.6	100.1
10–20 years	12.7	34.5	52.7	99.9
More than 20 years	11.9	33.3	54.7	99.2
Lifetime	5.2	31.0	63.8	100
All respondents	11.9	37.1	50.8	99.8

Note: Numbers are percents.
* Some totals are rounded off.

Table 6.8. Respondent Environmental Orientation and Length of Time Living in Their County of Residence

Length of time respondents have lived in their county Chi-square=5.28, p=.260	Environmental Orientation		
	Environmentalist: No	Environmentalist: Yes	Total*
Less than 5 years	46.7	53.3	100
5–10 years	38.1	61.9	100
10–20 years	45.0	55.0	100
More than 20 years	44.0	56.0	100
Lifetime	53.4	46.6	100
All respondents	43.8	56.2	100

Note: Numbers are percents.
* Some totals are rounded off.

population expansion from inmigration is probably not altering the mix of these characteristics in the voting population. However, over time the voting population is likely to get younger, wealthier, and better educated. Consequently, because education tends to have a positive effect on perceptions of threats related to local population expansion and on support for zoning, a relative increase in more highly educated voters could increase support for measures that mitigate and control the effects of growth. On the other hand, a younger voting population has mixed results. Younger voters, according to our analysis above, perceive threats from growth, but older voters support zoning and steering growth to towns, although younger voters do support protection of wildlife and ecosystems (figures 6.4–6.8; tables 6A.1–6A.2). A wealthier voting population would also result in increased support for zoning. So increased wealth and education bring forth support for zoning while youth detracts from zoning and steering population growth to existing towns.

CONCLUSION

The most important conclusion to be drawn from the Sierra Business Council Survey is that the voting public strongly supports measures to protect the natural environment and open space and is willing to support zoning and policies that direct development to existing towns and limit suburban-style sprawl. This support is forthcoming even though voters as a group are predominantly political conservatives. Moreover, at the margin, economic growth itself is resulting in increased support for measures to mitigate the effects of growth, especially for zoning. In short, growth is increasing the already relatively substantial support for growth controls. Given voter support for growth control measures, it is a little surprising that counties haven't moved more aggressively to establish countywide zoning and open space protection policies. Of course voters in a democratic society are not always, and perhaps rarely, able to directly dictate public policy. Special interest groups with the resources to devote to political activity and lobbying are often able to substantially influence the activities of government. As Timothy Duane suggests, land use practices at the county level are often slow to change because of special interest control of the land use planning process.[23] Eventually, countervailing interest groups can form and even gain the upper hand, but this takes time. The real danger is that too little open space and natural habitat will be left for protection by the time reforms can be instituted.

APPENDIX

Statistical Analysis of the Survey Results

Environmental Orientation: More on the Analytical Framework

Before moving ahead with the statistical analysis, the concept of an environmental orientation as something that can shape respondent attitudes and potential voter behavior needs to be addressed more fully. While the literature on environmental attitudes is extensive, there is no widely accepted theoretical framework for relating basic environmental beliefs and values to support for specific policies. Much of the literature deals with social and demographic variables that affect environmental concerns.[24] Environmental concern is an all-encompassing concept that includes environmental beliefs and values as well as attitudes toward specific environmental policies and actual environmental behaviors.[25] Some of the literature addresses the more specific concept of environmental orientation—a self-declaration of environmental beliefs.[26] Someone who has an environmental orientation responds positively to inquiries about whether they consider themselves to be an environmentalist. Environmental orientation is addressed in the Sierra Nevada survey with the question: "In terms of your philosophy, do you consider yourself to be an environmentalist?" Those who express an environmental orientation are found also to favor certain environmental policies in at least one study.[27]

The connection between beliefs and values and attitudes toward specific policies has been addressed relatively successfully by the psychological theory of planned behavior.[28] The theory postulates that a behavioral intention, such as an intention to vote for growth controls at the county level, is predicted by attitudes toward the object of the intention or the act, subjective norms, and perceived behavioral control. Attitudes toward the act refer to the degree to which the person has a favorable or unfavorable evaluation of the behavior in question. Subjective norms refer to social pressure to support the behavior. Behavioral control refers to the perceived difficulty of performing the behavior. All three together are hypothesized to predict behavioral intention and actual behavior.

Since the Sierra Nevada survey addresses only attitudes toward policies, not specific intentional behaviors, only the part of the planned behavior theory that addresses attitudes is useful. Essentially, the theory suggests that basic beliefs and values predict specific attitudes. Environmental orientation, for example, is a measure of beliefs that could predict specific attitudes toward policies.[29] Political orientation is also a measure of beliefs that could predict attitudes toward specific policies. In the Sierra Nevada survey, the political orientation of respondents is measured using the following question: "In terms of your philosophy, do you consider yourself to be a Conservative, Moderate, or Liberal?" While not explicitly employing the theory of planned behavior, the conclusions of others on the role of beliefs and values in predicting attitudes appears to be consistent with the theory.[30] Finally, demographic characteristics of respondents are also likely to play a role in the shaping of attitudes toward environmental threats and policies to address those threats.[31] Older respondents could well have different values than younger; the rich have a greater ability to pay for environmental measures that increase taxes or other costs than the poor, or the rich may have a different philosophical outlook toward the role of government than the poor; and the more highly educated may have different information or different values than the less educated.

Intervening between basic attitudes toward local environmental policies are likely to be beliefs about the extent of threats to the local environment.[32] A respondent is unlikely to favor local policies to protect the environment if an apparent threat is lacking. Hence, the extent of an environmental threat is likely to predict the extent of support for environmental protection.[33] Moreover, basic values and beliefs, such as environmental and political orientation, are in turn likely to influence the perception of an environmental threat.

In sum, the theory of planned behavior suggests that attitudes toward specific policies to limit growth and protect the local environment will be predicted by demographic variables, environmental and political orientation, and perceived threats. In addition, perceived threats are likely to be influenced by actual population growth, if indeed actual growth is observed to threaten the quality of the local environment. Perceived threats are also likely to be predicted by demographic variables and environmental and political orientation.

The Statistical Analysis and Results

To establish the effect of demographic variables, political and environmental outlooks, and growth on respondent perceptions of threats to their local community (as described in table 6.1), a procedure very much like regression analysis can be used. Because the responses to survey questions are categories rather than continuous numbers, multivariate regression analysis can't be used as it was in chapter 3. Instead, multinomial logit analysis is the appropriate statistical approach. Although at first glance it seems more complicated than simple regression analysis, multinomial logit analysis provides the same kind of information that regression analysis did in chapter 3. The procedure will tell us whether a particular independent variable has a statistically significant effect on a dependent variable where the latter is now equal to the probability that a respondent gives a particular answer to a survey question. Those who are uninterested in the details of the statistical technique can skip the next paragraph.

For multinomial logit analysis, the dependent variable is a positive whole number ranging from 0 to N–1 where N is the number of categories. The procedure provides an estimate of the probability of respondents choosing a particular category as determined by independent variables. The equation estimated using maximum likelihood procedures is the following:

$$(1)\ Prob(choice\ j) = \frac{\exp\beta_j\, {}^{\backprime}x_t}{\Sigma_{j=0}^J \exp\beta_j\, {}^{\backprime}x_t}$$

where there are $J+1$ possible categorical outcomes, β_j is a vector of estimated regression coefficients, and ${}^{\backprime}x_t$ is a vector of independent variables that are characteristics or beliefs of the individuals making the choices. Multinomial logit estimates N equations for N+1 categories. For example, if there are three categories, equations for categories 1 and 2 will be estimated but not for category 0. In the above equation, the components of β_j for j=0 are set equal to zero to normalize the equation and permit identification of the parameters. The regressors themselves don't represent the marginal effects of a particular independent variable since equation (1) is nonlinear and contains independent variables in both the numerator and denominator. The marginal effects of independent variables must be obtained by taking first derivatives of equation (1). The statistical package, *Limdep Version 7.0*,[34] does this for mean values of independent variables and reports marginal effects and their t-statistics for all independent variables and categories. Both the regression coefficients for equation (1) and the marginal effects will be presented in the tables for this appendix.

Threats to Respondent Communities

A multinomial logit analysis was conducted for the four questions addressing threats in table 6.1 and the results are reported in tables 6A.1.[35] A multinomial logit model estimates an equation that predicts the probability of a given response to a survey question for specified values of the independent variables. For example, the predicted probability of a respondent perceiving a decline in the natural environment to be very much of a threat for mean sample values is equal to .291 (table 6A.1). Different magnitudes for the independent variables lead to a different predicted probability for a particular question response. An environmental orientation, for instance, is a statistically significant predictor of threats perceived by respondents from a decline in the natural environment, the loss of open space, and rapid population growth, but not poor land use planning (table 6A.1). Estimated coefficients for environmental orientation in the "poor planning" equations are not statistically different from zero but are so in the other equations. The coefficients provide a measure of how environmental orientation affects threat perceptions. For example, a respondent who has an environmental orientation will have an increased probability at the margin (equal to approximately .10) of perceiving a declining quality of the natural environment as very much of a threat. Simply put, an environmentalist has a 10 percent greater probability at the margin than a non-environmentalist of perceiving declining quality of the natural environment as a threat.

Among the demographic variables, respondent income has no apparent impact on environmental threats. Its coefficients are relatively small in the threats equations, and statistically they are not different than zero (table 6A.1).[36] Age, however, does appear to have a statistically negative effect on perceptions of threats. In the case of "poor planning," a one-unit increase in the age category (roughly 10 years) results in a decline in the probability of a respondent perceiving poor land use planning as very much of a threat to their local community by .041. In short, older respondents are less likely to perceive threats to their local community than younger respondents.[37] Education appears to have a statistically significant positive effect on perceptions of each threat, either by reducing the probability of a respondent choosing the "not too" much of a threat category or increasing the probability of choosing the "very much" of a threat category, depending on the specific threat.[38] For instance, a one-unit increase in the education category results in an increased probability of a respondent choosing the "very much" of a threat category for poor land use planning equal to .063 (table 6A.1). Finally, political orientation appears to play a role in the perception of threats. In general, a move on the political orientation scale from liberal, to moderate, to conservative results in a decline in the probability that a respondent will perceive a threat to the environment.[39] Conservatives are less likely to perceive environmental threats than moderates or liberals.

Finally, net density growth is indeed a significant predictor of perceptions of threats for all four threat questions (table 6A.1). The coefficients are statistically important for all four threats. Although the marginal effects of population density growth appear to be fairly small, their impact on respondent probabilities of perceiving threats can actually be fairly substantial. For example, an increase in population density of 20 persons per thousand acres (the average increase faced by respondents in 1985–94) increases the predicted probability of perceiving a declining quality of the natural environment as very much of threat by .12 (.006 x 20). The same calculation for other threats yields similar results. Growth itself does substantially influence perceptions of threats to the local environment.

Land Use and County Government Policy

The results in table 6A.2 show that property rights are favored by political conservatives, while zoning is supported by environmentalists, older residents, those with higher incomes, and the more educated. In addition, perceptions of a threat to the community from poor land use planning and the experience of net population density growth increase the support for zoning as opposed to property rights. All variables are statistically significant. Once again, the coefficient is relatively small on net density growth, but if we multiply it by the average growth faced by respondents of 20 per thousand acres, then the increase in the probability of favoring zoning at the margin is equal to .06 (.003 x 20). Growth does have a positive and direct impact on zoning support, as well as a positive and indirect impact on zoning support through the threat posed by poor land use planning. Growth increases the likelihood that a respondent will see poor land use planning as a threat, and this perception increases the likelihood of respondent support for zoning. While the indirect effect is fairly modest, population growth does have a relatively substantial direct effect on zoning support.[40]

In addition to favoring zoning as a general land use control measure, respondents who claim to be environmentalists also support the protection of the

Table 6A.1. Multinomial Determinants of Threats to the Future of the Respondent's Community

	Poor Planning:			Decline in Quality of Natural Environment:		
	Not too threatening	Somewhat threatening	Very threatening	Not too threatening	Somewhat threatening	Very threatening
	Regression Coefficients					
Constant		−0.637	−0.219		−0.495	−0.828*
		(−1.45)	(−0.57)		(−1.19)	(−2.03)
Environmentalist		0.219	0.343		0.519*	0.689*
		(1.01)	(1.80)		(2.50)	(3.40)
Age		−0.110	−0.213*		−0.297*	−0.126
		(−1.19)	(−2.65)		(−3.45)	(−1.49)
Household Income		0.040	−0.049		−0.020	−0.031
		(0.33)	(−0.46)		(−0.17)	(−0.28)
Education		0.044	0.278*		0.318*	0.304*
		(0.30)	(2.14)		(2.23)	(2.22)
Political Orientation		−0.162	−0.235		−0.328*	−0.487*
		(−1.04)	(−1.73)		(−2.22)	(−3.48)
Net Density Growth: 1985–1994		0.021*	0.034*		0.024*	−0.033*
		(3.09)	(5.92)		(3.86)	(5.48)
	Marginal Effects					
Constant	0.87	−0.092	0.006	0.167*	−0.033	−0.134
	(1.08)	(−1.30)	(0.07)	(1.98)	(−0.46)	(−1.67)
Environmentalist	−0.070	0.007	0.062	−0.151*	0.048	0.104*
	(−1.71)	(0.22)	(1.50)	(−3.41)	(1.29)	(2.55)
Age	0.041*	−0.001	−0.041*	0.051*	−0.047*	−0.004
	(2.32)	(0.00)	(−2.36)	(2.76)	(−2.97)	(−0.25)
Household Income	0.004	0.012	−0.015	0.006	−0.001	−0.001
	(0.17)	(0.60)	(−0.67)	(0.27)	(−0.07)	(−0.23)
Education	−0.045	−0.018	0.063*	−0.076*	0.038	0.039
	(−1.63)	(−0.75)	(2.19)	(−2.58)	(1.50)	(1.49)
Political Orientation	0.049	−0.007	−0.042	0.102*	−0.026	−0.076*
	(1.66)	(−0.29)	(−1.43)	(3.21)	(−1.04)	(2.80)
Net Density Growth: 1985–1994	-0.007*	0.001	0.006*	−0.007*	0.002*	0.005*
	(−4.76)	(0.50)	(4.75)	(−4.90)	(1.97)	(4.04)
	Statistics					
Chi-Square	66.42*	66.42*	66.42*	101.15*	101.15*	101.15*
Predicted Probability	.373	.230	.397	.454	.255	.291
Sample Size	689	689	689	695	695	695

Note: The figures in parentheses are t-statistics; an asterisk indicates statistical significance at the 5 percent level or better. The independent variables are categorical and are defined as follows: Age—1. 18–29, 2. 30–39, 3. 40–49, 4. 50–64, 5. 65+; Household Income—1. $20,000 or less, 2. $20,000–40,000, 3. $40,000–75,000, 4. $75,000+; Education—1. High School, 2. Some College, 3. College Graduate; Political Orientation—0. Liberal, 1. Moderate, 2. Conservative; Environmentalist—0. No, 1. Yes.

Table 6A.1. Continued

	Loss of Open Space:			Rapid Population Growth:		
	Not too threatening	Somewhat threatening	Very threatening	Not too threatening	Somewhat threatening	Very threatening
	Regression Coefficients					
Constant		−1.236*	−1.214*		−0.964*	−0.684
		(−2.79)	(2.99)		(2.17)	(−1.73)
Environmentalist		0.246	0.465*		0.188	0.570*
		(1.13)	(2.30)		(0.86)	(2.94)
Age		−0.152	−0.218*		−0.204*	−0.196*
		(−1.67)	(−2.61)		(−2.23)	(−2.41)
Household Income		−0.041	0.135		0.097	−0.039
		(−0.34)	(1.19)		(0.78)	(−0.36)
Education		0.429*	0.258		0.047	0.329*
		(2.84)	(1.87)		(0.31)	(2.48)
Political Orientation		−0.166	−0.304*		−0.181	−0.299*
		(−1.08)	(−2.16)		(−1.14)	(−2.18)
Net Density Growth: 1985–1994		0.018*	0.037*		0.040*	0.040*
		(2.72)	(6.19)		(5.93)	(6.74)
	Marginal Effects					
Constant	0.305*	−0.136	−0.169*	0.192*	−0.112	−0.080
	(3.61)	(−1.87)	(2.10)	(2.27)	(−1.55)	(−0.96)
Environmentalist	−0.092*	0.015	0.077*	−0.103*	−0.014	0.116*
	(−2.13)	(0.44)	(2.00)	(−2.40)	(−0.41)	(2.76)
Age	0.047*	−0.013	−0.034*	0.048*	−0.019	−0.029
	(2.58)	(−0.92)	(−2.17)	(2.62)	(−1.37)	(−1.71)
Household Income	−0.014	−0.014	0.029	−0.003	0.020	−0.017
	(0.60)	(−0.75)	(1.35)	(−0.13)	(1.02)	(-0.74)
Education	−0.083*	0.562*	0.027	−0.054	−0.019	0.072*
	(−2.78)	(2.25)	(1.04)	(−1.85)	(−0.79)	(2.50)
Political Orientation	0.061*	−0.010	−0.050	0.062*	−0.007	−0.054
	(1.98)	(−0.44)	(−1.90)	(1.99)	(−0.29)	(−1.89)
Net Density Growth: 1985–1994	−0.007*	0.001	0.006*	−0.010*	0.004*	0.006*
	(−5.02)	(0.87)	(4.73)	(−5.90)	(3.27)	(4.59)
	Statistics					
Chi-Square	88.36*	88.36*	88.36*	105.85*	105.85*	105.85*
Predicted Probability	.525	.208	.267	.412	.224	.364
Sample Size	682	682	682	694	694	694

Note: The figures in parentheses are t-statistics; an asterisk indicates statistical significance at the 5 percent level or better. The independent variables are categorical and are defined as follows: Age—1. 18–29, 2. 30–39, 3. 40–49, 4. 50–64, 5. 65+; Household Income—1. $20,000 or less, 2. $20,000–40,000, 3. $40,000–75,000, 4. $75,000+; Education—1. High School, 2. Some College, 3. College Graduate; Political Orientation—0. Liberal, 1. Moderate, 2. Conservative; Environmentalist—0. No, 1. Yes.

Table 6A.2.   Multinomial Determinants of Respondent's Views on Land Use Policy

	Favor Zoning	Favor Property Rights	Favor neither Property Rights nor Zoning	Protect Wildlife Habitat, Ecosystems: Agree	Protect Open Space: Agree	Steer Development to Existing Towns: Agree
			Regression Coefficients			
Constant		1.036*	−5.034*	3.751*	1.688*	0.606
		(2.52)	(−4.21)	(5.97)	(3.18)	(1.55)
Environmentalist		−0.420*	0.053	1.046*	0.742*	0.728*
		(−2.16)	(0.11)	(4.15)	(2.93)	(3.84)
Age		−0.242*	−0.142	−0.209*	0.099	0.171*
		(−2.97)	(−0.74)	(−1.98)	(0.93)	(2.15)
Household Income		−0.507*	0.083	−0.001	−0.052	−0.112
		(−4.49)	(0.31)	(−0.01)	(−0.36)	(−1.04)
Education		−0.459*	0.365	0.034	−0.126	−0.117
		(−3.43)	(1.03)	(0.19)	(−0.69)	(−0.87)
Political Orientation		0.518*	1.143*	−1.247*	−0.383	−0.152
		(3.52)	(2.55)	(−4.91)	(−1.84)	(−1.06)
Threat		−0.398*	−0.398	0.382*	1.369*	0.396*
		(−3.35)	(−1.52)	(2.42)	(5.71)	(3.47)
Net Density Growth: 1985–1994		−0.019*	0.012	−0.007	−0.010	−0.004
		(−3.04)	(0.92)	(−0.92)	(−1.30)	(−0.78)
			Marginal Effects			
Constant	−0.089	0.216*	−0.127*	0.305*	0.122*	0.106
	(−1.13)	(2.81)	(−2.13)	(6.68)	(3.05)	(1.57)
Environmentalist	0.072*	−0.076*	0.004	0.085*	0.054*	0.128*
	(2.02)	(−2.09)	(0.34)	(4.17)	(2.89)	(3.89)
Age	0.045*	−0.043*	−0.002	−0.017*	0.007	0.030*
	(2.94)	(−2.73)	(−0.43)	(−1.98)	(0.93)	(2.16)
Household Income	0.087*	−0.092*	0.005	−0.001	−0.004	−0.020
	(4.10)	(−3.86)	(0.74)	(−0.01)	(−0.36)	(−1.04)
Education	0.073*	−0.085*	0.011	0.003	−0.009	−0.021
	(2.94)	(−3.18)	(1.16)	(0.19)	(−0.69)	(−0.88)
Political Orientation	−0.111*	0.087*	0.025	−0.101*	−0.028	−0.027
	(−3.99)	(2.99)	(1.56)	(−5.82)	(−1.84)	(−1.06)
Threat	0.072*	−0.065*	−0.007	0.031*	0.099*	0.069*
	(3.47)	(−2.98)	(−1.06)	(2.43)	(7.63)	(3.52)
Net Density Growth: 1985–1994	0.003*	−0.003*	0.0004	−0.001	−0.001	−0.008
	(2.69)	(−2.86)	(1.13)	(−0.92)	(−1.30)	(−0.78)
			Statistics			
Chi-Square	124.81*	124.81*	124.81*	81.14*	73.28*	42.58*
Predicted Probability	.739	.236	.025	.911	.920	.804
Sample Size	689	689	689	695	682	694

Note: The figures in parentheses are t-statistics; an asterisk indicates statistical significance at the 5 percent level or better. The independent variables are categorical and are defined as follows: Age—1. 18–29, 2. 30–39, 3. 40–49, 4. 50–64, 5. 65+; Household Income—1. $20,000 or less, 2. $20,000–40,000, 3. $40,000–75,000, 4. $75,000+; Education—1. High School, 2. Some College, 3. College Graduate; Political Orientation—0. Liberal, 1. Moderate, 2. Conservative; Environmentalist—0. No, 1. Yes.

natural environment, the preservation of open space, and the steering of development to existing towns to a greater degree than non-environmentalists (table 6A.2). The marginal effects are relatively high for an environmental orientation and are statistically significant for all three policy measures. Age has a negative effect (at a statistically significant level) on the probability of supporting protection of wildlife habitat and ecosystems, but age has a positive (and statistically significant) effect on the probability of support for steering development to existing communities (table 6A.2). Perceptions of environmental threats to the community have a relatively substantial positive (and statistically significant) effect on the probability of support for protecting wildlife habitat and ecosystems, preserving open space, and steering development to existing towns (table 6A.2). Population density growth, however, fails to have a statistically significant direct marginal effect on the probability of respondent support for the protection of wildlife habitat and ecosystems, the protection of open space, and the steering of development to existing towns, but it does have an indirect positive effect through threats to the community, although the magnitude of the indirect effects are comparatively modest.[41]

NOTES

1. Timothy P. Duane, "Human Settlement: 1850–2040," in *Status of the Sierra Nevada, Volume II: Assessment and Scientific Basis for Management Options*, Sierra Nevada Ecosystem Project, Final Report to Congress (Davis, Calif.: Centers for Water and Wildland Resources, University of California, Davis, 1996), 235–360; and Sierra Business Council, *Planning for Prosperity: Building Successful Communities in the Sierra Nevada* (Truckee, Calif.: Sierra Business Council, 1997).

2. See the discussion in chapter 1.

3. Kenneth T. Jackson, *Crabgrass Frontier: The Suburbanization of the United States* (New York: Oxford University Press, 1985), 6–10.

4. See the discussion of the antigrowth revolt in chapter 1.

5. Eugene C. Hargrove, "Anglo-American Land Use Attitudes," *Environmental Ethics* 2 (1980): 121–148.

6. Douglas R. Porter, *Managing Growth in America's Communities* (Washington, D.C.: Island Press, 1997); and Jim Howe, Ed McMahon, and Luther Propst, *Balancing Nature and Commerce in Gateway Communities* (Washington, D.C.: Island Press, 1997). Controlling growth is by no means a new issue for suburbs and is addressed in a rather extensive literature (Mark Baldassare, *The Growth Dilemma* [Berkeley: University of California Press, 1986]; "Suburban Support for No Growth Policies: Implications for the Growth Revolt," *Urban Affairs* 12 [1990]: 197–206; "Suburban Communities," *Annual Review of Sociology* 18 [1992]: 475–494; Mark Baldassare and Georgeanna Wilson, "Changing Sources of Suburban Support for Local Growth Controls," *Urban Studies* 33 [1986]: 459–471; Charles E. Connerly, "Growth Management Concern: The Impact of Its Definition on Support for Local Growth Controls," *Environment and Behavior* 18 [1986]: 707–732; C. Connerly and James E. Frank, "Predicting Support for Local Growth Controls," *Social Sci-*

ence Quarterly 67 [1986]: 572–585; David E. Dowall, *The Suburban Squeeze* [Berkeley: University of California Press, 1984]; and Mark Skidmore and Michael Peddle, "Do Development Impact Fees Reduce the Rate of Residential Development?" *Growth and Change* 29 [1998]: 383–401).

7. Baldassare and Wilson, "Changing Sources of Suburban Support."

8. The results of the survey are reported in Sierra Business Council (*Planning for Prosperity*).

9. According to Duane (*Shaping the Sierra: Nature, Culture, and Conflict in the Changing West* [Berkeley: University of California Press, 1999]), J. Moore Methods is a highly respected political polling firm. The survey, however, was not designed for academic research purposes. Instead it was designed as a policy tool for the Sierra Business Council. I am simply evaluating the survey results after the fact and did not participate in the survey design.

10. Alicia M. Gebhardt and Greg Lindsey ("Differences in Environmental Orientation Among Homeowners," *The Journal of Environmental Education* 27 [1995]: 4–13) find that environmentalists are more likely to be voters than non-environmentalists.

11. Sierra Business Council, *Planning for Prosperity*. Blocks of 40 randomly selected voters with telephone numbers were used, and voters were called in each block until a positive response was obtained. The sample was demographically adjusted to compensate for voters without phones by J. Moore Methods.

12. See the appendix for a more detailed discussion of the theoretical framework behind the analysis of voter attitudes.

13. The counties are divided into high- and low-growth using mean growth as the dividing line strictly for illustrative purposes.

14. As discussed in the appendix, the positive effect of education and the negative effect of age on the predicted proportion of the population claiming poor land use planning to be a threat are both statistically significant, while being an environmentalist or a conservative are not although their coefficient signs are in the predicted direction.

15. Age and a conservative political orientation do indeed have a statistically significant negative effect on the proportion of respondents who perceive these threats, while being an environmentalist or college graduate have statistically significant positive effects (see the appendix).

16. See the appendix for a discussion of the statistical evidence supporting the hypothesis that the experience of population density growth affects perceptions of threats to communities.

17. Although residents over fifty support zoning at about the same percentage as all residents, the statistical analysis in the appendix indicates that age has a statistically significant positive effect on the predicted proportion of supporters for zoning.

18. This is true of older residents as well even though they don't believe poor land use planning to be a threat. See the discussion in the appendix.

19. Population density growth is virtually identical for those who agree with the statements in table 6.3. Also, as noted in the appendix, population density growth is not a statistically significant determinant of the predicted probability of agreement for any of the statements in table 6.3. See the appendix for a more detailed discussion of the indirect effect through threats of growth on predicted proportions of supporters for the three measures.

20. These results differ from those found in research on the suburban antigrowth movement (Baldassare and Wilson, "Changing Sources of Suburban Support"). In the case of the Sierra Nevadas, environmental orientation and political outlook are key predictors of

sentiments for measures that limit growth whereas in suburban antigrowth research they are not. Moreover, in the Sierra Nevada the actual experience of growth positively affects perceptions of threats to the local community and support for zoning and has positive indirect effects on attitudes toward other regulatory measures through perceptions of threats, contrary to results in the suburban antigrowth literature.

21. Since population growth as a whole in the Sierra Nevada counties is being driven by inmigration according to Duane ("Human Settlement: 1850–2040"), movement between counties is likely to be modest and is therefore unlikely to bias the results much.

22. A Chi-square test was performed for each cross tabulation to test the hypothesis that the two variables are unrelated. A statistical significance of p = .05 or greater indicates that the hypothesis cannot be rejected and that the two variables are likely to be related.

23. Duane, *Shaping the Sierra*, esp. 337–385.

24. Gebhardt and Lindsey, "Differences in Environmental Orientation"; Paul Mohai, "Public Concern and Elite Involvement in Environmental-Conservation Issues," *Social Science Quarterly* 66 (1985): 820–838; Paul Mohai, "Men, Women, and the Environment: An Examination of the Gender Gap in Environmental Concern and Activism," *Society and Natural Resources* 5 (1992): 1–19; Paul Mohai and Ben W. Twight, "Age and Environmentalism: An Elaboration of the Buttel Model Using National Survey Evidence," *Social Science Quarterly* 68 (1987): 798–815; and Diane M. Samdahl and Robert Robertson, "Social Determinants of Environmental Concern: Specification and Test of the Model," *Environment and Behavior* 21 (1989): 57–81.

25. Norman W. H. Blaikie, "The Nature and Origins of Ecological World Views: An Australian Study," *Social Science Quarterly* 73 (1992): 144–165; Riley E. Dunlap and Kent D. van Liere, "The 'New Environmental Paradigm': A Proposed Measuring Instrument and Preliminary Results," *Journal of Environmental Education* 9 (1978): 10–19; Kent D. Van Liere and Riley E. Dunlap, "The Social Bases of Environmental Concern: A Review of Hypotheses, Explanations, and Empirical Evidence," *Public Opinion Quarterly* 44 (1980): 181–197.

26. Gebhardt and Lindsey, "Differences in Environmental Orientation," and Daniel Krause, "Environmental Consciousness: An Empirical Study," *Environment and Behavior* 25 (1993): 126–142.

27. Gebhardt and Lindsey, "Differences in Environmental Orientation."

28. Icek Ajzen, "The Theory of Planned Behavior," *Organization and Human Decision Processes* 50 (1991): 179–211; and Icek Ajzen and B. L. Driver, "Contingent Value Measurement: On the Nature and Meaning of Willingness to Pay," *Journal of Consumer Psychology* 1 (1992): 297–316.

29. Environmental orientation is a relatively crude measure of beliefs. Those respondents with an environmental orientation could easily range from those who believe that nature is valuable for its own sake, as argued in much of the literature on environmental ethics (Holmes Rolston III, "Values in Nature," *Environmental Ethics* 3 [1981]: 113–128; and J. Baird Callicott, "Intrinsic Value, Quantum Theory, and Environmental Ethics," *Environmental Ethics* 7 [1985]: 257–273), to those who see nature as valuable only for human purposes (Bryan G. Norton, "Why I Am not a Nonanthropocentrist: Callicott and the Failure of Monistic Inherentism," *Environmental Ethics* 17 [1995]: 341–358). For evidence that many people do value nature for its own sake, see William Kempton, James S. Boster, and Jennifer A. Hartley, *Environmental Values in American Culture* (Cambridge, Mass.: MIT Press, 1995).

30. Frederick H. Buttel, "Age and Environmental Concern: A Multivariate Analysis," *Youth & Society* 10 (1979): 237–256; Gebhardt and Lindsey, "Differences in Environmental Orientation"; Mohai, "Public Concern and Elite Involvement"; Mohai and Twight, "Age and Environmentalism"; Samdahl and Robertson, "Social Determinants of Environmental Concern"; Paul C. Stern, Thomas Dietz, and Linda Kalof, "Value Orientations, Gender, and Environmental Concern," *Environment and Behavior* 25 (1993): 322–348.

31. Edmond Constantini and Kenneth Hanf, "Environmental Concern and Lake Tahoe: A Study of Elite Perceptions, Backgrounds, and Attitudes," *Environment and Behavior* 4 (1972): 209–242; Gebhardt and Lindsey, "Differences in Environmental Orientation"; Mohai, "Public Concern and Elite Involvement," "Men, Women, and the Environment"; Samdahl and Robertson, "Social Determinants of Environmental Concern"; Van Liere and Dunlap, "The Social Bases of Environmental Concern"; Blaikie, "The Nature and Origins of Ecological World Views."

32. Valarie J. Gunter and Barbara Finlay, "Influences on Group Participation in Environmental Conflicts," *Rural Sociology* 53 (1988): 498–505, and Samdahl and Robertson, "Social Determinants of Environmental Concern."

33. Perceptions of the seriousness of environmental problems and the threats they bring likely influence attitudes toward environmental policies, according to Donald W. Hine and Robert Gifford, "Fear Appeals, Individual Differences, and Environmental Concern," *Journal of Environmental Education* 23 (1991): 36–41, and Samdahl and Robertson ("Social Determinants of Environmental Concern").

34. William H. Green, *Limdep Version 7.0* (Plainview, N.Y.: Econometric Software, 1998).

35. Perceptions of threats to the local environment were addressed many years ago in survey research on the Lake Tahoe basin. Threats found to be relatively urgent among those expressing environmental concern included deforestation, degradation of water quality, visual pollution, loss of open space, air pollution, and traffic congestion (Constantini and Hanf, "Environmental Concern and Lake Tahoe").

36. Results in the literature are mixed on the effect income has on environmental attitudes. Some find income to have a positive effect on environmentalists (Mohai, "Men, Women, and the Environment"; Gebhardt and Lindsey, " Differences in Environmental Orientation") and some perceive income as a negative effect (Samdahl and Robertson, "Social Determinants of Environmental Concern"). Most agree that the effect of income is modest at best (Van Liere and Dunlap, "The Social Bases of Environmental Concern"). Mohai ("Public Concern and Elite Involvement") found that social class does not influence support for environmental protection but does affect both political and environmental activism. A study in the Lake Tahoe area found income to be negatively correlated to environmental concern (Costantini and Hanf, "Environmental Concern and Lake Tahoe").

16637. Blaikie ("The Nature and Origins of Ecological World Views") points out that a middle-aged cohort now exhibits a relatively high level of environmental concern. The findings of other researchers on the role of age in affecting environmental attitudes is mixed. Gebhardt and Lindsey ("Differences in Environmental Orientation") and Samdahl and Robertson ("Social Determinants of Environmental Concern") find that age is positively correlated to environmental concern, while most studies find a negative relationship (Mohai and Twight, "Age and Environmentalism"; Van Liere and Dunlap, "The Social Bases of Environmental Concern").

38. The measure of education used in the survey lumps together those who completed high school and those who attended high school but did not complete it.

39. Education and political outlook are among the two most consistently mentioned statistically significant explanatory variables in the literature on environmental concern (Costantini and Hanf, "Environmental Concern and Lake Tahoe"; Gebhardt and Lindsey, "Differences in Environmental Orientation"; Mohai, "Men, Women, and the Environment"; Samdahl and Robertson, "Social Determinants of Environmental Concern"; and Van Liere and Dunlap, "The Social Bases of Environmental Concern").

40. This indirect effect can be estimated by multiplying the mean population density growth (20 per thousand acres) by the marginal effect of population density growth on a respondent's probability of seeing poor planning as a threat (i.e., the Marginal Effects coefficient for Net Density in the Poor Planning/Very Much column, table 6A.1), and by multiplying this result by the marginal effect of the threat on a respondent's probability of supporting zoning (i.e., the Marginal Effects coefficient on Threat in the Favor Zoning column, table 6A.2). The result will be a fairly small .009 (.006 x 20 x .072). The indirect effect doesn't amount to much.

41. Assuming the average increase of 20 in net population density per thousand acres, the marginal effect of the net population density increase on the probability of a respondent being in the "Decline in Quality of Natural Environment: Very Much" category is 20 x .005 or .10 (table 6A.1). Multiplying this times the marginal effects of the "Threat" variable on "Protect Wildlife Habitat, Ecosystems: Agree" category in table 6A.2, the result is .10 x .031 = .003. A similar calculation for the indirect effect of an increase in net population density on the expected probability of a respondent being in the "Protect Open Space: Agree" category is equal to .012. Finally, a comparable calculation for "Steer Development to Existing Towns: Agree" yields .008. These indirect effects of net density growth on support for county-level policies are, consequently, fairly modest.

7

~

Saving the Landscape:
Environmental Change and the
Land Trust Movement in the
Mountain West

The conclusions reached so far are conceptually fairly simple. Population is spreading into many counties of the mountain West at a relatively rapid rate. Population growth is not driven by expansion of the traditional mountain economy, suggesting a new foundation for growth. This new foundation includes the spreading of employment to mountain West counties in such a way as to cause their economic structure to look more like that of urban areas. Spreading of both population and employment has been enabled by new kinds of technologies that increase the ease and reduce the cost of communication and transportation. Moreover, rising affluence has increased the feasibility of moving to the mountain West for many people. Unfortunately, population spreading and rural sprawl appear to be causing ecosystem degradation and added stress to certain rare and endangered species in mountain counties. Such stresses are often occurring on top of those already present as a consequence of the enduring effects of the old economy extractive industries. Finally, voters of mountain counties in the Sierra Nevada have expressed concern about the loss of open space and natural habitat caused by residential development and population spreading. In particular, these voters have indicated strong support for measures that limit and guide growth, such as zoning, open space preservation, and natural habitat conservation, and the concentration of development in existing towns.

In some instances, county and municipal governments have responded to population expansion and residential development by instituting new land use plans and zoning regulations, placing moratoriums on further development, and purchasing open space. Limitations on development, however, have also been delayed and reduced in scope by the efforts of property owners and developers who benefit from local economic expansion and who are often active in local politics.[1]

169

In reaction to threats caused by development pressures and, in some cases, the failure of local government to act, land trusts have been created by community residents in many high-growth counties for the purpose of preserving open space, farm and ranch land, and natural areas. Because land trusts offer a potential vehicle for addressing problems caused by rapid local population growth, they clearly ought to be included in any discussion of local reactions to development pressures.

Land trusts are nonprofit, voluntary conservation organizations that accept donations of property or easements or raise money to purchase property or easements. A conservation easement is a legally binding agreement between a property owner and a land trust that restricts property development rights but allows the landowner to retain ownership. These rights are essentially donated to the land trust, and, if the land trust qualifies as a nonprofit in the eyes of the IRS, the donor can take a tax deduction for the appraised value of the rights. In addition to qualify for a tax deduction, restrictions of development rights must have a public benefit, such as the preservation of open space or natural habitat. The easement agreement is recorded as part of the deed and applies in perpetuity to all future owners of the property. The role of the land trust is to monitor and enforce the easement agreement. A land trust is thus a vehicle for voluntary action to limit development for the purpose of preserving open space, natural areas, and traditional land uses such as ranching and farming.[2]

Population spreading into rural mountain counties accelerates residential and commercial development and road construction, potentially threatening open space and natural areas. In the valley bottoms, the subdivision of ranch lands not only threatens open space but reduces land devoted to traditional economic activities and thus permanently alters local rural culture. Do such changes stimulate the formation of land trusts in rural mountain counties? Once formed, what is the primary emphasis of land trust activities? Is it to preserve open space and scenic vistas, local recreational opportunities, working ranches and the rural way of life? Or, is the conservation of natural habitats and rare and threatened species a matter of primary concern?

Two methods will be used to address these questions. First, a statistical analysis of land trust location patterns will be offered to establish whether land trust activity is related to local population expansion. Second, a series of short case studies of land trusts will be presented and analyzed for the purpose of determining why land trusts form and what priorities they follow in land conservation decisions. These case studies are based on personal interviews of staff and board members for key land trusts in Colorado and Montana. Before proceeding to these tasks, a conceptual framework is needed for understanding the difficulties land trusts face in getting organized.

THE POLITICAL ECONOMY OF LAND TRUSTS

Open space, beautiful views, natural habitats, healthy ecosystems, and the continuation of a rural way of life can all be viewed as what economists call "public goods." The enjoyment of such goods by one does not normally detract from the enjoyment by others. These are goods that commonly benefit many simultaneously. It may even be the case that some people who never materially benefit from these goods will support their provision out of a sense of duty to potential beneficiaries in future generations and perhaps even to nonhuman species who reside in local natural habitats. In short, material benefit is not a necessary reason for an individual to support protection of the public goods dimension of a given landscape.

Since public goods of the kind land trusts seek to protect are simultaneously desired and enjoyed by many, they must be collectively provided or protected. If nearly all ranchers go out of business in a mountain valley, the rural way of life will likely disappear. If most ranches are sold for development, open space and natural habitat will suffer. To prevent such occurrences requires some kind of collective action. Someone who desires a freshly baked loaf of bread or a bottle of fine wine will have little trouble purchasing such items. However, someone of modest means who wants to preserve a relatively pristine mountain valley is unlikely to have the same option. To put together the economic resources needed for such a task requires cooperation with other like-minded individuals. Such a voluntary effort, however, will have to contend with what is known as the "freerider" problem. If the effort to preserve a pristine mountain valley is ultimately successful, those who don't contribute to it will nonetheless enjoy the benefits. A beautiful mountain valley is freely and openly available to all of its residents and visitors. Moreover, if there are several thousand potential beneficiaries, the contribution of any individual would be such a small part of the total as not to matter for the success of the effort. Whether any given individual contributes economic resources to valley preservation won't make a difference. Consequently, few individuals who follow their self-interest are likely to join in voluntary preservation efforts.

One means for overcoming the freerider problem in the provision of a public good is political. Local politicians may well recognize the demand for such a good and institute measures to bring about its provision. Elected county politicians, for instance, could put in place land use regulations that would prevent the subdividing of a mountain valley by development projects. This solution would not work, however, if there are powerful local interest groups arrayed against it, such as landowners and developers.

If local regulatory measures are ruled out for political reasons, then the only option left would be voluntary efforts through organizations such as land trusts. Even though the freerider problem is undoubtedly a hindrance, voluntary organizations such as land trusts do manage to get organized and carry out landscape conservation programs. This suggests that human behavior is not confined to the strictly self-interested mode presumed by the freerider problem. People do voluntarily contribute time and money to conservation organizations. They most likely do this out of a sense of commitment to the goals of such organizations.

To put it differently, individuals who come together to form voluntary organizations such as land trusts engage not in the calculus of a private rationality, but in what the philosopher John Searle refers to as "collective intentionality."[3] In the case of collective as opposed to individual intentionality, the individual does not see herself as separate from the group. Group members simply internalize the goals and purposes of the group. Just as individual intentionality is a primitive form of behavior in some circumstances, so is collective intentionality in others. Where different individuals have a common vision to which they feel bound to contribute, then collective intentionality is a likely outcome. Of course, not everyone will feel so strongly, and not everyone who benefits from the goods created or preserved by a group such as a land trust will voluntarily contribute. But the potential for overcoming the freerider problem through voluntary collective efforts is a distinct possibility. The evidence for this is a relatively extensive land trust movement in the mountain West. The experience of population growth in pristine areas, I will now argue, is a causal force in mobilizing those who feel a commitment to the landscape to form land trusts.

LAND TRUSTS AND DEVELOPMENT PRESSURES

As of 1998, the Land Trust Alliance listed 33 local land trusts in its national directory that operate in 37 of the 86 mountain West sample counties.[4] In 1998 the average age of these land trusts was 7.6 years, and the oldest had been in existence for 31 years. Land trusts in the mountain West, consequently, are a relatively new phenomenon.

If the formation of land trusts is indeed stimulated by the actual experience of growth, the presence of land trust operations in a county should correlate with growth. A statistical analysis reveals that net population density growth from 1985 to 1997 and the number of ski areas present in the county in 1997 both have a positive impact on the number of land trusts operating in a given county.[5] According to the statistical results, an increase in population density of 100 per thousand acres would result in the creation of one land trust operating in the county. An increase in county ski areas by about three would result in the creation of a land trust. Obviously, many factors that can't be accounted for statistically determine whether a land trust is put into operation in any given county. It is true, however, that the number of land trusts in operation is positively related to population density growth. It is also the case that the presence of land trusts is positively related to the number of ski areas operating in a county. As noted in chapter 3, ski areas attract both vacation homes and employment and thus the development that goes with them. Ski areas along with their associated development could well be viewed as threatening to open space and natural areas by local residents and thus be a stimulus to land trust activity. In short, population density growth is not the only indicator of development pressures. In high mountain valleys near ski resorts, extensive construction of vacation homes, commercial tourist facilities, and part-time residences can also be a source of considerable development pressures.

LAND TRUST CASE STUDIES

In order to put meat on the above "statistical bones," a series of personal interviews with land trust directors or key board members was conducted in August and September of 2000. The purpose of each interview was to gather information on the motivations for forming the land trust, the nature of the development pressures facing the land trust, and the criteria used in the land trust's decisions to acquire or accept donations of conservation easements or fee simple title to properties. Was the formation of the land trust in fact motivated by economic development pressures? What is the nature of those development pressures? And does the land trust consider threats to specific ecosystems and species in its conservation decisions? These are the key questions the following case studies address. The interviews were open ended, except for a few Likert-style scale questions asked at the conclusion of each interview to allow for a quantitative summary of responses. The land trusts interviewed were chosen for geographic coverage and also for the amount and importance of the lands they have conserved. In an area where more than one local land trust operates, the larger one was selected for the interview on the presumption that the more active land trust would have increased experience to draw upon and would better reflect the local community land trust experience.[6] The key characteristics of the land trusts and the key demographic data for the counties they primarily operate in are presented in table 7.1.

The land trusts selected for interviews are clearly not located in counties that are representative of the 86 sample counties as a whole, as the demographic data in table 7.1 suggests. While the average density growth for the land trust counties is about the same as for all 86 sample counties, the land trust counties are clearly more affluent and have more vacation homes. The per capita income for land trust counties is about $3,000 more than for all sample counties as a whole, and the percentage of second homes is 7 percent greater. Moreover, all land trust counties except one have ski areas (Custer County, where the San Isabel Foundation is located, lacks a ski area). The land trust counties are clearly more oriented toward ski area and vacation home development than the sample as a whole. They are also relatively more affluent than the sample as a whole.

The Crested Butte Land Trust

The Crested Butte Land Trust operates in the East River Valley near the former mining town of Crested Butte (population 868) located in Gunnison County.[7] The area is a popular destination for skiers in the winter and outdoor recreationists in the summer, and, consequently, the local economy is heavily dependent on tourism. Moreover, the beautiful East River Valley is developing rapidly with ranchettes and subdivisions. While many of the new homes being constructed are vacation retreats, the valley appears to be attracting increasing

Table 7.1.   Land Trust Characteristics

	Land Trust Average	Crested Butte	Yampa	Grand	Eagle	San Isabel	La Plata	Mesa	Five Valleys**	Gallatin
Land Trust Data										
Year founded		1991	1992	1995	1989*	1995	1992	1980	1989	1990
Number of members or supporters		800	600	200	300	200	200	200	500	1,125
Estimated percentage of funds raised from vacation or second homeowners		50	50	60	75	50	5	0	5	?
Total acres protected through easements and land donations or purchases (Sept. 2000)		1,850	20,000	424	4,500	4,000	5,600	21,000	23,000	8,300
County Demographic Data										
Population Density Growth: 1985–1997 (Sample av.=6.2/1000 acres)	6.0	1.1	1.8	1.1	16.3	2.5	6.6	10.9	6.6	7.4
Second Home Percent Share: 1990 (Sample Average=16.8)	23.6	36.2	4.8	57.4	33.1	55.7	13.7	1.6	3.4	6.2
Per Capita Income 1997 (Sample Average=$19,766)	$22,984	$19,150	$28,361	$23,523	$31,890	$17,123	$23,163	$20,593	$21,496	$21,556

*Reorganized in 1995 with new mission.
**Excludes Rock Creek Trust data.

numbers of affluent retirees and families who have sufficient assets to live on without having to work. There are also a few consultants, stock brokers, and other telecommuters moving into the area who are able to continue their business connections with clients and customers outside the local area. The recent construction of a new high school has increased the attractiveness of the Crested Butte community to families. Because the rest of Gunnison County is heavily agricultural, the demographics of the county as a whole are not very representative for Crested Butte which is clearly a relatively affluent community. Gunnison County does have a somewhat high proportion of second homes, many of which are likely located in the East River Valley. The population density growth figure for the county as a whole is not a very accurate representation of development pressures around Crested Butte.

The Crested Butte Land Trust was founded in 1991 by a local builder (who is also an avid environmentalist), the town planner, and the town attorney. These individuals were concerned about the nature and pace of development occurring in the area and were involved in the creation of a town plan that addressed development issues. At about the same time, the town of Crested Butte passed a three percent real estate transfer tax of which half is available for the purchase of open space in the town. Any nonprofit, such as a land trust, could apply for these funds to defray the cost of open space purchases. Nonprofits could also apply for funds from a Gunnison County program that designates a portion of its sales tax revenues for open space acquisitions. These turned out to be major funding sources for some of the Crested Butte Land Trust acquisitions along with state funding for open space preservation from Great Outdoors Colorado.

The primary criterion for selection of land purchases or easements by the Crested Butte Land Trust is the preservation of open space. However, protection of natural habitat is a critical element in the project selection process as suggested by Crested Butte's Mission Statement reproduced in figure 7.1. Clearly, preservation of ecosystems and wildlife are key elements of the mission statement along with open space protection and preservation of traditional land uses such as ranching. The specific goals outlined in the mission statement are incorporated in the land trust's acquisition rating system used in decision making on proposed easements and land purchases.

The first major accomplishment of the land trust was the purchase of two parcels in 1992 along the Slate River, a tributary of the East River. The Slate River watershed contains some of Colorado's highest quality wetlands according to a local hydrologist and has continued to be a major focus of the land trust's conservation efforts. Conserving the Slate River is not only important for the protection of natural habitat, but, because it runs through the town of Crested Butte, the river is a major visual resource and contributes substantially to the scenic beauty of the local landscape. A second major goal of the land trust is to preserve open space in the so-called "Gothic Road" corridor between Crested Butte

Crested Butte Land Trust

The purpose of the Crested Butte Land Trust is the preservation and protection of open space lands within Gunnison County considered to be of a particular value to our heritage and quality of life by the:

- preservation or restoration of natural areas;
- preservation of water resources in their natural state;
- protection of flood plains;
- preservation of scenic areas and view corridors, wildlife habitats and fragile ecosystems;
- protection of agriculture and ranching uses;
- enhancement of access to public lands;
- utilization of non-urban land for spatial definition of urban areas; and
- preservation of land for its aesthetic or recreational value.

The Yampa Valley Land Trust

Yampa Valley Land Trust conserves natural, scenic, agricultural, historic and open land resources in Northwest Colorado, including but not limited to Routt, Moffat, Jackson, Grand, and Rio Blanco Counties, with a focus on the Yampa River Basin in Routt County. The Land Trust promotes land stewardship through public education and technical assistance.

The Grand County Land Conservancy

The purpose of the Grand County Land Conservancy is to aid and encourage our community to preserve the visual quality, agricultural lands, biological diversity, and historical heritage of Grand County.

Figure 7.1: Land Trusts Mission Statement

and Mt. Crested Butte. To this end, the land trust purchased a 154-acre parcel of ranch land in 1997 at a cost of $1.2 million. One of the land trust's crowning achievements has been the purchase, at a cost of approximately $1.8 million, and the reopening of the Lower Loop parcel to the public, an area that had traditionally been heavily used for recreation because of its proximity to key hiking trails in the area. A variety of other purchases and easements brings the total acres protected by the land trust to approximately 1,850 acres. The amount of land protected is small in comparison to other land trusts because land is so costly in the Crested Butte area.

The amount of land purchased by the Crested Butte Land Trust and the amount of money spent on these purchases is somewhat unusual. Many land trusts rely more heavily on easements. The ability to make large purchases in part stems from the availability of a variety of funding sources. To reiterate, the Crested Butte Land trust has been successful in obtaining open space funds from the town of Crested Butte's real estate transfer tax fund, the Gunnison County open space program, and Great Outdoors Colorado, a state agency that promotes open space conservation and gets funding from the state lottery. In addition, a one-percent program has been successfully instituted locally where merchants voluntarily contribute one percent of their sales to land trusts, and successful donor drives have been undertaken to match grant funds. The high cost of the land purchased is directly related to the popularity of the area among the relatively affluent for second and primary home construction. The land trust was established after development pressures had already increased land prices.

Although the conservation of biological diversity is a key part of the land trust's mission, the preservation of open space is clearly the dominant theme. This is undoubtedly related in large part to the availability of funding for open space preservation. It is also related to the interests of second home owners who make up a large portion of the land trust's 800 members and who are also major donors. Second home owners have a strong interest in seeing views preserved and development limited, both for aesthetic reasons and for the preservation and enhancement of their own property values. Second home owners in the Crested Butte area are both a part of the problem and a part of the solution. They illustrate the proposition that growth and development in themselves foster opposition to further development. Those who have gained their piece of paradise don't want to see it spoiled by further development.

In sum, the Crested Butte Land Trust was formed largely in response to local development pressures and considers natural habitat preservation to be a major goal, although its primary focus has been on the protection of open space.

The Yampa Valley Land Trust

The Yampa Valley is located in the northern Colorado Rockies and includes a popular ski resort and tourist destination, Steamboat Springs.[8] The valley itself is open and expansive, includes significant riparian habitats, and is framed by rolling uplands as well as forested mountains. The initial motivation for organizing the land trust in 1993 was a development proposal for the Catamount Lake area south of Steamboat Springs. The owner wanted 25 million dollars for the land, and developers wanted to put in a large ski run and connected residential and commercial development that could have doubled the population of the Steamboat area. The Cantamount project as originally conceived would have included a new ski resort that could accommodate 12,000 skiers per day, 3,700 new dwellings, 1,000 hotel rooms, and 250,000 square feet of retail space. After a recession in the 1980s, the community was sharply divided over the project. Some saw it as a vehicle for economic recovery; others were concerned about how it would change Steamboat Springs and the local way of life. Some residents feared that the local community would suffer from a homogenizing style of development typical of large metropolitan suburbs. The project would have substantially reduced open space in the southern approach to Steamboat Springs. The Yampa Valley Land Trust (YVLT) was able to negotiate a modified development proposal that put much of the land in a conservation easement and reduced the development to a lodge and 40 home sites.

While the formation of the YVLT was motivated by the Cantamount development proposal, double-digit population growth in the Steamboat Springs area is a looming threat to open space and natural areas that the YVLT also seeks to address. Although Steamboat Springs and the surrounding area is experiencing a surge of growth, population density growth in Routt County as a whole remains fairly modest (table 7.1) primarily because of a remaining large amount of undeveloped land in the county as a whole. Routt County, however, is relatively affluent with a comparatively high per capita income ($28,361). Affluence is thus a potential contributor to the pace of local development. Ironically, while Steamboat Springs is known primarily for its skiing, it is not skiing activity as such that is driving growth. Skiing, as measured by the number of lift tickets sold, is on the decline locally. This of course doesn't preclude skiing as an attraction for people who build primary residences or second homes in the area. While those who visit Steamboat Springs for skiing may be shrinking in number, tourism in general is doing well because the area has become a year-round tourist destination. Nonetheless, those who move into the area don't typically rely on tourism for employment, although retirees with more modest incomes sometimes take part-time jobs in the ski industry to supplement their income. As was the case for the Crested Butte area, some residents below retirement age who have recently moved to Yampa Valley and built large expensive homes on subdivided land have sufficient accumulated wealth to live on without working. People who rely on computers to deal with clients outside the area—the so-called "lone eagles"—are also growing in number. Some commute to jobs outside the area or travel extensively in connection with their work. Vacation or second homes are responsible for roughly half of new housing construction in recent years, although in 1990 the proportion of second homes was relatively modest (table 7.1). Again, as with Crested Butte, the Yampa Valley Land Trust receives significant support from vacation homeowners.

In Colorado, landowners are allowed to sink a well and build a house on a lot with a minimum of 35 acres without any kind of special permit. Consequently, in rural counties lacking growth controls, there are no special provisions to limit subdivision development. In general, where population and growth pressures are strong, as in the Steamboat Springs area, there isn't much to prevent the carving up of large ranches into smaller ranchettes except conservation easements and land trusts.

While many residents are second home owners, supporters of the Yampa Valley Land Trust come from a range of occupations, including ranchers. The board members are active in the land trust because of their passion for land conservation and their desire to preserve the local way of life. This is apparent in the mission statement reproduced in figure 7.1. The land trust purchases and accepts donations of easements, but land is not purchased outright. Roughly 75 percent of easements are donated, and the rest are purchased. Great Outdoors Colorado has been a significant source of funding for easement purchases. Routt County provides some of the land trust's operating funds, and the land trust has worked with the city of Steamboat Springs on a number of open space conservation projects. Moreover, both county and city governments are committed to open space conservation, and the county has an open space tax. Members of YVLT (600 total) are also a major source of support. Although the land trust can operate in five counties, it concentrates on the Yampa Basin. Lands proposed for easements are judged for acceptance by YVLT according to their wildlife, natural habitat, and scenic values and their connectivity to other preserved landscapes. The preservation of open lands and agriculture are goals of the land trust in addition to ecological considerations. While much of the land preserved in easements (20,000 acres) is valley bottom, some is foothill lands as well, both forests and shrublands. A number of species in the Yampa Valley are benefited by easements, including elk, mule deer, mountain lions, black bear, coyote, red fox, badger, nesting sandhill cranes, great blue herons, bald eagles, Columbia sharp-tailed grouse, sage grouse, and four threatened Yampa River fish. Preservation of elk wintering and calving grounds are particularly important considerations that get widespread support among valley residents. Habitat types protected by easements include rare riparian areas, spruce forests, aspen stands, hay meadows, open meadows, scrub oak uplands, and trout streams.

In sum, the Yampa Valley Land Trust was created as a response to a particular development project as well as to larger development pressures. While preserving open space and the agricultural way of life are key themes, the conservation of natural values is of critical importance in the land trust's conservation efforts. Wealth accumulation and new technology enabling the spreading of human population to remote locations appear to be important forces behind Yampa Valley population expansion.

YVLT's success is partly the result of the good relations it has with both city and county government and the commitment of both to open space conservation. As was the case for the Crested Butte Land Trust, YVLT has a strong interest in preserving natural habitat and came into existence largely in response to development pressures.

Grand County Land Conservancy

The Grand County landscape encompasses high mountains that include a popular ski area, a piece of a high mountain open valley known as North Park, and the headwaters of the Colorado River.[9] The combination of these landscape features has made the area popular for second home development. The Grand County Land Conservancy was formed in 1995 largely as reaction to fragmentation of the local landscape resulting from the development of second homes in the 1990s. The county itself has zoning and a growth management plan, but county commissioners have rendered the plan ineffective by approving property owner variance requests. The land trust founders felt that population growth in the area was out of control. The recession of the 1980s and the economic hardship it brought to Grand County caused second home and other residential development to look increasingly attractive to those in the community seeking improved local economic opportunities. Since the early 1990s, second home development has been a principle force behind income and employment expansion in the county, not only through expansion of the construction industry, but also because of the increased demand for retail and services that second home owners bring to the area. While its population density growth is not especially large because of extensive areas of remaining open space, the county does have a very high proportion of second homes (57 percent), and its per capita income is comparatively high ($23,573).[10] Grand County has developed later than some of the other resort communities, partly because of its remoteness and harsher climate.

The boom in second home ownership has been driven by an influx of individuals from California with sufficient funds from home sales to purchase both a residence in Denver and a second home. The runup of stock market values and the resulting increase in personal wealth has also contributed to elevated second home purchases. While second home construction is the dominant force in the local economy, some retirees, a few telecommuters, and some residents below retirement age who have sufficient capital income to live on without having to work are moving to the area despite the harsh climate. Because of the harsh climate, retirees choosing to live in Grand County tend to be in good health and are especially interested in the outdoor recreation opportunities in the area. These individuals are relatively affluent and contribute to the local demand for new housing. In addition, there is a modest expansion in tourism employment in the local economy, although these jobs are not normally very high paying. While some members of the community look on residential development favorably because of the local economic benefits it brings, others have expressed concern with the resulting loss of open space in valley areas and damage to riparian habitats along the Colorado River. New home construction benefits the local economy, but it is also a key threat to the local environment. Moreover, since second home owners are the source of about half the support for the Grand Valley Land Conservancy, they again seem to be a part of both the problem and its solution.

The loss of open space, agricultural lands, and natural habitat are of equal consideration in motivating the Conservancy's formation and its easement acquisitions. This is apparent from the mission statement reproduced in figure 7.1. A group of three community members was instrumental in the Conservancy's initial formation. Some Conservancy board members focus on habitat preservation while others are more interested in preserving the existing rural way of life. Consequently, the preservation of ranch land is just as important as open space in the Conservancy's easement acquisitions. Because of limited financial resources, the land trust focuses on contributed easements as opposed to land or easement purchases. Since Grand County includes the headwaters of the Colorado River, the Conservancy's board feels that it has a special responsibility for threatened riparian areas along the river and attempts to focus its efforts on river-related conservation projects. Preserving wildlife habit is an important goal in the Conservancy's decisions on easement selection. The one group in the community that is suspicious of the Conservancy's activities is ranchers. They fear the land trust will somehow figure out a way to get their property rights away from them. For this reason, the Conservancy doesn't have the total support of the local community. As already noted, comparatively wealthy second home owners are the land trust's primary supporters. Relatively wealthy landowners not dependent on ranching income are the ones contributing easements and supporting the land trust with donations. The Conservancy's easements (424 acres) include both valley bottom ranch land and riparian areas. The sage grouse is a species of concern in protecting habitat in the area and in easement selection decisions. Otherwise, the focus in easement decisions is on wildlife habitat, as opposed to individual species, as well as view corridors and agricultural land protection. The mission statement is taken seriously as a basis for conservation decisions. Because the land trust is fairly young, the total amount of land preserved is below other land trusts interviewed.

In sum, the Grand County Land Conservancy was formed in direct response to the increased subdividing of valley bottom and riparian lands for residential construction. While second home construction is the predominant force behind local economic expansion, local growth is also being stimulated by an increasing number of retirees, telecommuters, and the independently wealthy who are building new homes on subdivided rural land. In the Conservancy's decisions on easements, the preservation of wildlife habitat and threatened species is a key goal.

Eagle Valley Land Trust

Eagle County encompasses some of Colorado's most scenic mountains, including the Mount of the Holy Cross and the Gore Range, as well as river valleys and shrubby uplands.[11] The county also includes the well-known ski resort, Vail. The Eagle Valley Land Trust was founded in 1981 for the purpose of preserving agricultural land. The original founders saw accelerating development in the area as a threat to agriculture. The one person most responsible for the land trust's founding worked in agricultural real estate and was a strong advocate for the preservation of the agricultural sector in the mountain West. However, before the land trust got off the ground, the sharp recession of 1982 brought development to a halt making a land trust unnecessary for the moment. The land trust took on new momentum in 1992 in response to increased development along the Interstate 70 corridor. Vail, of course, is at the center of this development, containing some of Colorado's most expensive rural real estate. The primary economic force behind growth is second home construction by the wealthy. The extension of I–70 through Vail in the 1970s as well as the development of a substantial regional airport rendered Vail an extremely attractive location for affluent second home owners. Denver is roughly one and a half hours away by car. Vail's attraction is not just skiing since second homes are used year-round. Affluent homeowners in Vail seem to have attracted still more affluence. In the I–70 corridor, traditional ranching no longer exists. Old ranches have been developed, or else they have been taken over by affluent owners who operate them essentially as hobby ranches and vacation getaways. There are a few telecommuters, but most newcomers in the area have enough money to live on without having to work. Retirees settling in the area are fairly modest in numbers. Because of the scale of development activity, the local economy is also beginning to diversify. The scale of the economy is sufficient to support more specialized services. Construction has been the mainstay of the economy in the past, but the employment base appears to be shifting to services. Because of the shortage of available land and incredible land prices in the Vail area, development is being pushed downvalley to the west. The I–70 corridor itself is almost completely developed. Since only the rich can afford Vail, moderate-income residents are relegated to downvalley real estate. Traditional ranching is confined to a few remote corners of the northern part of the county. The rest of agricultural lands in the county are largely in the hands of affluent hobby farmers. Since these individuals are not inclined to subdivide their land, the natural features are in effect being conserved, at least for the moment. In short, Eagle County features rapid population density growth, a large proportion of second home owners, and an unusually high level of affluence.[12]

The loss of open space and wildlife habitats in the I–70 corridor are the two key issues that motivated the rejuvenation of the Eagle Valley Land Trust (EVLT) in the early 1990s, although the loss of agricultural lands continues to be a critical issue for land trust board members. The predominant goal of the land trust is the protection of open space, especially in the I–70 corridor. Board members fear the creation of a strip city through the full length of the corridor in Eagle County. Although the land trust's mission statement in figure 7.2 clearly indicates that open space protection is its primary goal, the conservation of wildlife habitat is an important consequence of its activities. The trust holds a number of easements on local ranches that protect wildlife habitat. There are some locations in the county where sage grouse leks are found, and some of these have disappeared as a consequence of development. One of EVLT's easements protects

The Eagle Valley Land Trust

The Eagle Valley Land Trust is dedicated to the preservation and enhancement of open space in Eagle County and surrounding areas. The Trust seeks to accomplish its mission by
- identifying key lands deserving of open space protection;
- educating residents and visitors about the benefits of open space and providing information and expertise on conservation tools for landowners, public agencies and other interested parties;
- acting as a holding agent or steward of lands which may be given to or purchased by the Trust;
- serving as a facilitator for those wishing to convey land to qualified government agencies or other private conservation entities;
- raising funds to purchase open space for permanent preservation and conservation.

The San Isabel Foundation

The purpose of the San Isabel Foundation is to provide a local resource or partner for local landowners to facilitate the stewardship and preservation of agricultural lands, wildlands and wildlife habitat, open space, water, scenic beauty and other natural and historic resources for now and future generations.

The La Plata Open Space Conservancy

La Plata Open Space Conservancy (LPOSC) incorporated as a private, nonprofit land trust in 1992 to protect open lands in Southwest Colorado that have important agricultural, wildlife, scenic, historical, archaeological, and/or recreational value.

The Mesa County Land Conservancy

Mesa County Land Conservancy (MCLC) is a private nonprofit land trust. Our mission is to protect agricultural land, open space, and wildlife habitat. We do this through the use of conservation easements.

Figure 7.2:   Land Trusts Mission Statement (Continued)

such a lek. Moreover, EVLT facilitated the public sector acquisition of key natural habitat on Brush Creek south of Eagle, a town to the west of Vail on the I–70 corridor. Brush Creek State Park is a winter range for elk and mule deer and is a summer habitat for black bears and raptors. East and West Brush Creeks are important trout streams and are bordered by important riparian habitats.

In its efforts to conserve I–70 open space, EVLT was instrumental in brokering a land purchase by Eagle County near Gypsum in the I–70 corridor. The land is composed primarily of gypsum hillsides and sagebrush flats and is a key buffer between communities along the interstate. One of the land trust's goals is to keep some open space areas between communities along the interstate free of development. To date EVLT has been responsible for preserving about 4,500 acres in the county through its activities as a land deal broker and easement holder.

EVLT is supported primarily by a relatively small number of large donors, three-fourths of whom are second home owners in the area. The few remaining old-time ranchers are suspicious of EVLT and its activities. However, most ranches in the county today are really hobby ranches owned by wealthy individuals. These landowners don't seem to be much inclined to do easements, seeing themselves as decent stewards of the land. Consequently, EVLT has encountered some resistance outside the I–70 corridor regarding conservation easements.

Although EVLT's mission statement emphasizes open space, it just recently had the Colorado Natural Heritage Program conduct an inventory of rare and threatened species and natural communities. The purpose of the inventory was to identify ecologically significant landscapes. The survey recorded 53 significant plant communities and identified 29 rare and threatened species including the bald eagle, northern goshawk, boreal toad, Townsend's Big-eared Bat, Colorado River cutthroat trout, and Harrington's beardtongue. Getting landowner cooperation for the survey was tough. Fearing that they might come under regulation if threatened species were found on their property, landowners often refused entry to survey members. Nonetheless, a number of sensitive habitats and rare and threatened species were identified, and a priority system for habitat preservation was worked out. Rare and threatened species in the area are small in number primarily because Eagle County is at high elevations where there tend to be fewer species in total than at lower elevations. While mule deer and elk were not emphasized in the Natural Heritage study, they are of major concern to local residents. These animals are an integral part of the local culture. The Canada lynx is also not discussed much in the Natural Heritage study, although the lynx is a major source of concern for some and was a major issue in a recent ski area expansion. Backcountry skiing causes snow compaction and opens up lynx habitat to coyotes who compete for the same prey base, posing a threat to the lynx.

The Eagle Valley Land Trust faces the not insignificant challenge of protecting land in one of the most highly traveled highway corridors in Colorado. The incredible costs of land in this corridor, caused by the attraction of wealth to Vail, increases this challenge, although this same wealth also increases the land trust's ability to raise funds from a relatively small number of donors. For all intents and purposes, cattle ranching in the county is no longer feasible as a means for earning a living, and affluent hobby ranchers that have taken over much of the old ranch lands are not inclined to negotiate conservation easements. For these reasons, the environment for land deals faced by EVLT is different and in some respects more challenging than in many other areas in Colorado. Although Eagle County has land use plans and zoning, variances are frequently given to landowners that cumulatively repudiate the intentions of the plans. Given the wealth in the county and the marked decline in open space that has occurred, it is surprising that the Eagle Valley Land Trust seems to be the only effective force in the county for open space conservation.

San Isabel Foundation

The San Isabel Foundation is a land trust operating in the beautiful Wet Mountain Valley, bounded by the Arkansas River to the north, the San de Cristo Mountains to the west, the Wet Mountains to the east, and the Spanish Peaks to the south.[13] The San Isabel Foundation (SIF) was founded in 1995 by local homeowners concerned with the residential development and subdivision of ranch lands occurring around Westcliff, Colorado, and in Custer County generally. The founders are mainly people who moved to the area within the last 20 years. Their key concern is with the subdividing of valley bottom ranches as well as the construction of homes on ridge lines. The driving goal of SIF is to preserve open space, although the protection of wildlife habitat is also of substantial importance as expressed in the organization's mission statement (figure 7.2). The founders have a strong interest in preserving ranching in the area and the rural way of life that goes with it.

Even though SIF is clearly interested in preserving working ranches, local ranchers, who often trace their roots back to the early days of Anglo-American settlement, are somewhat mistrustful of SIF because most of its board and supporters are relative newcomers to the valley. However, traditional ranchers are clearly concerned with development trends in the valley. Ranchers were behind Custer County zoning regulations instituted some 25 years ago that require a minimum parcel size of 80 acres per residential structure on valley bottom lands as opposed to state regulations requiring only 35 acres without a special permit. At the time this measure was instituted, ranchers were expressing concern about development pressures in the area. Despite their own support for county-level land use regulations, ranchers are mistrustful of SIF because they feel that easements will ultimately lead somehow to a form of government regulation outside their control, something they fear deeply. Ranchers nonetheless participate in SIF workshops on conservation easements, although they express considerable cynicism about the approach. A cultural divide that is difficult to bridge exists between ranchers whose families have been in the valley more than a hundred years and relative newcomers. To allay their fears while at the same time participating in efforts to limit development, ranchers have formed their own land trust, the Custer Heritage Committee. In this way they are able to insure control, but at the same time they are able to work with SIF. The ultimate goal of the Heritage Committee is to collect funds for the purchase of easements from ranchers. SIF helped them get started and has helped them with projects including the raising of matching funds.

The critical dilemma for land trust members who want to pursue easements on ranch lands is that contributed easements don't provide immediate economic benefits to ranchers. Ranchers don't earn enough to take advantage of the tax breaks, although in the long run reducing their estate taxes by diminishing the marketable value of their property can be important to them. This allows a large ranch to be passed on to descendants without having the burden of heavy estate taxes, the payment of which might require the subdivision and sale of the property. In the short run, however, ranchers are just barely making it; raising cattle is simply not a very profitable business. The importance of ranching to conservation in the Wet Valley cannot be underestimated. It is the ranchers' land that has the greatest conservation value, and it is the ranchers who can least afford to give away conservation easements. Consequently, in order for land trusts to obtain easements from ranchers, they must be purchased, and such purchases require outside funding. A saving grace for ranchers is, ironically, horse owners who have recently moved to the area and need hay for feed. Ranchers now make more money selling hay to horse owners than they do raising cattle. All of SIF's easements so far have come from individuals not dependent on ranching income who could afford to contribute an endowment for monitoring purposes and who could take advantage of the resulting tax breaks.

Wet Valley ranchers are seen locally as good stewards of the land. They don't graze in the national forests. They do allow cattle in streams, but they are willing to fence off some riparian areas. The main species of local concern are elk and blacktail deer. Elk hunting is a popular activity among valley residents. Elk winter range and calving grounds occur in the valley bottom areas and are threatened by development. SIF and others in the community are very interested in preserving these areas. SIF, with the help of various government agencies, did do a local natural resource inventory, although the Colorado Natural Heritage Program has not yet been invited in for a more detailed survey because of rancher concerns. Ranchers don't want anyone finding spotted owls on their property. Again they fear the potential for regulation.

Along similar lines, some locals who are benefiting from development trends in the valley are suspicious of cost-of-services studies that show development results in increased local taxes. A cost-of-services study was undertaken for Custer County, and the author found that development would indeed result in higher taxes. Advocates of development questioned the legitimacy of the study because it was undertaken by a farmland conservation organization. Controversy over the study illustrates a split in the community between those who benefit from development and favor it, and those who are concerned about the scenic and environmental effects of development.

Residential development and subdivision of ranch lands in the Wet Valley are being driven by an influx of newcomers, including some who have enough money to live without working, some retirees, and a fair number of telecommuters. Many new residents have done well in the stock market, and some continue to engage in consulting jobs after leaving full-time positions elsewhere. Some Wet Valley citizens are commuters to Pueblo or Colorado Springs. Oddly, newcomers frequently don't stay for more than four or five years. Once they have built their houses, they seem to get bored with the local way of life and move on. There are always a fair number of used homes on the market in the Valley. Second home construction is also an important force in the area. The construction industry has been a big beneficiary of these new economic trends. Average income for Custer County as a whole is low because of the continued dominance of ranching. The same phenomenon explains the relatively modest growth in population density. On the other hand, second home ownership is relatively high (56 percent of all units), suggesting that vacation homes are the predominant source of new development in the area.[14]

The Wet Valley, in comparison with other areas of Colorado, is in the early stages of the development cycle. Development is sufficiently threatening to motivate conservation efforts by local residents, but it has not proceeded so far as to significantly impair open space or critical habitats. This is an increasingly rare set of circumstances in Colorado.

La Plata Open Space Conservancy

The La Plata Open Space Conservancy (LPOSC) operates in southwestern Colorado in the Durango area and was incorporated as a private nonprofit land trust in 1992.[15] The La Plata County landscape includes a mixture of fairly dry valley bottoms, forested foothills, and high mountains, and the area is a popular destination for tourists and outdoor recreationists. The land trust originally was instituted in the 1980s as a branch of the La Plata County government. However, because of its governmental connection, it was unable to generate private donations, and county funding was insufficient. Consequently, board members pushed its nonprofit status so that it could operate with a greater degree of independence and secure private contributions.

Since 1992, the organization has succeeded in preserving over 5,500 acres in La Plata, Montezuma, and Dolores Counties with 7 parcels in fee simple purchases and 40 in conservation easements. The goal of the organization is to protect open space for its scenic, wildlife, agriculture, recreational, historical, and archeological values. Although open space is a dominant theme in LPOSC's mission statement (figure 7.2), wildlife conservation is considered to be an important goal by the organization. Most LPOSC projects involve two or more goals in the mission statement. Land has been preserved from development by LPOSC through easements or purchases specifically to protect elk migration corridors and winter range, deer habitat, Gunnison sage grouse habitat, and riparian habitats of benefit to songbirds, waterfowl, and birds of prey. Deer populations are declining in La Plata county, and both elk migration routes and winter range are substantially threatened in the Durango area by development. The La Plata Open Space Conservancy has tried to link properties to form larger habitat patches and migration corridors, particularly in two locations, the Pine River Valley east of Durango and the Texas Creek Valley northeast of Durango. The North Texas Creek Valley is located in the middle of one of the largest winter migration corridors for big game animals in La Plata County, and the combination of several easements protects a big game route and habitat. The area also provides seasonal habitat for black bears and mountain lions. In addition, LPOSC holds rare riparian riverfront land along the Animus River that has significant habitat value for bird species. At least 60–75 percent of the land trust's easements are valley bottom lands.

Community support for LPOSC is widespread, and no one is antagonistic to the organization, although a few are skeptical, especially older residents in ranching. Only a handful of people still make their living in full-time ranching. Agriculture is extensive, but most who work in it have jobs in town as well. The composition of the LPOSC board is a mixture of both old-timers and newcomers.

The key threat to open space and wildlife habitat in the Durango area is residential development. Large ranches are being divided into smaller parcels that are sold as residential sites. The demand for such properties is driven largely by wealthy urban refugees building second homes or primary residences. The Durango area is a popular location for second home construction by the relatively affluent, although second homes in the aggregate are a small part of the total housing stock.[16] Some newcomers who are building second homes or permanent residences are independently wealthy and don't have to work.[17] Telecommuters who have business connections outside the area are also a part of the influx of new residents, although their numbers are hard to estimate. Turnover in the luxury housing market is high. Apparently, many new residents discover that the area doesn't have what they really want only after they have moved in. While ski area development is a threat in the northern part of La Plata county, Durango is not really considered to be a ski community in the same sense as Aspen or Telluride. Nonetheless, focal points for development include the local ski area north of Durango as well as the Animus Valley connecting Durango with the ski area and the mountains to the north. The Pine River Valley east of Durango is also a nucleus for rural subdivision and ranchette development.

Unlike other areas of the state where working ranches predominate, landowners in the Durango area are willing and able to donate easements, and, for this reason, only contributed easements are accepted by LPOSC. Some fundraising is undertaken, however, to cover transaction costs for landowners who can't afford to do so. More easement deals could be done, but there is only one full-time staff person, limiting the pace of transactions. Because working ranches in the Durango area have largely been sold off to more affluent landowners, the potential for contributed easements is greater than otherwise. The Durango area is farther along the development curve with fairly high population density growth than, for example, the Wet Valley.[18] Newcomers who have found their paradise in La Plata County are frequently active against further development efforts. Unfortunately, some parts of the county, particularly the Animus River Valley north of Durango, are already extensively subdivided. Since the county lacks zoning, it is the LPOSC that is the only real vehicle for limiting and guiding development.

Mesa County Land Conservancy

Mesa County Land Conservancy (MCLC) is one of the oldest land trusts in the state and operates in and around Grand Junction, Colorado.[19] Mesa County sits on the Colorado River plateau and contains a broad agricultural valley around Grand Junction as well as a portion of the Rocky Mountain's west slope to the east. Mesa County also includes important riparian areas along the Colorado and Gunnison Rivers in addition to the canyons and mesas of the Colorado National Monument. MCLC was started by orchard owners back in the early 1980s for the purpose of preserving agricultural land. Development pressure was moving out from Grand Junction to the east into orchard country. In the 1980s, landowners feared that oil shale development in the area was going to cause a boom in residential construction and suburban sprawl. While MCLC's primary goal continues to be preserving agricultural lands, the preservation of open space and wildlife are increasingly important objectives (figure 7.2). Because it operates in close proximity to an expanding medium-sized urban center, MCLC's activities differ somewhat from strictly rural land trusts. MCLC not only attempts to limit rural exurban sprawl, as many land trusts do, but it also attempts to limit suburban sprawl and the loss of orchards to the east and west of Grand Junction. By taking easements on orchards that have little natural value but are critical for preserving open space, the objective of limiting sprawl is being pursued by Conservancy members. MCLC is also working with local governments to establish "separators" or buffer zones between Grand Junction and Fruita to the west of the city and Clifton and Palisade to the east by using easement purchases. Because zoning is not used to protect buffer areas, the only tool available is easements. The plan is to pursue grant funds from Great Outdoors Colorado and other sources to pay for easement purchases in the buffer zones.

　　MCLC also has projects in rural areas of the county including Plateau Valley to the east of Grand Junction and Glade Park near the Colorado National Monument. In these areas the goal is not only to protect open space, but to conserve wildlife habitat and plant communities as well. Key wildlife issues in these areas include the protection of migration routes and winter range for elk, deer habitat, and sage grouse habitat, all of which are threatened by ranchette-style housing development. The Plateau Valley is ranch land with a small amount of irrigation for hay, and Glade Park is ranch land as well. Easements and purchases of development rights in Glade Park protect elk and deer winter range and migration corridors, riparian wetlands, Gunnison sage grouse habitat, cottonwoods, sagebrush, pinyon pine and juniper, as well as native plant communities including Gallete grasslands, Grand Junction milkvetch, Grant helleborine, and dropseed grass. In the Plateau Valley, MCLC provided a vehicle to express community opposition against development on the My Way Ranch. The owner wanted to develop 200 homes on the ranch but ran into local complaints. The landowner compromised by accepting some MCLC easements and reducing housing units by over 150. In this area, the Farmer's Home Administration foreclosed on several ranches a number of years ago and placed easements on them before reselling. MCLC took on some of these easements and raised funds for monitoring. The market price of these ranches to the new landowners was less than usual because of the easements. Easements thus have the potential to make agricultural land more affordable for new ranchers. The ranch land easements in these areas tend to be relatively large in comparison to the orchard easements near Grand Junction. The land trust has protected 21,000 acres in total under 44 easements.

The Grand Valley surrounding Grand Junction is largely agricultural with patches of riparian habitat. In the Grand Valley, MCLC is involved in wildlife habitat restoration and management projects in riparian areas sponsored by government agencies. In these projects, MCLC manages wildlife restoration projects in return for a fee from government wildlife agencies. These projects have the financial virtue of contributing to the land trust's overhead costs.

The key threat to open space and natural areas in Mesa County is an influx of new residents, especially from California. These are primarily people who made big capital gains from selling their homes and have plenty of money left after they buy a new one in Mesa County. At one point in the early 1990s, the Grand Junction Economic Development Council was even advertising in California for people to move to the area. Sprawl driven by population growth is a real concern to the communities near Grand Junction, as is the subdividing of agricultural lands for residential development. The influx of new residents was not composed of just retirees because the schools were soon bursting at the seams, suggesting that younger families were moving into the area as well. Population density growth is relatively substantial in Mesa County, although the per capita income is not much above the sample average.[20]

Because MCLC was started by local agriculturists who were long-time local residents, the land trust has wide support in the local community, although a few older ranchers seem skeptical. The land trust has successfully navigated the slippery slope of both receiving contributed easements and purchasing development rights. The latter was accomplished with the help of Great Outdoors Colorado grants and funds from the Nature Conservancy and the county. The purchasing of development rights or easements has the potential to dampen enthusiasm for contributed easements, although as already noted, working ranch owners cannot always afford to donate easements. In sum, the formation of Mesa County Land Conservancy was motivated more by urban as opposed to rural sprawl, although a good portion of its easements are currently in rural areas subject to development pressures. More recently, habitat conservation has played a growing role in the land trust's conservation activities.

Five Valleys and Rock Creek Land Trusts

The Five Valleys Land Trust (FVLT) operates in the major river valleys of western Montana.[21] While the higher elevations in this area are predominantly in public ownership, the valley bottoms are largely in private hands. Five Valleys originally formed in 1972 as the Five Valleys River Parks Association, and it focused its energies initially on the creation of riverfront parks in Missoula, Montana. In 1989 the organization was transformed into a land trust to operate in Missoula, Ravalli, Mineral, Lake, Lewis and Clark, Sanders, and Granite Counties. Most of its easements, however, are in Missoula County. The goals of the land trust, as noted in figure 7.3, are to protect wildlife habitat, riparian areas, agricultural lands, and scenic and historic places in the seven county area.

The land trust first received public attention for its efforts to preserve land on Mt. Jumbo from development in the early 1990s. This mountain is visible from Missoula and is recognized by the large "L" emblazoned on its surface. Popular support for preserving the mountain was driven in part by the ability to see elk on the mountain from the city in winter. The elk population in the

---

The Five Valleys Land Trust

The Five Valleys Land Trust is a not-for-profit regional community-based organization dedicated to protecting wildlife habitat, riparian areas, agricultural lands, and scenic and historic places throughout Missoula, Ravalli, Mineral, Sanders, Lake, Lewis and Clark, and Granite Counties.

The Gallatin Valley Land Trust

The Gallatin Valley Land Trust is a nonprofit membership organization dedicated to the conservation of open space, agricultural land, wildlife habitat and the creation of public trails in and around Gallatin County.

Figure 7.3: Land Trusts Mission Statement (Continued)

area is under threat because of development in its historic winter range. More recently FVLT has been instrumental in preserving land on Mt. Sentinel (recognized by a large white "M" on its surface) also visible from Missoula. Land deals currently engineered by FVLT will protect the backside of the mountain from development and will tie in with other easements in Pattee Canyon adjacent to the mountain.

FVLT has brokered land deals and received easements that protect over 21,000 acres in the Five Valleys area. Most of these easements are intended to protect either valley bottom agricultural lands, riparian areas, or highly visible ridge lines. More recently FVLT is attempting to take a proactive and strategic approach to easement acquisition. To this end it is working with other organizations and government agencies on the Clark Fork River corridor to assess the conservation needs for the upper Clark Fork and to inventory land ownership. The project will identify threats along the corridor as well as potential conservation opportunities in riparian areas and adjacent uplands, and it will undertake landowner outreach and education in order to cultivate easement opportunities.

One of the difficult issues faced by western land trusts is gaining the confidence of older ranchers who want to see their way of life continue but are generally mistrustful of outsiders and anyone they see as connected in some way with the government. To foster better relationships with its easement holders and with ranchers in particular, FVLT has hired a land conservation specialist to monitor easements and make suggestions to owners about beneficial improvements in agriculture practices, such as fencing off riparian areas. The specialist eases these discussions by making suggestions only and indicating how funding might be pursued. This is referred to as soft stewardship, and the approach is taken to gain landowner confidence and to foster voluntary landowner cooperation in land stewardship efforts. Because easements ultimately can only set the broad parameters of good conservation, a more active form of monitoring may be needed to achieve conservation goals, something FVLT hopes to accomplish with its land conservation specialist.

Another critical issue facing land trusts in the West is that lands with the greatest conservation value are often found on ranches whose owners are very close to retirement age. The only asset these people have to fund their retirement is the land they own; they are land rich but cash poor. Consequently, they cannot afford to contribute easements and can only participate in easement deals if they are paid for relinquishing the development rights to their property. If land trusts are to move in the direction of purchased easements, they need to raise funds and they may well suffer a reduction in donated easements from landowners who perceive that land trusts can afford to buy easements. FVLT has yet to go down the slippery slope of easement purchases but recognizes that to be effective it may well have to do so in the future. So far, its 11,800 acres of easements have been contributed, though in some cases fundraising has been undertaken to cover some transaction costs and easement monitoring endowments. The availability of federal funds through the Conservation and Recreation Act in the future could well cause land trusts to move in the direction of purchased easements.

An unusual feature of FVLT is that it has a second land trust contained within it that focuses entirely on Rock Creek, a world-famous trout stream located to the east of Missoula. Rock Creek has its headwaters in the Anaconda-Pintlar Wilderness and flows north into the Clark Fork River. While the lower reaches are steep and narrow, open ranch country is found in the upper reaches. So far only the lower reaches have faced the threat of subdivision and development. The Rock Creek Trust is a project of FVLT and is focused entirely on the Rock Creek watershed. The Rock Creek Trust was created in 1986 as a part of the Department of Natural Resources and Conservation Services, but in 1995 Rock Creek decided to go private and became a part of FVLT. Because Rock Creek is a world-famous trout stream, funding for easement purchases has been readily forthcoming from various grant sources and from individual donors. A $1.5 million fundraising effort is nearing completion for the purpose of protecting an additional 7,700 acres and 13 miles of stream frontage. This enterprise would be on top of the 11.5 miles of stream and 4,500 acres that has already been protected since Rock Creek Trust's founding in 1986. As a matter of practice, Rock Creek Trust pays one-half of the easement's value for its purchases. Successful acquisition of easements on working ranches has been possible only because easements could be purchased. The goal of the Rock Creek Trust is to protect the riparian corridor itself and the open space around it. Obviously a key goal is to protect native trout species in the creek, but other species in the area are important in the watershed as well, such as mountain sheep and various riparian species.

Population and population density growth is relatively rapid in the Missoula area. Growth in the early 1990s was a key motivation for the formation of the FVLT and the expansion of the land trust's activities beyond the Missoula riverfronts. A big concern at the time was the effect of development on local elk herds. The immediate concern was with subdivision development on Mt. Jumbo in the Missoula Valley, a critical elk habitat and important scenic and recreation area. FVLT successfully obtained key easements and brokered a deal for a land purchase by the city that protected Mt. Jumbo from development, and the land trust as a consequence gained visibility in the community. Missoula County and the counties around it are growing rapidly and are experiencing substantial residential construction and subdivision of valley bottom lands. The big attraction is the quality of life, although in many ways new residents are recreating the suburban-style environment they thought they were leaving behind. This is particularly evident in the Bitterroot Valley to the south of Missoula. In Missoula County, the per capita income is only slightly above the sample average, and the share of second homes is quite low.[22] The development pressures here appear to by less driven by an influx of wealth than in some of the resort communities of Colorado. Missoula County growth seems to be the product of a more generalized population spreading to the mountain West than an influx of the wealthy with money to burn.

One exception to this view is occurring in the upper portion of the Rock Creek watershed where the very wealthy are buying up 5,000-acre parcels for hobby ranches. Open space is protected for the moment in this area by the size of these parcels, but there are adjacent areas where ranchette development is clearly a threat.

The whole issue of easements and property rights is a touchy one in a relatively conservative state like Montana. Easements walk a fine line between protecting scenic and natural values and telling the landowner how to manage their land. In a culture founded on property rights ideals, this is tough to do. Land use planning by counties and zoning is virtually nonexistent in the Five Valleys area, although subdivision review is required for parcels less than 160 acres in Missoula. Many requests for variances are granted, however. There really does seem to be substantial support in the Missoula area for land conservation, although there is surprisingly little pressure to do more land use planning at the county level. Land trusts are the only vehicle available at the moment in the area for what could be called a "backdoor form" of land use planning.

Gallatin Valley Land Trust

The Gallatin Valley Land Trust (GVLT) operates primarily in an expansive valley north of Yellowstone National Park that is bordered by the Madison Range to the west and the Gallatin Range and Bridger Range to the east.[23] The land trust emerged in response to the rapid population growth occurring in Gallatin County and the surrounding area in the early 1990s and has just celebrated its tenth anniversary. Local residents began to be concerned that agricultural lands, wildlife habitat, and recreation access to public lands were being lost as a consequence of development. The land trust's goals are conserving open space, agricultural lands, wildlife habitat, and public access to trails as can be seen in figure 7.3. A unique focus of the land trust is the Mainstreet to Mountains project establishing trail linkages from Bozeman, Montana, to the Bridger Mountains to the north and the Gallatin Range to the south. GVLT has worked closely with the Bozeman city government on this project and has gained considerable community visibility as a consequence. The trails are popular and heavily used by city residents.

In the past 10 years GVLT has also focused on obtaining easements in Gallatin County's valley bottoms that protect riparian areas, wildlife habitat, and agricultural lands. Riparian areas are viewed as being of special importance in evaluating potential easements, and connectivity to other easements and public lands is of special significance in easement selection. The land trust has protected a total of 8,300 acres in easements in Gallatin, Madison, Park, and Jefferson Counties. All of its easements are donated, although it has raised funds to cover transaction costs, the baseline study, and the easement monitoring endowment. Ranchers in the Gallatin Valley are sometimes unable to afford the contribution required to cover costs. This is a dilemma faced by GVLT in performing easements with working ranches. As in other mountain valleys of the western United States, ranchers in the Gallatin area are land rich and cash poor, and ranch owners are frequently older and need to liquidate some of their land value for retirement. In the next 20 years, half the private land in Montana will be changing hands because of population aging. Although easements provide significant estate tax benefits, the charitable deduction is not always valuable to ranchers because of their low income levels. Deals should be proposed that would provide ranchers with some cash. This will ultimately require GVLT and other land trusts to move away from strictly donated easements.

While GVLT was essentially reactive in its early days and still responds to easement inquiries, it is taking a more strategic approach to acquisitions by focusing on key wildlife corridors. An important goal is to keep corridors open through easements from Yellowstone northward to help in the larger effort of maintaining habitat connectivity from Yellowstone to the Yukon. As a part of this project, GVLT is focusing easement acquisition efforts on the corridor linking the Gallatin and Bridger Ranges, one that is unfortunately bisected by Interstate 90. GVLT is also working at acquiring easements in key wetland areas and riparian corridors in the valley bottoms of the Gallatin area, and it is attempting to connect existing easements to form larger habitat blocks and to acquire easements bordering public lands for buffering purposes. Wildlife of special concern to GVLT include elk, mule deer, west slope cutthroat trout, wolves, and grizzlies, although at present grizzlies occur only in one area and wolves are being kept within Yellowstone National Park. GVLT is working hard in the Paradise Valley along the Yellowstone River to limit development and the resulting stream channel modification that is occurring at a furious pace. The land trust has recently launched an outreach project in the Paradise Valley in order to acquire easements and limit sprawl in the area. GVLT is also working on some high-elevation easements around the Big Sky ski area development where population growth is especially rapid. Some critical high-elevation habitat has been preserved as a result.

While it has wide community support, GVLT faces some skepticism from ranchers who think land trusts are too closely allied with environmentalists, although some ranchers have indeed accepted GVLT as an organization that works for them. Some ranchers who are not trustful of GVLT do look to their own organizations at times for easements. Thus there does seem to be a strong community-wide sentiment in favor of open space and agricultural land conservation. Both old-timers and newcomers favor limiting growth in some way. However, there is no county-level mechanism for limiting growth outside of municipal boundaries, although Gallatin County is working on a master plan. The county currently lacks significant countywide zoning requirements in rural areas. Nonetheless, local zoning districts can be formed if there is sufficient support by landowners. Sixteen of these zoning districts currently exist in the county. This approach to open space conservation will be discussed in more detail in the final chapter. Apart from these zoning districts, GVLT is the only other mechanism at present for land and open space conservation.[24]

Rapid growth in Gallatin Valley and the surrounding counties is driven by an influx of outsiders attracted by the local quality of life. There is an increasing belief that some are moving into the area who rely on computer technology to serve customers located elsewhere. Essentially, some newcomers may be bringing their means of earning a living with them. Development projects such as Big Sky, a large ski area and resort complex, are indeed only for the very wealthy. Most development at Big Sky is for second homes, and some projects elsewhere in the county appeal specifically to affluent second home owners as well. This influx of outside wealth creates some resentment among many Montanans who have a below average standard of living. Gallatin County, like Missoula, features a fairly modest per capita income slightly above the sample average and a limited second home development in the aggregate, but a relatively high level of growth in population density.[25] Gallatin County thus appears to be experiencing the consequences of a generalized spreading of population to rural areas offering significant amenities.

The real problem with growth and the residential construction that it brings in places like Gallatin County is that most of it is occurring outside of existing communities and is resulting in the loss of agricultural land and wildlife habitat. Ranches and productive farmlands are being taken out of production and subdivided into smaller parcels for a ranchette style of development. One result of low-density development in Gallatin County is increased costs for local public services. Development is also a major threat to wetlands and is causing groundwater contamination from septic systems in some localities.

SUMMARY AND DISCUSSION

The thesis that land trusts are created in response to residential development pressures and rural sprawl is strongly supported in the interviews. The key reasons land trusts form, as noted in table 7.2, include the loss of open space, natural areas and wildlife habitat, and farmland as a consequence of residential construction. Threats to the rural way of life from residential development and rapid population growth are also important reasons land trusts come into existence. Growth and sprawl is a concern of all the land trusts interviewed.

The major concrete issue facing most of the land trusts interviewed is the subdividing of large ranches into ranchettes and housing developments. According to the opinions of land trust interviewees expressed in table 7.3, urban refugees are able to move to the remote valleys of the mountain West in part because they have accumulated substantial wealth through stock market and housing market

Table 7.2. Importance of Reasons for Forming a Land Trust and Acquiring Easements

	Crested Butte	Yampa	Grand	Eagle	San Isabel	La Plata	Mesa	Five Valleys	Gallatin	Average
Importance of the following in motivating the formation of the land trust.										
Loss of open space as a consequence of residential construction.	10	10	9	9	9	10	8	8	9	9.1
Loss of natural areas and threats to vegetation and wildlife as a consequence of residential construction.	10	10	9	9	9	10	8	8	9	9.1
Loss of farmland or ranch land as a consequence of residential development.	9	10	7	7	9	10	10	4	10	8.4
Threats to a rural way of life from residential development and rapid population growth.	8	10	7	6	10	10		8	9	8.7
Importance of the following in the decision to acquire land or accept easements.										
The preservation of open space and scenic vistas.	10	10	8	10	9	10	8	8	9	9.1
The preservation of natural areas, wildlife, or rare and threatened plant and animal species.	10	10	8	8	9	10	9	8	9	9.0
The preservation of farmland or ranch land.	10	10	8	8	10	10	10	8	10	9.3
The protection or expansion of outdoor recreation opportunities.	10	2	1	3	2	8	?	6	8	5.0

Note: The response scale is 0 to 10 with 0 meaning not at all important and 10 meaning very important. Averages have been rounded to nearest decimal point.

Table 7.3. Land Trust Interviewee Opinions on Development Trends in Area of Operation and Local County Population Density Growth

Development Trends	Crested Butte	Yampa	Grand	Eagle	San Isabel	La Plata	Mesa	Five Valleys	Gallatin	Land Trust Average
Percentage of homes built over the past 15 years that are believed to be vacation or second homes.	50	60	80	60	50	13	5	5	?	40.4
Percentage of individuals moving into area over the past 15 years believed to be retirees.	25	50	10	15	50	13	25	7	?	24.4
Percentage of individuals moving into area over the past 15 years believed to be below retirement age and wealthy enough not to have to work.	40	30	8	20	20	5	3	10	?	17.0
Percentage of individuals moving into area over the past 15 years believed to be telecommuters or others using the Internet and similar new technologies to serve customers outside the local area.	15	40	20	20	20	10	7	10	?	17.8
Percentage of individuals moving into area over the past 15 years believed to have taken tourist-related employment.	85	?	50	25	40	20	30	10	?	37.1
Percentage of individuals moving into area over the past 15 years believed to have jobs outside the local area to which they commute.	5	10	10	10	40	1	0	0	?	9.5

Note: The response scale is 0 to 10 with 0 meaning not at all important and 10 meaning very important. Averages have been rounded off to the nearest decimal point.

financial gains, they can draw on retirement income, or they are able to take advantage of new technologies (such as the Internet) to serve customers in distant population centers from their homes or local offices.[26] Affluence and the ability to earn income through new technology in remote locations are thus among the forces apparently driving the spreading of population to the rural mountain West. Also driven by affluence is second home construction, another major force behind the subdividing of ranches according to interviewees. Some land trusts receive a significant amount of their financial support from second home owners wanting to preserve the quality of the environment attracting them in the first place. Having obtained their piece of a beautiful landscape, they don't want others to spoil it.

There is an apparent division in the forces behind economic expansion in the counties covered by land trust interviews. Growth in and around Colorado resort communities (such as Crested Butte, Steamboat Springs, and Vail) is driven predominantly by affluence and vacation home development. Growth in the Durango and Grand Junction areas in Colorado and around Missoula and Bozeman, Montana, appears to be a result of broader-based population spreading to the mountain West driven by the attraction of local amenities and the increased mobility of sources of earned income.[27]

In response to development pressures, land trusts have taken on the task of preventing the division of large ranches. This is a little ironic because grazing is frequently viewed by environmentalists as one of the significant destructive forces operating in the West to degrade natural habitats, and some people who have held this view in the past are now involved in the land trust movement. Land trust activists generally take a more benign view of ranching than the environmental community at large, noting that ranches provide winter habitat and calving grounds for ungulates as well as habitat for other species. The primary complaint against ranching, even by some land trust activists, is the degradation of riparian areas caused by cattle grazing in and near riparian habitats. While land trust activists generally agree that many ranchers could do a better job protecting riparian areas, most strongly agree that ranchers are on the whole good stewards of their own land and, with the proper incentives, can be motivated to address riparian issues. Development and the subdividing of ranch lands is seen as the bigger threat to wildlife. Moreover, working ranches are an obvious vehicle for achieving the open space protection goal that virtually all the interviewed land trust employees seek, not to mention the preservation of agricultural activity. For those who see ranching and agriculture as major threats to the natural environment, this sounds like a false rationalization. However, if the alternative is the separation of large ranches into small ranchettes and subdivisions, ranching is likely the lesser of the two evils in light of the consequences of rural sprawl discussed in chapters 4 and 5. Fencepost-to-fencepost cropping, however, is another matter, but this kind of agriculture is not very common in the high mountain valleys of the West.

The goals of the land trust members interviewed tend to be fairly universal and include protecting open space, agricultural lands, and wildlife habitat (table 7.2). In a couple of cases, facilitating outdoor recreation through trail access is a goal, but recreation is generally not a high priority for land trusts. Goals are often given equal weight in discussions, but open space seems to be a bit more important than the other issues. While some land trusts are simply reactive to landowners interested in easements, planning efforts that use the concepts of corridors, buffer zones, and core habitats are on the increase. A number of land trusts actively seek easements from properties in areas that fit into a larger conservation scheme. Land trusts are becoming a "backdoor" means for land use planning in a world where property rights are held to be sacred and where local government has frequently opted out of the land use planning process in favor of unfettered market forces.

Land trusts are both a vehicle for redistributing economic power away from those who favor development, such as real estate interests, developers, and some landowners, and a means for fostering dialogue in local communities about conservation issues. To an outsider, it seems odd that ranchers would oppose land trust activity since easement agreements are strictly voluntary. Moreover, one of the key ironies facing land trusts is that easements tend to increase the value of lands not under easements by reducing the supply of land subject to development. Nonparticipating landowners gain. One would think ranchers would support land trusts out of self-interest, and some may well do so. Nonetheless, ranchers remain suspicious. They believe that their land will somehow come under government regulation through land trusts. Their concerns may not be far off base if land trusts create informal networks of advocates for land use planning and zoning. In this situation, ranchers may legitimately fear a redistribution of political power away from themselves and regulations that reduce the value of their land and place restrictions on their agricultural practices.

As already noted, a principle irony of land trust activity is increased land values on lands not subject to easement restrictions. A cynic might say that this explains why land trusts receive substantial support from second home owners. Of course, second home owners may also offer their support because they simply want to preserve the landscape that they now own a piece of. Increased land values make it more difficult for land trusts to do their work. Contributed easements are less likely to be forthcoming, particularly from ranchers, when land values are on the rise. This means that in order for land trusts to be effective, they must venture to purchase easements. A move to easement purchases could well mean a reduction in contributed easements and a rising need to obtain foundation or government money to conserve large chunks of land needed for the preservation of populations of native plant and animal species. Given that ranchers are land rich but cash poor, the path of contributed easements has its limitations. Ranchers who need funds for retirement have to get at least some cash from their land in order to live. Purchased easements are potentially attractive to ranchers who want to remain on the land or want to pass it on to their descendants.

New residents, the driving force in the subdividing of ranch lands, don't always stay in mountainous areas. Once they have built their dream homes, they often cannot find much to do locally. New residents soon discover the rigors of the mountainous winter climate, and some may well miss urban amenities not locally available. Whatever the reason, turnover in new homes is quite high in some localities. Still, there always seems to be another prospective buyer to replace those that leave, although a serious recession and stock market crash could ultimately diminish the wealth that seems to be driving some rural real estate markets. Many land trust advocates would probably agree that the real goal of land use planning should be to encourage people to live within the present boundaries of existing urban concentrations. The land trust movement is essentially an attempt to apply the brakes to population spreading and rural sprawl and fill in the gap left by the absence of public sector land use planning. The big problem with the "backdoor" approach to planning that land trusts are attempting is that it can never be comprehensive. The danger that development will simply be diverted to parcels of land not under land trust easement or ownership will always exist. The end result could be a few patches of preserved land surrounded by a sea of development.

NOTES

1. Timothy P. Duane, *Shaping the Sierra: Nature, Culture, and Conflict in the Changing West* (Berkeley: University of California Press, 1999), 337–385.
2. Julie A. Gustanski and Roderick H. Squires, eds., *Protecting the Land: Conservation Easements Past, Present, and Future* (Washington, D.C.: Island Press, 2000).
3. John R. Searle, *The Construction of Social Reality* (New York: Free Press, 1995), 23–26.
4. Land Trust Alliance, *1998 National Directory of Conservation Land Trusts* (Washington, D.C.: Land Trust Alliance, 1998). Land trusts that operate statewide, regionally, or nationally are excluded. The goal is to consider local land trusts only because they are more likely to have formed in response to local development pressures.
5. The statistical technique used is multivariate regression analysis. For an explanation of the approach, see the appendix to chapter 3. The estimated regression equation is as follows:

$$\text{TRUSTSOP} = 0.2968 + 0.01490\text{POPDCH} + 0.03664\text{SKI97},$$
$$\qquad\qquad (3.01)\ (2.27)\qquad\quad (3.43)$$

where TRUSTOP is the number of trusts operating in a county, POPDCH is the change in population density on private lands between 1985 and 1997, and SKI97 is the number of ski areas in the county. The figures in parentheses are t-statistics which are all significant at 5 percent level, and the adjusted R-squared is equal to .20.

6. Time and budget limitations restricted the interviews to Colorado and Montana.

7. Interview with Vicki Church, Executive Director, 14 August 2000.

8. Interview with Susan Dorsey Otis, Executive Director, 19 September 2000.

9. Interview with Cindy Southway, Executive Director, 20 September 2000.

10. See table 7.1.

11. Interview with Brad Udall, Executive Director, 21 September 2000.

12. See table 7.1.

13. Interview with Alice and Charles Proctor, Board Members, 22 September 2000.

14. See table 7.1.

15. Interview with Katharine Roser, Executive Director, 25 September 2000.

16. See table 7.1.

17. The per capita income for La Plata County is about $4,000 above the sample average (see table 7.1)

18. See table 7.1.

19. Interview with Doris Butler, Board Member, Mesa County Land Trust, 26 September 2000.

20. See table 7.1.

21. Interviews with Wendy Ninteman, Executive Director, Five Valleys Land Trust, and Ellen Knight, Executive Director, Rock Creek Trust, 28 September 2000.

22. See table 7.1.

23. Interview with Debbie Deagen, Executive Director, Gallatin Valley Land Trust, 29 September 2000.

24. However, at the time of the interview, there was a bond measure coming up on the local ballot (November 7, 2000) that would fund purchases of development rights.

25. See table 7.1.

26. The opinions offered in table 7.3 are based on respondent impressions, not concrete data. Because questions were asked independently, the answers given don't always sum up to a figure lower than 100 percent for the different questions. Also, some respondents perceived overlap in the questions. For example, someone moving to the mountain West may have recently retired from a job at a relatively young age, be sufficiently wealthy so as to not need to work, but nonetheless continues working as a consultant from a home office using computer technology. In sum, these responses must be taken with a grain of salt. The respondents are experts on land trust activities, but not necessarily on economic trends.

27. It is important to recall from chapters 2 and 3 that earned income includes wage, salary, and proprietor's income.

8

≈⁀

The Environmental Ethics
of Rural Sprawl: Ecological
Cities and Biodiversity

The central thesis of this book is that human population is spreading into remote rural areas in the mountain West as a consequence of growing affluence and new technologies. Communication and transportation cost-shrinking
technologies and affluence are rendering residential location for many people a
matter of choice rather than a matter of necessity. Many can now choose to live
in rural places offering beautiful landscapes and abundant outdoor recreation opportunities without sacrificing their ability to participate in the global economy.
The predominant environmental effect of this phenomenon is to further stress
native flora and fauna already suffering from traumas created by the extractive
industries that once served as the foundation of the rural mountain economy.

In this and the final chapter, the basic thesis of the book will be taken as a
given, and the question of what ought to be done about population spreading and
rural sprawl will be examined presuming the acceptance of an environmental
ethic and a resulting public desire for the conservation of native plant and animal species. The essential conclusion of the arguments to follow is that a reinvigorated urban life is the answer to the problem of population spreading.

ENVIRONMENTAL ETHICS AND BIOLOGICAL CONSERVATION

In terms of academic disciplines, environmental ethics is a relatively new venture.[1] Participants have been largely concerned with establishing the philosophical foundations of an ethical attitude toward the natural environment. As might
be expected for a comparatively new field of inquiry, there is considerable disagreement over its basic premises. Many environmental philosophers accept

some form of the idea that elements of the natural world are valuable in their own right, but they often disagree on the philosophical foundation for this view. Some claim that individual organisms in nature have intrinsic value because they have interests.[2] Organisms pursue some end that is established by the nature of their being. Others argue that intrinsic value can be attributed to species and ecosystems as well.[3] The basic goal of an organism is to perpetuate its species through reproduction, and species themselves evolve in the context of ecosystems. Thus both have intrinsic value. Some critics object to the notion of intrinsic value as something internally determined by the nature of entities in themselves. We cannot fully know the natural world outside of our own perceptions; we cannot look at the world through eyes other than our own. Insofar as we know, only conscious subjects can confer value on other beings. Value doesn't exist in nature; rather it is granted by the human valuer.[4] Of course, the qualities we perceive in nature do matter. We care that natural beings appear to have interests, organisms appear to perpetuate their species, and ecosystems appear to serve as incubators for new species. As a consequence of our human capacity for empathy and the scientific recognition that human beings are the product of evolutionary processes along with all other species, we may see evolutionary processes, ecosystems, species, and individual organisms as valuable for their own sake. Whichever interpretation we accept, whether we look to objective features of the natural world, or whether we take a subjective approach to valuing nature, the natural world can be viewed as valuable for its own sake.

Not all environmental philosophers agree with this idea that nature has value in its own right.[5] Some argue that our views of the natural world are ultimately anthropocentric (human centered rather than biocentric or nature centered).[6] Under an anthropocentric environmental ethic, the full consequences of our actions for all human beings, present and future, in the broadest sense should be addressed, including the value-shaping function of nature. When considering whether or not to preserve a landscape such as a beautiful valley surrounded by mountains, a wide range of human-centered values ought to be addressed: preserving habitat for game animals; the nonconsumptive use of wildlife, such as bird watching; hunting and fishing opportunities; opportunities for hiking and the aesthetic appreciation of the surrounding environment; potential for scientific research; and the sequestering of carbon in valley vegetation. In addition, the ability of the landscape to influence the values of future generations should be considered as well. Future visitors may change their values and outlook forever in response to the natural beauty of what they see and may, as a consequence, be transformed into advocates for the conservation of the natural world.[7] A valley full of ranchettes and housing developments would be unlikely to have the same effect, however.

Whatever their reasoning on foundations, most environmental philosophers look to Aldo Leopold's "Land Ethic" as the inaugurating work of their discipline.[8] Leopold saw ethics in both historical and social terms. Historically, ethical standards evolve and alter their coverage. Socially, ethics rest upon membership in the community. Just as ethics evolved historically to include Odysseus's slave-girls, it can evolve to include the land. "The land ethic simply enlarges the boundaries of the community to include soils, waters, plants, and animals, or collectively the land." Moreover, according to Leopold, "a land ethic changes the role of Homo sapiens from conqueror of the land-community to plain member and citizen of it."[9]

In the end, this debate over ethical foundations is important in a democratic society only to the extent that the public participates in it. If environmental ethics is not a part of the larger public discourse, then debates among academics will have little effect in the world of social and political decision making.[10] Survey research does indeed suggest that individuals frequently express ethical concern for the natural environment and often do so on the grounds that nature is valuable for its own sake.[11] While some environmental philosophers are troubled by the concept of species rights, respondents to surveys frequently accept the notion that species have rights to exist even though they may not be of material benefit to human beings.[12] Aldo Leopold, however, has no trouble with rights language, claiming that "we have at least drawn nearer the point of admitting that birds should continue as a matter of biotic right, regardless of the presence or absence of economic advantage to us."[13] The path by which members of the public have acquired such attitudes is difficult to establish with any finality, but one can speculate that public exposure to environmental issues and ideas has played a role. Certainly, the publication of Rachel Carson's Silent Spring in the 1960s can be viewed as a watershed event.[14] In her book, the dangers of emitting toxins such as DDT into the environment were established by Carson in a manner that was at once eloquent and convincing, and yet frightening. While the human dangers were certainly a part of the story, the threat to wildlife from pesticides was the central theme. As an apparent consequence of rising public concern in the 1960s, a flurry of environmental legislation was voted into law in the 1970s, including the Endangered Species Act.[15] Since this point in time, periodic opinion surveys have found public concern for the environment to be comparatively high.[16] Events and experiences appear to influence basic attitudes and values as well as public policy. Environmental ethics do indeed seem to be a part of the public discourse.

ENVIRONMENTAL ETHICS AND CITIES

Cities and urban life are not given much attention in the environmental ethics literature as Alastair Gunn points out in a recent article. Gunn goes so far as to suggest that environmental ethics is misdirected because it largely ignores the phenomenon of urbanization and has little to say about environmental issues in an urban setting.[17] He argues that we have little choice but to give up on the

Leopoldian ideas of biological conservation embodied in the concept of a land ethic and turn to urban landscape planners, such as Ian McHarg, who take environmental considerations into account in their designs for urban living. Leopold has nothing to say about urban environments, where almost half of the world's population is now found, but McHarg does.

While dismissing the land ethic as irrelevant is too drastic, both the approach of McHarg and Leopold are needed to address the issue of declining biodiversity.[18] The central thesis offered here is that environmentally friendly cities of the kind envisioned by McHarg are essential to the conservation of biodiversity outside their borders as well as within. The design of urban landscapes and the health of city economies are of central importance for the protection of the environment and the conservation of biodiversity for three fundamental reasons: (1) attractive cities where decent living standards can be obtained are needed to limit the spreading of population into rural core habitat reserves, buffer areas, and natural corridors; (2) urban areas as currently constituted use the resources of nature unsustainably and place too large an environmental footprint on the world, one that can be shrunk only through environmentally sensitive urban design and consumption patterns; and (3) environmental values and the political will to conserve critical habitats needed for biodiversity conservation are more likely to occur in a society engaged in the practice of applying ecological principles to everyday urban life. In essence, urban populations need to internalize and practice environmental values of the sort offered by both Ian McHarg and Aldo Leopold in order to conserve environmental health within and biodiversity outside the physical confines of urban life. If the bulk of the world's human population lives in cities lacking in natural amenities and devoid of opportunities for contact with elements of nonhuman nature, then adequate political support for the conservation of biodiversity seems unlikely.

This view of the role of urban life in biological conservation offers an interpretation of the human-nature connection that could also help resolve the recent debate over historical conceptions of the wilderness. Critics, such as Callicott and Cronon, argue that the conventional conception of wilderness artificially separates human beings from nature. In the view of the critics, a wilderness untrammeled by human activity, where human beings visit but do not remain, is unrealistic and undesirable.[19] That human beings are indeed a part of nature cannot be denied nor can the pervasiveness of human impacts on the natural world. As Herman Daly emphasizes, the human economic system is embedded in and dependent upon a global ecosystem.[20] Yet for the sake of conserving biodiversity in the modern world, much human activity must be spatially separated from the activity of many wild species. This does not mean that the laws of nature no longer apply or that we are not a part of nature. It simply means that there must be a territorial separation between our own habitat and that of many other species if the latter are to survive.[21]

The dilemma of spatial separation is the possible lack of human connection to wild nature. If Alasdair MacIntyre is right, moral commitments arise from social practice.[22] If there are to be moral commitments to the conservation of biodiversity, and if the bulk of human population is concentrated in cities, then everyday urban life must somehow incorporate connections with the natural world and the practices of biological and environmental conservation. The problem is moving from the moral commitments of modern consumer capitalism—commitments that support perpetual urban expansion and the outward spread of population to the suburbs and beyond—to commitments supporting a physically limited city that uses the resources of nature in a stable and sustainable fashion and contains within it habitat patches that offer some connection with elements of wild nature. Cities as they exist today are by no means devoid of natural elements. Large urban areas are commonly found on migratory flyways, in or near river valley floodplains, and near biologically rich estuaries. Even though large expanses of terrestrial and aquatic habitats have disappeared because of urbanization, at a smaller landscape scale, many habitat patches and corridors supporting native flora and fauna frequently remain or can be restored.

THE HUMAN USE OF LANDSCAPES AND BIODIVERSITY

Landscapes fall on a spectrum of human use with wildlands at one end, where human influence is minimal, and cities on the other, where human use predominates. While humans are necessarily a part of nature—we rely for our sustenance on the resources and services of the natural world—the spectrum of land use reflects a divide between cultural and biological evolution. Human beings are subject to urban-oriented forces of cultural evolution, and so are other species who occupy the human end of the landscape spectrum. Species who inhabit landscapes at the wildlands end of the spectrum are more likely to be subjected to the forces of biological evolution.[23]

To conserve biodiversity and the processes of biological evolution, conservation biologists argue that immense, relatively wild core areas where human impacts are largely absent, need to be preserved. In addition, surrounding buffer zones, where human activity of a limited scope is permitted, are essential for protecting core reserves, and to link them, relatively natural corridors are needed in between. This form of habitat protection, conservation biologists argue, is essential for limiting further declines in biodiversity. Noss and Cooperrider argue that four fundamental objectives need to be pursued in order to protect biodiversity at a regional level:

1. Represent, in a system of protected areas, all native ecosystem types and seral stages across their natural range of variation.
2. Maintain viable populations of all native species in natural patterns of abundance and distribution.

3. Maintain ecological and evolutionary processes, such as disturbance regimes, hydrological processes, nutrient cycles, and biotic interactions.
4. Manage landscapes and communities to be responsive to short-term and long-term environmental change and to maintain the evolutionary potential of the biota.[24]

These goals are best accomplished with a system of core reserves that include all native ecosystem types and provide adequate habitat for all native species unable to survive in the interstices of human-dominated landscapes. A core reserve is to be maintained in a natural state, and, within the reserve, natural disturbance events (such as fire), are either "allowed to proceed without interference or are mimicked through management." Ideally, reserves should be big enough to accommodate recovery from disturbance events. A reserve that is too small, for example, may lack a sufficient undisturbed seed stock of native plants to recover from a catastrophic fire. Also, reserves should be of sufficient size or configured in such a way as to allow adaption to long-term changes, such as the northerly movement of habitat range boundaries for species from climatic warming.[25]

Multiple-use buffer zones surrounding core reserves serve several purposes, including amelioration of edge effects, enlargement of the effective size of the reserve for mobile species, and connectivity to other reserves. Buffer zone activities compatible with conserving native biodiversity could include nonmotorized recreation, selection forestry, light grazing, and small-scale agriculture. The subject of biological connectivity is complex and controversial. Basically, suitable landscapes or corridors are needed for seasonal migrations, dispersal to new habitat ranges, extension of the effective habitat area of core reserves for wide-ranging species, and for effective gene flow between subpopulations to maintain local genetic diversity. Connectivity can be served in some instances by well-placed habitat patches, landscapes with relatively low road densities, and specific habitat corridors such as riparian forests along streams and rivers. For large carnivores, such as black bears, grizzly bears, mountain lions, and wolves, home ranges are so large that no single reserve can encompass populations of sufficient size to avoid extinction in the long term. Consequently, networks of reserves are needed that are connected by regional-scale corridors.[26]

While these principles of conservation biology are of recent origin, they are compatible with Aldo Leopold's "Land Ethic." According to Leopold, "A thing is right when it tends to preserve the integrity, stability, and beauty of the biotic community."[27] While modern ecological language speaks more about disturbance and change in ecosystems, at a landscape level, where the objective is to maintain representative ecosystems, the goal Leopold offers and conservation biology seeks is essentially the same. More specifically, Leopold speaks not only of the tragic loss of wilderness, but also of the need to preserve remaining wilderness areas as refuges for wildlife and as a scientific norm for land health. In his discussion of wilderness for wildlife, he focuses on the plight of the grizzly bear in the western United States, pointing out that national parks are insufficient in size to offer adequate habitat for grizzlies, and that national forest lands surrounding the parks need to be preserved as wilderness to assure the long-term survival of the grizzly.[28] Leopold, in this discussion, recognizes the need for large core habitat areas, one of the cornerstones of modern conservation biology. As Callicott suggests, Leopold was also concerned with finding an appropriate balance on multiple-use lands between wildness and instrumental human use,[29] exactly the problem modern conservation biology faces in the buffer zones and corridors connecting wilderness core areas.

The conclusion that follows from this discussion of conservation biology is relatively simple: some physical separation between wild nature and modern human activity of the sort found in urban areas and rural landscapes devoted to an industrial-style agriculture is essential for conserving biodiversity. While small patches of habitat within the urban and agricultural land matrix may be essential for conserving local endemic species with relatively small-scale habitat needs, and while migratory corridors of seminatural habitat through such areas may be important, the conservation of biodiversity requires landscapes where modern human impacts—roads, housing developments, clearcut logging, mining, and intensive agriculture—are precluded.[30]

CITIES, THE MODERN ECONOMY, AND BIODIVERSITY

Although urban life and rural industrial agriculture are predominantly shaped by the forces of culture, they are still a part of nature. The practices of both occur in an ecological context, and both affect local and global ecological processes. Both urban life and rural industrial agriculture draw on local and global supplies of energy, water, and materials, and they emit waste products into the local and global environment affecting nutrient, carbon, and hydrological cycles. Moreover, both have historically expanded over the global landscape, taking over relatively wild landscapes and reducing the habitat of species intolerant of intense human activity.

A number of economic trends are at work influencing rural settlement patterns and pressures on remaining relatively wild landscapes. Industrialization in the United States and other western countries has resulted in most people living in urbanized settings.[31] Increased labor productivity (output per worker) in agriculture and natural resource-based industries, and in some instances the depletion of resource reserves such as mineral deposits and old-growth forests, have contributed historically to a relative decline in rural population. Modern industry and commerce rely heavily on the economies of close proximity or agglomeration found only in an urban setting. Cities are essential, as Jane Jacobs so eloquently argues, for the creation of material abundance.[32] The industrial revolution and its accompanying transformation of material living standards took place in cities. The proximity afforded by cities is the life's blood of an industrial and free market economy. The complex interactions of city life are the roots of technological and scientific innovation. The creation of wealth, to this point in our economic history, has been an urban affair. Moreover, Jacobs suggests that cities foster and shape rural economic activity rather than the other way around, as demonstrated so persuasively in Cronon's work on the effect of the growth and development of Chicago on the farmlands and forests of the upper Midwest.[33] In the modern developed world, economic life is predominantly urban, and the rural economy is largely an appendage to the urban economy. Urban areas, in short, are the primary source of modern economic prosperity.

Yet human attitudes toward cities are profoundly ambivalent as noted in chapter 1. The poor flock to cities in search of economic well-being, while the rich flee cities to escape environmental and social chaos. The Jeffersonian vision of a democratic society presumed that small landowning farmers, not city dwellers, would serve as society's political and cultural backbone. As Gunn reminds us in his article, Jefferson's views were fundamentally antiurban and anti-industrial.[34] Cities in nineteenth-century America, essential as they were to economic progress, were tainted not only by the pollution and unhealthy conditions created by a newly industrialized society, but also by the corruption of city government political machines. The good and moral life in this country was to be found in a rural setting, not an urban one. The rural ideal, as Sam Bass Warner articulates, includes enjoyment of the pleasures of family life, the security of small communities, and a proximity to the world of nature.[35] Since this ideal was impossible to obtain in an urban society, it was sought through location on the urban fringe by those who could afford to do so once the electric trolley made it possible. The invention of the motor vehicle essentially eliminated remaining constraints on the outward march of urban development and enabled the pursuit of the rural ideal for all except the very poorest in American society, who largely remain confined to neighborhoods in the inner city.[36]

As Sam Bass Warner observed early on, the suburban dream contains inherent flaws and contradictions. Suburban expansion itself destroyed any sense of connection to the rural landscape. The suburbs generally became independent political jurisdictions, but not intimate, close-knit communities. Of the three components of the rural ideal articulated by Warner, only the pleasure of family life in detached homes was assured in turn-of-the-century suburbs.[37] In the modern suburb, the security of home ownership in detached homes on relatively large lots and the desire for control over local schools and land use generally prevail, but suburban expansion has brought increasing costs for public facilities, increasing traffic congestion, growing pollution problems, and losses of open space.[38]

Such problems have resulted in a reaction against growth in some communities and, for some individuals, a search for more pleasant surroundings beyond urban boundaries. As suggested in earlier chapters, this has been facilitated by a weakening of the economic need for proximity as the result of recent technological innovations such as overnight delivery, the fax, the modem, cellular phones, and satellite television. As noted earlier, in recent years population growth in many rural areas featuring attractive natural landscapes has exceeded urban growth, threatening an invasion of sensitive natural habitats by the relatively wealthy.

While a backlash to urban living may be occurring in the United States, the predominant trend globally is toward increased urban concentration of population. In another 25 years, more than two-thirds of the world's population will likely live in urban areas, with as much as 90 percent of the growth in global urban population occurring in developing countries.[39] The urban population surge in developing countries is already creating appalling local environmental conditions that are a serious threat to human health, especially for the poor. In the cities of developing countries, these conditions offer a striking parallel to conditions in nineteenth-century industrial cities where poverty, high population densities, and industrial activity create substantial threats to human health from air and water pollution and dangerous accumulations of solid wastes. Urban development trends in the less affluent countries of the world today seem to be repeating the European and American experience of economic transformation during the industrial revolution.

Widespread global urbanization presents both opportunities and challenges for biodiversity conservation. With population increasingly concentrated in cities, the feasibility of conserving sensitive natural habitats in rural areas would appear to increase. There are, however, several challenges. One is to render cities sufficiently attractive to prevent the repopulation of rural areas and the invasion of critical natural habitats by the affluent in wealthy countries such as the United States. Another challenge is to prevent a reversal of the rural-urban shift in population in developing countries where successful urban economies will likely relieve development pressure on tropical rain forests and other sensitive habitats. Still a third challenge is to reduce the ecological footprint of cities, such as the need for agricultural land and natural resource extraction to support relatively affluent urban populations. An expanding ecological footprint associated with the economic demands of affluence will continue to put development pressure on remaining natural habitats.[40] Footprint reduction also involves global environmental stresses, such as the deterioration of the ozone layer, acid rain, global warming, and the release of persistent toxic chemicals, all problems that originate directly or indirectly from urban areas and pose a threat to species residing in relatively wild habitats. These kinds of global environmental problems are strongly associated with affluence and must be addressed to a greater degree by relatively wealthy countries if they are to be resolved. The challenge for cities in developing countries is to mitigate the problem of poverty and the environmental threats that go with it, not so much to reduce their ecological footprint, which is relatively low in comparison to the affluent cities of the world, but to provide a decent standard of living and environment to their residents as a matter of economic justice as well as to divert population pressures from sensitive habitats in rural areas.

Cities thus need to be both socially and environmentally attractive and need to use the resources of nature in a sustainable manner that allows not only for a decent standard of living and healthy local environment, but for the conservation of biodiversity as well. Jane Jacobs is one of our most eloquent contemporary advocates of socially attractive cities, while Ian McHarg is the same for environmentally attractive cities.

In her classic work, *The Death and Life of Great American Cities*, Jacobs offers powerful arguments for relatively high-density cities. Her emphasis is on the importance of vibrant neighborhoods. In her view city neighborhoods should have the following features: (1) They should serve more than one primary function, ideally more than two functions. (2) Most blocks should be short; the opportunity to turn corners should be frequent. (3) Neighborhoods should mingle buildings that vary in age and condition and should include older buildings. (4) The density of population must be sufficient to support the purposes for which people are attracted to a neighborhood.[41]

For streets and neighborhood parks to be successful and offer a sense of security and safety, people must appear in them at different times of the day. This is fostered by different primary uses. Neighborhood streets are active throughout the day, for example, if people work in the neighborhood in the morning, spill out onto the streets for lunch, and go home again at night. In between these hours, neighborhood residents shop in local stores. Perhaps in the evening, people are attracted to the area for the restaurants or entertainment. Streets that are used steadily are safe, can be used by children, and are attractive as a place to engage in casual or impromptu social interaction. Short blocks create a variety of paths through a neighborhood. Long blocks are isolating and are used less by neighborhood residents. A city needs a variety of older buildings to attract new businesses that can't afford very high rents. Older buildings with low rents often serve as incubators for new businesses. A variety of old and new buildings brings a multitude of building uses to a neighborhood. Older buildings can often be cleverly adapted to new uses. These are the features Jacobs envisions for a socially successful city.[42]

Jacobs sees the city as essentially a human artifact, one that ought to be shaped in such a way as to satisfy human social needs. While the human species is ultimately a natural being, according to McHarg, the city in which human beings reside cannot contain internally all of nature's processes:

The modern city is, in this respect, profoundly different in that major natural processes which sustain the city, provide food, raw materials for industry, commerce, and construction, resources of water, and pure air are drawn not from the city or even its metropolitan area but from a national and even international hinterland. The major natural processes are not intrinsic to the locus of the city and cannot be.[43]

Still, in McHarg's view, human beings should not live in a totally artificial environment. Nature in cities not only offers tangible values, such as wooded slopes that absorb moisture and prevent flooding and erosion, but also a variety of intangible values including stimulation of reflection on the source of human meaning: "Clearly the problem of man and nature is not one of providing a decorative background for the human play, or even ameliorating the grim city: it is the necessity of sustaining nature as source of life, milieu, teacher, sanctum, challenge, and, most of all, of rediscovering nature's corollary of the unknown in the self, the source of meaning."[44] While urbanization, as it is currently proceeding, is typically unresponsive to its natural setting, it need not be this way. McHarg argues for the preservation of natural processes in open spaces interfused with urban development. McHarg's vision is captured in the following quote:

> Indeed, in several cities, the fairest image of nature exists in these rare occasions where river, flood plain, steep slopes and woodlands have been retained in their natural condition. . . . If rivers, flood plains, marshes, steep slopes, and woodlands in the city were accorded protection to remain in their natural conditions or were retrieved and returned to such a condition where possible, this single device, as an aspect of water quality, quantity, flood and drought control, would ensure for many cities an immeasurable improvement in the aspect of nature in the city, in addition to the specific benefits of a planned watershed.[45]

While cities cannot fully embody their connections to nature within their boundaries, they can be designed so as to preserve critical elements of nature and natural processes.

A socially and environmentally attractive city of the kind described by Jacobs and McHarg will take us at least partway toward reducing the city's ecological footprint by using the resources of nature more efficiently. The relatively high population densities envisioned by Jacobs will reduce the consumption of energy for both transportation and space heating and the volume of materials required for housing construction. In densely populated cities, reliance on the automobile can be reduced and alternative, more energy-efficient forms of transportation can be utilized such as light rail, subway systems, or even bicycles. Moreover, in the mixed use neighborhoods described by Jacobs, moving around on foot to satisfy daily needs becomes a possibility. In short, disconnecting ourselves from the automobile, a source of many of our environmental problems, becomes a distinct possibility.[46] These same high population densities will support the preservation of local open space and natural processes McHarg advocates by limiting the spread of population into local natural habitats with significant natural value. Habitat patches and natural corridors in cities contribute to the conservation of local biodiversity and offer opportunities for human contact with natural ecological processes and wild species.

THE ECOLOGICAL CITY AND ENVIRONMENTAL VALUES

As Alasdair MacIntyre argues, moral commitments arise from social practice. A social practice, according to MacIntyre, is any "coherent and complex form of socially established cooperative human activity through which goods internal to that form of activity are realized."[47] Surely, an "ecological city," as described by Jacobs and McHarg, would qualify as a social practice. Internal goods are realized by "trying to achieve those standards of excellence which are appropriate to, and partially definitive of, that form of activity."[48] The internal good of the ecological city is its functioning in such a way as to preserve global environmental integrity and biodiversity, and the standards of excellence are the specific activities of urban living that leave the least feasible urban footprint consistent with a decent human life. If this is true, cities designed to function in accordance with ecological principles and the principles of sustainable resource use will require a commitment to environmental values among its residents, including respect for wild species and a desire to conserve biodiversity that lies within and outside urban boundaries. Moreover, the presence of natural habitat patches and wild species allow for an understanding of the values attributable to wild species of flora and fauna and ultimately allow for a commitment to the preservation of those values. In this view, the ecological city will generate its own value commitments. Values arise from experience and practice. As Leopold emphasized, "ecological comprehension" is a prerequisite to the internalizing of a land ethic by society,[49] and such comprehension can probably only come from contact with the land and its natural processes.[50]

Socially and environmentally friendly cities, designed using the principles of ecology, are desirable for the kind of human life they have to offer as well as for the sake of biological conservation. How we get from where we are now to the ecological city is the real problem. The primary barrier to a solution is the inability of modern economic institutions to either produce or support the value commitments required to create ecological cities. The global corporate economy is rooted in and promotes economic freedom, consumer sovereignty, and private property rights, all of which are values that underpin a high-consumption economy and the uninhibited spreading of population and economic activity over the landscape. The community-oriented urban and environmental practices required for the ecological city would necessarily constrain private property rights so near and dear to the hearts of modern economic institutions. The freedom to put a housing development on a forested ridgetop or to spread urban development over the landscape for as far as the eye can see would no longer be an option.

The practices of the modern economy and of the ecological city envisioned by McHarg are clearly at odds. If the preservation of natural habitats and unspoiled ecosystems depends on the ecological city, then this also means that modern economic practice and the conservation of biodiversity are at odds. A new, more environmentally friendly approach to urban life requires a shift in values, but dominant economic institutions and the value scheme they support are antithetical to environmental values. If it takes an ecological city to create environmental values, then we are indeed stuck.

Two philosophers, Rorty and MacIntyre, have offered ideas that may help us see the way out of this predicament. First, Rorty gives us the concept of "edifying discourse" which is essentially "the attempt to reinterpret our familiar surroundings in the unfamiliar terms of our new invention," as Rorty puts it.[51] This seems to be exactly what Leopold discusses in his "Land Ethic," and what Rachel Carson intends in her *Silent Spring*. Through edifying discourse we have the potential to remake ourselves, including our relationship to the natural environment. Second, MacIntyre suggests that systems of values and methods of thinking, or what he calls "traditions," can be confronted with epistemological crises, where trusted approaches are no longer adequate to address unresolved challenges. This leads to a new view of things which, according to MacIntyre, must "furnish a solution to the problems which had previously proved intractable" and provide an explanation of "just what it was that rendered the tradition, before it had acquired these new resources, sterile or incoherent."[52] This seems to be what the ecological way of thinking and the land ethic attempt to do. In the old way of thinking, individual properties were walled off. Owners used their property as they saw fit, ignoring consequences for others or the natural environment. Ecological thought tells us that properties are interconnected, and the land ethic suggests to us that property, or the land itself, may be of value in its own right. The old view fails to address the problems of the ecological crisis; the new view confronts those problems directly.

If the survey researchers are right, edifying discourse around environmental and ecological questions has already made its mark. Large majorities of people claim to be environmentalists, and some even maintain that nature is valuable for its own sake, independent of the material benefits it provides to human individuals.[53] Although the ecological city hasn't yet been needed to foster environmental values, our environmental values have not substantially shaped our practices. Even though the contradictions between economic practice and the conservation of biodiversity are widely recognized, the epistemological crisis of conventional thought has yet to cause a transformation of modern economic institutions. Why this is the case seems to have a fairly obvious answer. The interests of dominant economic institutions are, at least in the short run, contrary to the creation of ecological cities. By virtue of their wealth and power, these same institutions exert substantial influence on political institutions and the public media and means of mass communications. Those who believe that change is necessary suffer from the freerider problem and are thus unable to use the power of numbers to politically offset the power of wealth.

There are, nonetheless, positive signs. Property owners have in some instances recognized that uncontrolled urban expansion, and even uncontrolled rural expansion, can be self-destructive. This has resulted in political revolts against growth and local governmental measures to control it.

Alistaire Gunn suggests that if we need a patron saint of ecology, it ought to be Ian McHarg rather than Aldo Leopold. In light of the importance of ecological, friendly cities for the conservation of biodiversity, I would agree that McHarg's views are important. Cities are essential to limit destructive human impacts on other species. Without attractive, environmentally efficient cities, humans and their ecological footprints will spread far and wide across globe, exacerbating our current mass species extinction crisis. In the pantheon of ecological heroes, I would elevate McHarg to stand alongside Leopold. We need both. And maybe Jane Jacobs too.

CONCLUSION: URBANISM, LAND TRUSTS, AND BIOLOGICAL CONSERVATION

The task of creating ecological cities is obviously a long-term one, requiring major transformations in our social and economic institutions. Whether and how this will happen is by no means clear. One tangible response to population spreading has been the formation of land trusts. For this reason it is a useful exercise to speculate on the role that land trusts can play in containing population spreading and contributing to a reinvigorated urban life.

In terms of the language of conservation biology, land trusts operate mainly in the working landscapes of buffer areas and connecting corridors as opposed to core reserves. The challenge faced by land trusts is to prevent high-density development on agricultural landscapes that still retain habitats for native plant and animal species. A second challenge is to promote agricultural practices consistent with maintaining these habitats. The tools available to these voluntary organizations are clearly limited. Land trusts can offer the opportunity to landowners to take charitable deduction tax breaks, reduce inheritance taxes, and, in some cases, lower local property taxes in exchange for conservation easements. Moreover, easements can reduce the market value of agricultural land and thus make it easier for younger farmers and ranchers to enter into the business, although easements can have a negative effect on agricultural loan collateral by reducing the value of property that can be used to back up a loan. In some cases land trusts are able to raise funds from public and private sources to purchase conservation easements.

While all these tools are effective in slowing development, they probably are insufficient to bring rural residential sprawl and population spreading to a halt. Obviously, greater public sector funding from such sources as federal offshore oil lease revenues could significantly increase the capacity of land trusts to use their tools to forestall development pressures. With increased funding, land trusts would no longer be limited to accepting donations of easements and could purchase more easements. While sales of easements to land trusts would offer further economic incentives for farmers and ranchers to continue in their current line of work, maintaining ecologically compatible economic activity in buffer zone areas in the long run may well be infeasible—particularly for ranching in the mountain West, an economic activity already considered by many to be unprofitable and economically marginal. Easement acquisitions on working ranches may simply be a prelude to ultimate land trust or public ownership of ranch lands if other economic uses of the land cannot be found that are compatible with conservation easement provisions.

The rural commitment to property rights has inhibited land use planning to contain and redirect development to existing towns and cities. Land trusts have, in a sense, offered an alternative to planning through their easement and property acquisition activities. The more sophisticated land trusts actually engage in planning, establishing priorities to follow in acquisition and targeting properties for easements that best fit their priorities. Land trusts, one might say, engage in a "backdoor" form of land use planning without directly confronting local commitments to property rights.

While land trusts cannot transform the quality of life in urban areas, they currently serve as the only active line of defense in many localities against population spreading beyond urban boundaries. Moreover, in some cases land trusts are active within urban boundaries in the preservation of remaining habitat patches and corridors. Land trusts could thus play a bigger role in realizing McHarg's vision of conserving natural landscapes in urban settings. Land trusts frequently serve in an educational capacity, communicating to the public the importance of preserving local landscapes with scenic and natural values. Finally, land trusts, as conservative as they might seem to some environmental activists, are an interesting institutional experiment. They are a democratic, community-based vehicle for activists who want to get involved in efforts that lead directly to landscape conservation. Land trusts could ultimately serve as the basis for local movements in support of more extensive public measures to protect natural and seminatural landscapes on private lands. They could be participants in Rorty's process of "edifying discourse" that leads to larger social, and maybe even ecological, transformations.

While land trusts may be able to help limit sprawl beyond urban boundaries, they are not the only or final answer to the spreading of human population across the landscape. Ultimately, population spreading will require more substantial measures. To a discussion of such measures, we now turn.

NOTES

1. The journal *Environmental Ethics* began publishing in 1978.
2. Paul W. Taylor, *Respect for Nature: A Theory of Environmental Ethics* (Princeton: Princeton University Press, 1986).

3. Holmes Rolston III, "Values in Nature," *Environmental Ethics* 3 (1981): 113–128; and *Genes, Genesis, and God: Values and their Origins in Natural and Human History* (Cambridge: Cambridge University Press, 1999), 1–53.

4. J. Baird Callicott, "Intrinsic Value, Quantum Theory, and Environmental Ethics," *Environmental Ethics* 7 (1985): 257–273.

5. Bryan G. Norton, "Why I Am not a Nonanthropocentrist: Callicott and the Failure of Monistic Inherentism," *Environmental Ethics* 17 (1995): 341–358.

6. Some make a distinction between biocentric and ecocentric environmental ethics. Biocentric refers to individual organisms as valuable for their own sake while ecocentric refers to species and ecosystems as valuable for their own sake. See Gary K. Meffe and C. Ronald Carroll, *Principles of Conservation Biology* (Sunderland, Mass.: Sinauer Associates, 1994), 35.

7. Bryan G. Norton, *Why Preserve Natural Variety?* (Princeton: Princeton University Press, 1987), 185–213.

8. Aldo Leopold, *A Sand County Almanac* (New York: Ballantine Books, 1970).

9. Leopold, *A Sand County Almanac*, 237–240.

10. Some philosophers object to notions of the public as the final arbiter of a particular philosophical view. These philosophers point to historical instances of the public accepting philosophical ideas because of their immediate emotional appeal that in retrospect most would reject as repugnant. The classic example is the rise of the Nazis in Germany in the 1930s and the appeal to popular sentiments. Instead philosophical views should be subjected to the standards of reasoned inquiry and judged on this basis. While no one would deny the importance of reasoned judgement, it is still the case that moral standards have little practical value if they are not accepted by political and social decision makers. One hopes that the public, like philosophers, arrive at their basic values in a reasoned and rational manner. One also hopes that those with the power to make political and social decisions do so as well. See Hilary Putnam, *Reason, Truth, and History* (Cambridge: Cambridge University Press, 1981), 110–112 and 150–173.

11. William Kempton, James S. Boster, and Jennifer A. Hartley, *Environmental Values in American Culture* (Cambridge, Mass.: MIT Press, 1995). In this work, focus groups are used to establish the language actually employed by members of various interest groups as well as the public at large to describe a wide range of attitudes toward the environment. Survey questions were then formulated on the basis of focus group language. High levels of agreement (strongly agree, agree, slightly agree: 83–90%) with the following statements were found in a sample of the public at large:

> All species have a right to evolve without human interference. If extinction is going to happen, it should happen naturally, not through human actions.
>
> Other species have as much right to be on this earth as we do. Just because we are smarter than other animals doesn't make us better.
>
> Justice is not just for human beings. We need to be as fair to plants and animals as we are towards people.
>
> Our obligation to preserve nature isn't just a responsibility to other people but to the environment itself.

12. See Taylor, *Respect for Nature*, 219–255. The primary objection to rights language for species is that bearers of moral rights must be members of a community of moral agents and must be capable of asserting their rights against others. Species are obviously incapable of doing this. The term *rights* in the survey research by Kempton et al. (*Environ-*

mental Values in American Culture) seems to refer to an obligation by humans to avoid causing species' extinction. In short, respondents seem to accept the idea that humans have obligations to nonhumans expressed in terms of rights language. Rights language is simply a familiar way of stating a moral obligation. Such rights are not absolute. Human beings may well put the rights of the human species above other species. This is suggested by the low level of agreement (21 percent) by respondents in Kempton et al. (*Environmental Values in American Culture*) with the following statement:

> If any species has to become extinct as a result of human activities, it should be the human species.

13. Leopold, *A Sand County Almanac*, 247.

14. Rachel Carson, *Silent Spring* (Boston: Houghton Mifflin Company, 1962).

15. Anthony Downs, "Up and Down with Ecology—The 'Issue-Attention Cycle,'" *The Public Interest* 28 (1972): 38–50.

16. Riley E. Dunlap, "Trends in Public Opinion toward Environmental Issues: 1965–1990," *Society and Natural Resources* 4 (1991): 285–312.

17. Alastair S. Gunn, "Rethinking Communities: Environmental Ethics in an Urbanized World," *Environmental Ethics* 20 (1998): 341–360.

18. Ian L. McHarg, "The Place of Nature in the City of Man," in *Western Man and Environmental Ethics: Attitudes toward Nature and Technology*, ed. Ian G. Barbour (Reading, Mass.: Addison-Wesley Publishing Company, 1973), 171–186; and Ian L. McHarg, *Design With Nature* (Garden City, N.Y.: Natural History Press, 1969).

19. William Cronon, "The Trouble with Wilderness, or, Getting Back to the Wrong Nature," in *The Great New Wilderness Debate*, ed. J. Baird Callicott and Michael P. Nelson (Athens: University of Georgia Press, 1998), 471–499; and J. Baird Callicott, "The Wilderness Idea Revisited: The Sustainable Development Alternative," in *The Great New Wilderness Debate*, 337–366.

20. Herman E. Daly, *Steady-state Economics*, 2d ed. (Washington, D.C.: Island Press, 1991), 181.

21. The degree of separation required obviously depends on a society's economic practices. Aboriginals using their own technologies and living at modest densities on a landscape can be perfectly consistent with the continued survival of native species. The introduction of modern technologies and practices in such landscapes may well be inconsistent with the long-term survival of many native species.

22. Alasdair MacIntyre, *After Virtue: A Study in Moral Theory* (Notre Dame, Ind.: University of Notre Dame Press, 1984).

23. Donald M. Waller, "Getting Back to the Right Nature: A Reply to Cronon's 'The Trouble with Wilderness,'" in *The Great New Wilderness Debate*, 541–567; and Holmes Rolston III, *Genes, Genesis, and God: Values and their Origins in Natural and Human History* (Cambridge: Cambridge University Press, 1999), 108–159.

24. Reed F. Noss and Allen Y. Cooperrider, *Saving Nature's Legacy: Protecting and Restoring Biodiversity* (Washington, D.C.: Island Press, 1994), 89–90.

25. Noss and Cooperrider, *Saving Nature's Legacy*, 129–177.

26. Reed F. Noss, Michael A. O'Connell, and Dennis D. Murphy, *The Science of Conservation Planning: Habitat Conservation Under the Endangered Species Act* (Washington, D.C.: Island Press, 1997), 4–5.

27. Leopold, A Sand County Almanac, 262.

28. Leopold, A Sand County Almanac, 264–279.

29. Callicott, "The Wilderness Idea Revisited," 237–238.

30. This divide between landscapes where cultural and biological evolution would dominate seems to be at the core of the new wilderness debate. Those who criticize the wilderness idea, such as Callicott ("The Wilderness Idea Revisited") and Cronon ("The Trouble with Wilderness"), seem to believe that cultural evolution currently predominates, and landscapes largely untrammeled by human beings do not now and perhaps never existed. All that is feasible is the sustainable development of landscapes where as many species as possible are conserved in the interstices of human influence. Others, such as Rolston ("The Wilderness Idea Reaffirmed," in The Great New Wilderness Debate, 367–386) and David Foreman ("Wilderness Areas are for Real," in The Great New Wilderness Debate, 395–407), disagree, suggesting that in a modern context, the conservation of biodiversity and the forces of evolution in fact require landscapes where human influence is relatively minimal. While this seems to be the lesson of the discipline of conservation biology, there are dissenters within the discipline itself who argue for the conservation of many small habitat patches as a feasible alternative to large core reserves. This debate was known by its acronym, SLOSS, which stands for "single large or several small." Most conservation biologists would agree, however, that large core reserves have a better chance at doing the job than a collection of small habitat patches, particularly for wide-ranging large herbivores and carnivores. The conservation of biological evolution would seem to require some separation between human communities and wild flora and fauna. See Noss and Cooperrider (Saving Nature's Legacy) for a discussion of this debate.

31. World Resources Institute, World Resources, 1996–97: The Urban Environment (New York and Oxford: Oxford University Press, 1996), 3. By 1995, 70 percent of the population in Europe and North America was living in urban areas.

32. Jane Jacobs, The Economy of Cities (New York: Vintage Books, 1970).

33. William Cronon, Nature's Metropolis: Chicago and the Great West (New York: W. W. Norton, 1991).

34. Gunn, "Rethinking Communities."

35. Sam B. Warner Jr., Streetcar Suburbs: The Process of Growth in Boston, 1870–1900 (New York: Atheneum, 1974).

36. Kenneth T. Jackson, Crabgrass Frontier: The Suburbanization of the United States (New York: Oxford University Press, 1985).

37. Warner, Streetcar Suburbs, 153–166.

38. Baldassare, 1986, 1–32; and Anthony Downs, New Visions for Metropolitan America (Washington, D.C.: The Brookings Institution, 1994).

39. World Resources Institute, World Resources, 1996–97, 1–15.

40. See Mathis Wackernagel and William E. Rees (Our Ecological Footprint: Reducing Human Impact on the Earth [Gabriola Island, British Columbia: New Society Publishers, 1995]) for a discussion of the concept of an ecological footprint.

41. Jane Jacobs, The Death and Life of Great American Cities (New York: Vintage Books, 1961), 150–151.

42. Jacobs, The Death and Life of Great American Cities.

43. McHarg, "The Place of Nature in the City of Man," 180.

44. McHarg, Design With Nature, 19.

45. McHarg, "The Place of Nature in the City of Man," 183.

46. For more on the role of the automobile in cities, see Peter Newman and Jeffrey Kenworthy, *Sustainability and Cities: Overcoming Automobile Dependence* (Washington, D.C.: Island Press, 1999).

47. MacIntyre, *After Virtue*, 187.

48. MacIntyre, *After Virtue*, 187.

49. Leopold, *A Sand County Almanac*, 262.

50. In "Thinking Like a Mountain," Leopold suggests that his own views on conservation issues were profoundly influenced by his experience in nature; see Leopold, *A Sand County Almanac*, 137–141. The public apparently believes that contact with nature is important for the formation of environmental values. See Kempton et al., *Environmental Values in American Culture*, 56.

51. Richard Rorty, *Philosophy and the Mirror of Nature* (Princeton: Princeton University Press, 1979), 360.

52. Alasdair MacIntyre, *Whose Justice? Which Rationality?* (Notre Dame, Ind.: University of Notre Dame Press, 1988), 361–364.

53. Dunlap, "Trends in Public Opinion"; and Kempton et al., *Environmental Values in American Culture*.

9

~

Strategies for
Limiting Rural Sprawl

While the public expresses support for the conservation of biodiversity and may well be willing to limit the outward sprawl of population from urban centers, the immediate political desire to do so is more questionable. Powerful economic interests benefit from existing urban land use patterns. Nonetheless, there are signs of progress. The so-called smart growth movement supports measures to restrict urban sprawl and increase urban density along the lines suggested in the last chapter.[1] Moreover, something of an urban renaissance appears to be underway in many of our older central cities.[2] Consequently, we will take the public desire to limit both urban and rural sprawl as a given and lay out some of the possible strategies for increasing population densities, both in existing urban areas and rural areas experiencing population growth.

As outlined in the previous chapter, attractive, environmentally friendly urban centers are important for the conservation of biodiversity by limiting the spread of population to rural areas that still contain critical natural habitats. How to revitalize urban life is a massive topic in itself, and we can only begin to suggest the specific means for doing so here. A key ingredient for an environmentally friendly urban renaissance will no doubt be unhooking ourselves from the motor vehicle as the primary means of urban transportation. Consequently, this is the focus of the discussion to follow on creating ecologically sound urban landscapes.

An attractive urban life will, no doubt, staunch some of the population flow to beautiful but environmentally significant rural landscapes, but it will be unlikely to stop the flow completely. Consequently, measures are needed in these landscapes to increase population density and to pull development into existing towns or concentrate it in such a way as to protect natural habitats. Land trusts are one response to the problem of rural sprawl, but other measures will be

needed. The main shortcoming of land trusts is their inability to be comprehensive in their influence on land use patterns. Development will, in all probability,
be diverted to parcels outside the influence of land trusts. Thus land use control
measures will ultimately be needed to prevent sprawl.

LIMITING URBAN SPRAWL AND
CREATING ATTRACTIVE HIGH-DENSITY CITIES

Auto Dependency, Population Density, and the Environment

Let's begin by considering broad patterns of transportation energy consumption
in urban areas and their relationship to auto dependency.[3] In general, urban
transportation energy use, in terms of consumption per capita, declines as we
move from country to country in the following order: United States, Australia,
Canada, Europe, and Asia.[4] Not surprisingly, automobile use decreases as we
move from country to country in the above order, and public transit use increases. Auto use and mass transit use are thus inversely related, and auto use and
energy efficiency are inversely related as well. That is, auto-dependent cities use
more energy per capita in transportation. On the other hand, energy efficiency
and the use of mass transit are positively related. Transit-dependent cities use less
energy per capita. Despite the difference in dependence on public transit, the average time spent in commuting is stable across cities at around a half hour. Commuting by car is faster, but distances covered in commuting are greater, judging
by the larger volume of total travel in auto-dependent cities.

The central reason for auto dependency and longer commuting distances traveled in United States urban areas is their lower density of development. The average population density per hectare for large American cities is 14.2, while it is
28.5 for Canadian cities, 49.9 for European cities, and 161.9 for Asian cities. Because of lower population densities, Americans have to travel farther to get to
work, to shop, and to move around the urban landscape for other reasons. Also,
because of lower densities and the spread of destinations across the landscape,
the automobile is the most popular means for getting around. Public transportation on fixed routes is incapable of efficiently serving a public whose jobs and residences are spread out in a highly decentralized fashion.

Because of the relatively direct connection between fossil fuel energy consumption and greenhouse gas emissions, per capita emissions for the residents of
large U.S. cities are dramatically higher than for other cities in the world. The per
capita emissions rate in the United States is about 2.4 times that of the typical urban resident in a large European city, and about 5.4 times that of a typical Asian
urban resident.[5] The higher level of greenhouse gas emissions for the United
States is attributable in part to the higher use of the automobile in urban areas,
and this higher use in turn is related to low-density urban development. Per capita

emissions for other types of urban air pollutants from motor vehicles, such nitrogen oxides and volatile organic compounds, are also higher on average in large U.S. cities than for comparable cities elsewhere. The automobile is clearly a major source of urban air pollution problems in the United States today.

Auto dependency has other environmental consequences as well. Extensive use of the automobile leads to a relatively high level of impervious surfaces such as paved streets and parking lots. These same impervious surfaces collect a variety of toxins from motor vehicles that get washed into local streams and rivers during storms. Moreover, such surfaces result in high volumes of runoff during storm episodes that quickly end up in streams and rivers rather than being absorbed in soils and slowly making their way into groundwater reserves. The net result is an increase in the frequency and intensity of flooding.[6] Auto dependency thus creates significant water pollution and flooding problems in addition to global warming and various air pollution problems.

Apparently the longstanding trend to lower urban density in the United States is continuing. According to a recent report, between 1982 and 1997, urbanized land in the United States increased by 47 percent from 51 to 76 million acres while population only increased by 17 percent.[7] This suggests auto dependency is expanding rather than contracting.

Subsidizing the Automobile

While the story of the shift to the automobile as the major mode of transportation in the United States is an interesting one, it would take us beyond the scope of our discussion here. Nonetheless, it is important to note that the shift was not a matter of consumer choice but the result of public policy. Public policy created the national interstate highway system and its associated scheme of urban freeways from city to suburb. Without these, urban transportation would have remained less auto dependent, and public transportation would probably have been expanded instead. Certainly, the dismantling of the system of urban and inter-urban trolleys in many metropolitan areas after World War II would probably not have occurred.[8] The building of freeways and the resulting development of sprawling suburbs benefited a diverse array of interests including the motor vehicle, petroleum, and construction industries, all of which had powerful lobbies in Congress. Certainly, suburbanization was a primary engine of economic growth after World War II and, for that reason, found strong political support.

Behind suburbanization is an abundance of subsidies to both the automobile and suburban-style housing.[9] We will focus here on subsidies to the automobile since they are most closely related to the issue of automobile dependency. These subsidies take the form of external costs caused by individual auto ownership and use but actually borne by others. When I drive my car, I pay for fuel, fuel taxes, insurance, depreciation, and maintenance, but I don't directly pay for the full costs of road maintenance and construction, traffic

control, congestion, accidents, parking spots, or air, water, and noise pollution. Some roads are paid for through fuel taxes, but some fall on the property
and other local taxes, as do the costs of traffic control. The estimates for annual external costs per year for a car range from around $2,200 to $4,200. Obviously, if owners paid the full cost of using their cars, they would probably
choose to reduce their usage by shifting to public transportation for the purpose of commuting.

Getting Rid of Subsidies

An obvious measure for reducing automobile dependency would be to get rid of
the external subsidy by instituting, for example, an equivalent gasoline tax. Residents of European cities pay much more for gasoline than Americans simply because of substantially higher rates of taxation. Thus a gas tax would be a simple
and effective means for steering the public away from auto use and toward alternative forms of transportation.

Unfortunately, there is little assurance that a gas tax itself would accomplish
less auto dependency and a shift to denser urban areas. The problem is that gasoline prices and income differences don't fully explain variances in automobile use
and population densities from city to city. According to Newman and Kenworthy, across global cities only about half the difference in gasoline use can be explained by differences in income and prices.[10] In Toronto, for example, prices and
income are not that different from the United States, but the use of public transit is much higher and per capita gasoline consumption lower simply because
high-quality mass transit is available. The response to higher gasoline taxes in
the United States could be a modest increase in efficiency through the selection
of more fuel-efficient models over the long run, but not much reduction in automobile dependency.

Increasing Density and the Quality of Urban Life

In the eyes of advocates for cities like Jane Jacobs, the key to a decent quality of
life is relatively high urban density and mixed urban use. Mixed urban uses allow
a variety of functions to performed within a local neighborhood. A single neighborhood in a reasonably dense urban setting can serve not only as a place to live,
but also can offer opportunities for employment and shopping, all within walking distance of one another. Not everyone can live and work in the same neighborhood, but some can, and many can do their daily shopping on foot. Neighborhoods with sufficiently high density and mixed use can offer the kind of street
life that makes urban areas socially attractive. Neighborhoods need to be connected, and in a relatively high-density urban area this can be efficiently accomplished by public transportation. Automobiles are still an important part of
the urban matrix, but their needs must be balanced against the needs of pedes-

trians and bicyclists. One means for doings this is traffic calming, something that can be accomplished with wider sidewalks, center islands on streets and boulevards, and traffic circles. Traffic calming can be combined with landscaping on the widened sidewalks, center islands, and traffic circles to make streets increasingly attractive to pedestrians. One reason people have left auto-dominated central cities for the suburbs is that city life has often been given over to the automobile. Long unbroken streets with high-speed traffic, narrow sidewalks, and a lack of landscaping are unappealing to pedestrians, as are acres of parking lots or large, noisy freeway structures. Conversely, high-density, pedestrian-friendly cities combined with convenient public transportation are likely to win converts back to a less auto-oriented way of life. This doesn't mean giving up cars completely, it just means depending on them less for urban transportation.

Although it would help, simply raising the cost of driving is unlikely to stimulate the development of more high-quality, pedestrian-friendly urban environments. In addition, public transportation needs to be expanded and improved, and land use practices need to be changed. Development should be clustered at higher densities along public transit routes, and the long established practice of segregated zoning by use needs to be abandoned. Of course the added tax revenues from a larger gas tax could be funneled to improvements in public transportation and land use planning. As U.S. citizens, we need to make our cities look more like Europe's and Canada's. To constrain sprawl and redirect development to the central city, urban growth boundaries beyond which urban development is precluded may well be needed where outward growth is not otherwise constrained.[11]

Greening the City

A relatively new urban ecology movement suggests that urban ecosystems can be made to function more like natural ones.[12] For example, the urban water cycle can be transformed so that it functions more like a natural water cycle. This involves restoring streams and wetlands to their natural condition so they are better able to absorb flood episodes and cleanse streamwaters of pollutants, increasing the extent of soft surfaces and reducing urban sprawl so stormwater can be absorbed more effectively into the water table, increasing storage of stormwater for recharging local aquifers and nonpotable usage (such as lawn watering), undertaking localized water treatment and recycling of nutrients and organic materials, and increasing the use of water-efficient appliances.

A variety of other ecologically friendly steps can be undertaken as well. These include more energy-efficient buildings, renewable energy projects, expanded green areas and the planting of more vegetation (including urban gardens), promotion of pedestrian and bicycle transportation, the recycling of household wastes and building materials, and the use of natural building materials. The basic goals are to reduce energy and materials metabolism in urban areas, reduce waste output, and create an urban setting with more natural features. Urban ecology in this way incorporates the practices of an environmental ethic into everyday life. At the same time, the greening of the city and reduced auto dependency make urban settings more attractive and thus lessen inclinations to relocate outside urban areas in habitats necessary for the conservation of biological diversity.

Can Americans Give Up the Rural Ideal?

All this presumes that at least some Americans can give up the rural ideal of a home on a relatively large piece of land in a rural or semi-rural setting. As a practical matter, the suburbs with their increasing congestion and intensity of development in most cases offer a rather poor imitation of the rural ideal. Still, the attraction of the detached single-family dwelling, the idea of local political control over schools, and the homogeneity of the local population in the suburbs is still attractive to many.

On the other hand, affluent Europeans have adapted to high-density cities and the attractions of urban life. Wealth and auto dependence at the global level are not correlated.[13] Even in the United States, the most prestigious and expensive places to live are in the high-density downtown areas of such cities as New York, Boston, and San Francisco. Numerous examples of appealing, high-density cities exist globally, including Singapore, Hong Kong, Zurich, Copenhagen, Stockholm, Toronto, and Vancouver, Canada.[14] In the United States, Portland, Oregon, is known for its growth boundaries, encouragement of high-density development, and development of a popular light rail system. A recent revival in downtown housing construction in many central cities in the United States suggests that some of our most affluent citizens are voting with their feet in order to take advantage of the amenities offered by high-density urban living.[15]

Summary: Limiting Urban Sprawl and Creating Attractive High-Density Cities

Eliminating the hidden subsidy to the automobile will not be enough to create high-density, attractive cities. The existing scheme of land use planning and controls needs to be reworked to encourage mixed use and higher-density development, and public transportation needs to be reshaped and improved. To avoid the leapfrogging of development beyond urban boundaries, all this needs to be done on a regional basis. The primary barrier to a regional scheme of planning and zoning is the unwillingness of local governments to give up their control over land use. Historically, this control has been employed in suburban communities to keep out low-income housing and insure socioeconomic homogeneity. For decent and equitable land use arrangements in cities, exclusive local control of land use will have to be forgone in order to achieve the larger goal of a socially just and environmentally friendly urban life.[16]

LIMITING RURAL SPRAWL

Increasing the attraction of existing urban centers will likely slow the population flow to places of natural beauty in the mountain West, but it is unlikely to bring that flow to a halt. Consequently, strategies are needed to mitigate the effects of population growth and development in rural mountain West counties. Land trusts in the mountain West are a significant vehicle for preserving natural habitat and open space. However, the critical problem facing land trusts is the requirement of either voluntary fundraising for easement and property purchases or the need for voluntary landowner contributions of easements or properties. Not all land trusts can raise enough funds to compete with developers in the local property market, and not all owners of critical natural habitat are willing to contribute easements or land. Consequently, development will be diverted to lands outside the sphere of land trust influence. Only a portion of the landscape will be subject to the "backdoor" form of land use planning available to land trusts.

Other means are available to local communities concerned with the prospect of rural sprawl, including comprehensive land use planning and zoning, local government purchases of development rights and land acquisitions for conservation purposes, the creation of transferable development rights, and the creation of local zoning districts where countywide zoning is infeasible. In addition, local cost-of-services studies are a useful tool to demonstrate that residential development often costs more (in terms of the expense of added government services) than it delivers (in terms of added tax revenues at the local level). These studies help mobilize support for land use management efforts that limit development and require developers to bear some of the added public sector costs resulting from residential expansion.

Comprehensive Land Use Planning

In the rural mountain West, a vehicle for protecting open space and natural habitat is county-level land use planning and zoning. Through land use planning, sensitive landscapes can be identified and mapped, and through zoning, the density of development can be limited on such sites. As an alternative, the density of development can be limited for all existing agricultural and undeveloped lands. Custer County in Colorado, for example, took this approach by limiting development to one house per 80 acres for valley bottom ranch land, higher than the state restriction of one per 35 acres. County-level zoning, however, is not always acceptable to local landowners who fear restrictions that could impinge on their current land use or reduce its market value. Zoning and land use planning at the county level, consequently, are not always politically feasible in the absence of other measures. Ranchers who are land rich but cash poor in mountain West valleys are not going to give up the right to develop their land very easily.

An alternative approach likely to be more acceptable to landowners is a scheme of zoning regulations that allow residential construction at higher densities in exchange for the clustering of development and the preservation of a certain amount of open space.[17] For example, the owner of a 100-acre parcel, normally restricted to the construction of a single dwelling by zoning regulations, might be allowed to build more units if development is concentrated on, say, a 20-acre site and the remaining 80 acres is left as open space. This arrangement would be more attractive to landowners concerned with the market value of their property. Routt County, the location of the skiing and resort community of Steamboat Springs, has a provision for conservation subdivisions that allow development in exchange for open space conservation. In practice, however, this provision acts like a normal subdivision law and has been a vehicle for facilitating development in the Steamboat Springs area.[18]

Open Space Taxes

Another approach to open space and natural habitat protection taken by counties and other units of local government is to institute open space taxes for the purpose of purchasing land or easements. The funds collected are often used to help pay for land preservation projects undertaken by local land trusts or other nonprofit organizations. The town of Crested Butte instituted a real estate transfer tax to be used for open space purchases as early as 1979. More recently, the tax rate was increased and the funds were a big help to the Crested Butte Land Trust in making some key land purchases in the local area.[19] Both Gunnison and Routt Counties in Colorado have open space taxes, and both make funds available for specific land conservation project proposals submitted by land trusts.[20] The limitation of this approach to land conservation are the same as those facing land trusts. Development can leapfrog over lands in conservation ownership or under easements.

Transferable Development Rights

In combination with a countywide land use plan that identifies critical habitat for conservation, transferable development rights (TDRs) are a flexible tool that can garner landowner support for zoning that limits the density of development in key localities. Under a TDR program, landowners can transfer development rights from areas where development is restricted to areas where development is permitted. For example, suppose the normal density limit in the zoning law is one dwelling per 20 acres and that all landowners are allocated one development right per 20 acres. Under a TDR scheme, development is restricted in some areas of a county, but in other areas the density of development can be increased by purchasing development rights from landowners in the restricted area. The restricted locations are sending areas for development rights while the unrestricted locations are receiving areas. TDRs can be purchased in the sending areas to increase the density of development in the receiving areas.[21] While land in sending areas cannot be developed, landowners can nonetheless realize economic value from their land by selling their development rights. The net result is the concentration of development in less environmentally sensitive locations. Such a scheme should reduce landowner opposition to zoning restrictions because all landowners can benefit from development even though it cannot occur everywhere.

Zoning Districts

As noted in chapter 7, countywide zoning is not very popular in the mountain West. However, Montana state law permits the formation of zoning districts at a sub-county level. A zoning district can be established if at least 60 percent of the landowners sign a petition for such a district and if fewer than 40 percent of the landowners who in total own less than 50 percent of the land enter written protests against the district. An advisory committee of landowners then works with the local County Planning Board and Commission to prepare a draft zoning regulation for adoption by the County Commission after public hearings.[22] In Gallatin County, 16 of these zoning districts are currently in existence.

One of the more interesting examples is the Springhill Zoning District located just north of Bozeman, Montana, near the Bridger Range. The community is composed of around 140 individuals equally split between ranchers, retirees, and people who have home businesses or commute to Bozeman for employment. The Springhill Community includes approximately 19,000 acres of which 11,000 is national forest land. The area includes 88 parcels of land with 51 residential dwellings. In 1989 a petition was successfully circulated for the establishment of a zoning district with the same boundaries as the local elementary school district. Seventy percent of the landowners supported formation of the district. Landowners were concerned with a residential subdivision constructed in the area in 1989, and local residents wanted to maintain the character of the existing landscape and limit the extent of new residential development. By 1992 a land use plan and zoning regulations were established.

The goals of the Springhill land use plan include preserving the existing rural agricultural community, protecting riparian areas, preventing development on steep slopes and in wetlands, preserving the natural vegetation, and conserving wildlife habitat. The principle means for accomplishing these goals are to limit residential development and to cluster it on a limited amount of land. The primary vehicle in the zoning regulations for limiting and clustering residential development is a system of transferable development rights. In the Springhill Zoning District, one residential dwelling unit is allowed as a matter of right per 160 acres or per parcel existing at the time the zoning law was adopted in 1992. In addition, landowners are allowed one additional development right for every 80 acres within an original parcel subject to obtaining a conditional use permit. The owner of a 200-acre parcel, for example, would have a total of three development rights, two of which would require a conditional use permit. These could be used to construct three dwellings, or the development rights could be sold. Any development right can be transferred through sale to any other parcel within the zoning district. Transferable development rights are consequently a marketable entity that can be separated from the original property. Transferable development rights as well as development rights arising from the 80-acre provision, however, can only be used on 15 percent of the original parcel area. The remaining 85 percent must be permanently preserved as open space. In this way, development will be limited and much of the district will be preserved in its current open space status. For example, an owner of a 200-acre parcel with one dwelling on the property could purchase an additional three development rights for a total of five subject to conditional use (two development rights are from the 80-acre provision), but development of the five units would have to be confined to subdivided parcels totaling no more than 30 acres.[23]

In at least one case, a zoning district has been organized partly to facilitate wildlife conservation for a particular species. The specific purposes of the Middle Cottonwood Zoning District include the following: "to prevent the overcrowding of land and undue concentration of population; to ensure the quality and adequate quantity of ground water; to preserve wildlife habitat; to preserve and maintain agricultural land; to preserve the scenic resources of the district; and to limit density as a primary method of achieving the foregoing purposes."[24] In the Cottonwood plan, mule deer winter range is delineated and affects density requirements. Within the winter range, a minimum of 40 acres is required for a single-family detached dwelling, while outside the winter range, only 20 acres is required. In this way the Zoning District offers some protection to mule deer populations.

The primary limitation of zoning districts is that they cover only a part of the county. Since much of Gallatin County remains unzoned, development is readily diverted to unzoned areas.

Cost of Services from Residential Development

Different kinds of land use generate varying amounts of local tax revenues and place differing burdens on the provision of local government services such as education, highway construction and maintenance, and public safety. Education, the most costly of local government services, is impacted entirely by the number of residents with children, not by the volume of agricultural or commercial activity in a local area. Commercial and agricultural business ventures, however, make use of local roads and highways as do local residents. The same is true for public safety services and the services of general government, such as zoning and planning or property value assessment.

The American Farmland Trust has developed and applied a framework for estimating the relative contribution of tax and other revenues from different land uses and the relative burden of those same land uses on expenditures for local government services. The resulting studies are know as cost-of-community-services studies and generate the ratio of expenditures to revenues attributable to different land uses. These land use ratios indicate the amount of expenditure for a particular land use type. For example, a study for Custer County, Colorado, found that $1.16 was spent on local services to residential property occupants for every dollar raised from residential property owners and occupants in taxes and other local revenues. The comparable amounts for commercial/industrial property and for agricultural/open space property were respectively $.71 and $.54 in the Custer County study. Consequently, residential property results in a net expenditures burden that is borne by revenues from other types of property for Custer County. The notion of increasing cost of services associated with residential population expansion is supported anecdotally by recent growth in road traffic in Custer County requiring elevated spending on various road maintenance and improvement projects.[25] A similar study for Gallatin County in Montana found the ratio of spending on local services for residential property to equal $1.45 for every dollar of local government revenue raised from residential property owners and occupants. The comparable amounts for agricultural and open space, industrial, and commercial property are $.25, $.07, and $.18.[26] Clearly, services to residential property in Gallatin County are being paid for in part by owners of other types of property just as they are in Custer County.

Such studies must be taken with a grain of salt. The process of allocating payments to different types of property for some expenditure categories is fairly arbitrary. Also, commercial property owners may well benefit indirectly from services provided to residential property owners. Local businesses, for example, benefit from a well-maintained road system that allows their customers to travel to town for shopping. Also, everyone in the local community may benefit from a well-educated public whose presence in the community increases the quality of local life in both the public and private sphere.

Nonetheless, cost-of-services studies are useful in offering local residents some idea of the costs of different kinds of new development in the local community. Clearly, residential development is likely to increase the local costs of education, road maintenance, and public safety. A survey of 58 studies in 17 states found that the expenditure-revenue ratios don't vary dramatically and averaged $1.15 for residential land use, $.37 for agricultural and forest land use, and $.29 for commercial and industrial land use.[27] Given the relatively high cost of public school education, the results are intuitively reasonable despite any shortcomings in the underlying methodology for deriving the figures. There is some danger in applying the ratios at the margin. The added cost of a housing development for retirees will likely differ from one for families with young children who will enter the local school system. Nonetheless, cost-of-services studies do raise red flags about the impact of new development. Unless residential development is accompanied by an expansion of local commercial facilities, the resulting addition to the cost of municipal services may well exceed the added revenues generated. If so, then the end result may be an increase in local tax rates. If local residents are aware of the full costs of development, then they may be more inclined to support land use planning, zoning, and other measures to control local growth. As we saw in chapter 6, the residents of the Sierra Nevada Mountains appear ready to support land use control measures that limit local growth and mitigate its harms.

CONCLUSION

All this boils down to a rather simple point: to conserve naturally occurring flora and fauna in the mountain West, the density of development needs to be increased in both urban and rural areas. Denser, pedestrian-oriented cities are more attractive than low-density, auto-oriented cities, and more attractive cities will entice population and limit outward spreading to rural areas. A similar dynamic may be at work in rural areas as well. Residents of such towns as Bozeman, Montana, may have the best of two worlds. They live in an attractive community with a vibrant street life and a system of trails that connects them to wilderness in the mountains beyond. In the Bozeman area, one doesn't need to live on a large piece of land outside city boundaries to enjoy the beauties of the natural landscape. Moreover, living at higher densities in towns like Bozeman leaves more habitat available for nonhuman species. Finally, living at relatively high densities in attractive cities that limit sprawl and provide decent public transportation, such as Portland, Oregon, serves to limit the human ecological footprint on the global environment and, in the process, helps to conserve biodiversity on a global scale.

NOTES

1. Phyllis Myers, "Livability at the Ballot Box: State and Local Referenda on Parks, Conservation, and Smarter Growth, Election Day 1998," (Discussion Paper, The Brookings Institution, Center on Urban and Metropolitan Policy, Washington, D.C., 1999).

2. Rebecca R. Sohmer and Robert E. Lang, "Downtown Rebound," (Fannie Mae Foundation Census Note, Washington, D.C.: Fannie Mae Foundation and Brookings Institution Center on Urban and Metropolitan Policy, 2001).

3. This section is based almost entirely on Peter Newman and Jeffrey Kenworthy, *Sustainability and Cities: Overcoming Automobile Dependence* (Washington, D.C.: Island Press, 1999). Their book is a must read for anyone who is interested in environmental issues that affect cities. This section has benefited from classroom discussions of sustainability and cities in an interdisciplinary course I teach at Marquette University, *The Environment and the City*.

4. Newman and Kenworthy, *Sustainability and Cities*, 68–126.

5. Newman and Kenworthy, *Sustainability and Cities*, 121.

6. Vladimir Novotny and Harvey Olem, *Water Quality: Prevention, Identification, and Management of Diffuse Pollution* (New York: Van Nostrand Reinhold Company, 1994).

7. William Fulton, Rolf Pendall, Mai Nguyen, and Alicia Harrison, "Who Sprawls Most? How Growth Patterns Differ Across the U.S." (Washington, D.C.: The Brookings Institution, Center on Urban & Metropolitan Policy, Survey Series). http://www.brookings.edu/es/urban/publications/fulton.pdf, 2001 [accessed 12 January 2002].

8. See Kenneth T. Jackson, *Crabgrass Frontier: The Suburbanization of the United States* (New York: Oxford University Press, 1985) for the full story on suburbanization in the United States and the role of transportation in it.

9. Single-family homes are subsidized through the mortgage interest income tax deduction and through various government programs that reduce mortgage interest rates. See Jackson, *Crabgrass Frontier*, for a full discussion of these.

10. Newman and Kenworthy, *Sustainability and Cities*, 79.

11. Large cities in the western United States, for instance, are frequently constrained from outward expansion by geographical barriers, such as mountain ranges, or by the presence of public lands. As a consequence, western metropolitan areas are actually denser than their eastern counterparts.

See Fulton et al., "Who Sprawls Most?" Of course such a constraint could cause a leapfrogging over the barriers to the rural areas of the mountain West. In the East, Midwest, and South, sprawl and population spreading can simply proceed outward from existing urban centers. In any case, constraints on outward sprawl do increase density.

12. See Newman and Kenworthy, *Sustainability and Cities*, 128–239.

13. Newman and Kenworthy, *Sustainability and Cities*, 113.

14. Newman and Kenworthy, *Sustainability and Cities*, 128–239.

15. Sohmer and Lang, "Downtown Rebound."

16. For an excellent summary of this issue, see Anthony Downs, "Dealing Effectively with Fast Growth," *Policy Brief 67* (The Brookings Institution, Washington, D.C.) http://www.brook.edu/comm/policybriefs/pb067/pb67.pdf, 2000 [accessed 12 January 2002]. Anywhere growth controls are instituted, either in an urban or a rural setting, the issue of affordable housing for low- to moderate-income families will come up. Local control of zoning has confined low-income residents to the central city in most urban areas. Regional systems of assistance for low-income housing could be established where each local municipality takes on a fair share burden of low-income housing construction or rehabilitation. To facilitate low- to moderate-income housing construction, developers as a group could be required to construct or rehabilitate a certain proportion of new housing units for low- and moderate-income residents. This could work through a regional system of housing development rights where developers earn transferable development rights through low- and moderate-income housing construction. These rights could then be used or sold to other developers and would be needed to construct upscale housing units. Something similar could be established in rural areas experiencing strong development pressures. Growth controls tend to increase land costs, but this can normally be offset by the efficiencies associated with the construction of housing at higher densities.

17. Jim Howe, Ed McMahon, and Luther Propst, *Balancing Nature and Commerce in Gateway Communities* (Washington, D.C.: Island Press, 1997), 56 and 74.

18. Phone conversation with Susan Dorsey Otis, Director of the Yampa Valley Land Trust, July 2001.

19. See chapter 7 for a discussion of the Crested Butte Land Trust.

20. In these programs the term *purchase of development rights* (PDR) is often used. Basically, PDRs are the same as conservation easements where the right to develop the land is purchased and retired by either a nonprofit (such as a land trust) or a unit of local government.

21. Howe et al., *Balancing Nature and Commerce*, 80–83.

22. Gallatin County Planning Board, *Zoning District Model* (Bozeman, Mont.: Gallatin County, 1996), 1–5.

23. Gallatin County Planning Department, *Springhill Planning and Zoning District* (Bozeman, Mont., 1992); and a conversation with Jim Madden of the Gallatin Valley Land Trust, July 2001.

24. Gallatin County Planning Board, *Zoning District Model*, 8–9.

25. Mark Haggerty, "The Cost of Community Services in Custer County, Colorado" (Tucson, Ariz.: Sonoran Institute, 2000).

26. Mark Haggerty, "The Fiscal Impact of Different Land Uses on County Government and School Districts in Gallatin County, Montana" (Bozeman, Mont.: Local Government Center, Montana State University, 1996).

27. Haggerty, "The Fiscal Impact of Different Land Uses."

Bibliography

Agee, James K. *Fire Ecology of Pacific Northwest Forests.* Washington, D.C.: Island Press, 1993.

Aiken, Katherine. "Western Smelters and the Problem of Smelter Smoke." In *Northwest Lands, Northwest Peoples: Readings in Environmental History*, edited by Dale D. Goble and Paul W. Hirt, 502–522. Seattle: University of Washington Press, 1999.

Ajzen, Icek. "The Theory of Planned Behavior." *Organization and Human Decision Processes* 50 (1991): 179–211.

Ajzen, Icek, and B. L. Driver, "Contingent Value Measurement: On the Nature and Meaning of Willingness to Pay." *Journal of Consumer Psychology* 1 (1992): 297–316.

Albrecht, Don E., Gordon Bultena, and Eric Hoiberg. "Constituency of the Antigrowth Movement: A Comparison of Urban Status Groups." *Urban Affairs Quarterly* 21 (1986): 607–616.

American Rivers. "Yellowstone River Named One of Nations Most Endangered Rivers." http://www.amrivers.org/pressrelease/pressmeryellowstone1999.htm, 1999 [accessed 12 January 2002].

Anglin, Roland. "Diminishing Utility: The Effect on Citizen Preferences for Local Growth." *Urban Affairs Quarterly* 25 (1990): 684–696.

Baldassare, Mark. "Suburban Communities." *Annual Review of Sociology* 18 (1992): 475–494.

———. "Suburban Support for No Growth Policies: Implications for the Growth Revolt." *Urban Affairs* 12 (1990): 197–206.

———. *The Growth Dilemma.* Berkeley: University of California Press, 1986.

Baldassare, Mark, and W. Protash. "Growth Controls, Population Growth, and Community Satisfaction." *American Sociological Review* 47 (1982): 339–346.

Baldassare, Mark, and Georjeanna Wilson. "Changing Sources of Suburban Support for Local Growth Controls." *Urban Studies* 33 (1986): 459–471.

Barkley, David L. "The Decentralization of High-Technology Manufacturing to Non-Metropolitan Areas." *Growth and Change* 19 (1988): 13–30.

Barkley, David L., and John E. Keith. "The Locational Determinants of Western Non-metro High Tech Manufacturers: An Econometric Analysis." *Western Journal of Agricultural Economics* 16 (1991): 331–344.

Beesley, David. "Reconstructing the Landscape: An Environmental History." In *Status of the Sierra Nevada, Volume II: Assessment and Scientific Basis for Management Options*, Sierra Nevada Ecosystem Project, Final Report to Congress, 3–24. Davis, Calif.: Centers for Water and Wildland Resources, University of California, Davis, 1996.

Berry, Kristin H., Laura Stockton, and Tim Shields. "18 Years of Change in Protected and Unprotected Desert Tortoise Populations at the Interpretive Center, Desert Tortoise Research Natural Area, California." Paper presented at the twenty-third annual meeting and symposium of the Desert Tortoise Council, Tucson, Ariz., April 1998.

Beyers, William B. "Trends in Service Employment in Pacific Northwest Counties: 1974–1986." *Growth and Change* 22 (1991): 27–50.

Blackwood, Larry G., and Edwin H. Carpenter. "The Importance of Anti-Urbanism in Determining Residential Preferences and Migration Patterns." *Rural Sociology* 43 (1978): 31–47.

Blaikie, Norman W. H. "The Nature and Origins of Ecological World Views: An Australian Study." *Social Science Quarterly* 73 (1992): 144–165.

Booth, Douglas E. "Spatial Patterns in the Economic Development of the Mountain West." *Growth and Change* 30 (1999): 384–405.

Brattstrom, B. "Social Behavior and Habitat Requirements of Desert Reptiles." In *Herpetology of the North American Deserts: Proceedings of a Symposium*, edited by Philip R. Brown and John W. Wright, 127–142. Special Publication No. 5, Southwestern Herpetologists Society, October 1994.

———. "Habitat Destruction in California with Special Reference to *Clemmys marmorato.*" In *Proceedings of the Conference on California Herpetology*, edited by H. F. De Lisle, P. R. Brown, B. Kaufman, and B. M. McGurty, 13–24. Southwestern Herpetologists Society, 1988.

Brown, James H. *Macroecology*. Chicago: University of Chicago Press, 1995.

Buttel, Frederick H. "Age and Environmental Concern: A Multivariate Analysis." *Youth & Society* 10 (1979): 237–256.

California Native Plant Society. *California Native Plant Society's Inventory of Rare and Endangered Vascular Plants of California*. Sacramento, Calif.: California Native Plant Society, 1994.

Callicott, J. Baird. "The Wilderness Idea Revisited: The Sustainable Development Alternative." In *The Great New Wilderness Debate*, edited by J. Baird Callicott and Michael P. Nelson, 337–366. Athens: University of Georgia Press, 1998.

———. "Intrinsic Value, Quantum Theory, and Environmental Ethics." *Environmental Ethics* 7 (1985): 257–273.

Canfield, Jodie E., L. Jack Lyon, J. Michael Hillis, and Michael J. Thompson. "Ungulates." In *The Effects of Recreation on Rocky Mountain Wildlife: A Review for Montana*, coordinated by Gayle Joslin and Heidi Youmans, 6.1–6.25. Committee on Effects of Recreation on Wildlife, Montana Chapter of the Wildlife Society, 1999.

Carey, Cynthia. "Hypothesis Concerning the Causes of the Disappearance of Boreal Toads from the Mountains of Colorado." *Conservation Biology* 7 (1993): 355–362.

Carson, Rachel. *Silent Spring*. Boston: Houghton Mifflin Company, 1962.

Chang, Chi-ru. "Ecosystem Responses to Fire and Variations in Fire Regimes." In *Status of the Sierra Nevada, Volume II: Assessment and Scientific Basis for Management Options*, Sierra Nevada Ecosystem Project, Final Report to Congress, 1071–1099. Davis, Calif.: Centers for Water and Wildland Resources, University of California, Davis, 1996.

Claar, James J., Neil Anderson, Diane Boyd, Ben Conard, Gene Hickman, Robin Hompesch, Gary Olson, Helga Ihsle Pac, Tom Wittinger, and Heidi Youmans. "Carnivores." In *The Effects of Recreation on Rocky Mountain Wildlife: A Review for Montana*, coordinated by G. Joslin and H. Youmans, 7.1–7.63. Bozeman: Committee on Effects of Recreation on Wildlife, Montana Chapter of the Wildlife Society, 1999.

Clark, David E., and William J. Hunter. "The Impact of Economic Opportunity, Amenities, and Fiscal Factors on Age-Specific Migration Rates." *Journal of Regional Science* 32 (1992): 349–365.

Cleveland, Harlan. "The Twilight of Hierarchy: Speculations on the Global Information Society." *Public Administration Review* 45 (1985): 185–195.

Coleman, Melissa. "The High End of Home Economics: Aspen's Trophy Home Phenomenon." *High Country News* 30–15 (August 17, 1998): 12.

Colorado Natural Heritage Program. *Colorado Rare Plant Field Guide*. Fort Collins, Colo.: Colorado Natural Heritage Program. http://ndis.nrel.colostate.edu/ndis/rareplants/cover.html, 2000 [accessed 12 January 2002].

———. "The Natural Heritage Methodology." Ft. Collins, Colo. http://www.cnhp.colostate.edu/docs/methodology.html [accessed 5 July 2001].

Colorado State University. "Boreal Toad." *Natural Diversity Information Source*. Ft. Collins, Colo. http://ndis.nrel.colostate.edu/escop/doc/borealtoa/borealtoad.html, 1999 [accessed 12 January 2002].

———. "Northern Leopard Frog." *Natural Diversity Information Source*. Ft. Collins, Colo. http://ndis.nrel.colostate.edu/escop/doc/aaric/northernleopardfrog.htm, 1999 [accessed 12 January 2002].

———. *Natural Diversity Information Source*. Ft. Collins, Colo. http://ndis.nrel.colostate.edu/escop/, 2000 [accessed 12 January 2002].

Congdon, Justin D., Arthur E. Dunham, and R. C. Van-Loben-Sels. "Demographics of Common Snapping Turtles (*Chelydra serpentina*): Implications for Conservation and Management of Long-Lived Organisms." *American Zoologist* 34 (1994): 397–408.

Connerly, Charles E. "Growth Management Concern: The Impact of Its Definition on Support for Local Growth Controls." *Environment and Behavior* 18 (1986): 707–732.

Connerly, C., and James E. Frank. "Predicting Support for Local Growth Controls." *Social Science Quarterly* 67 (1986): 572–585.

Cook, Annabel K., and Donald M. Beck. "Metropolitan Dominance versus Decentralization in the Information Age." *Social Science Quarterly* 72 (1991): 284–298.

Cordell, H. Ken, and Susan M. McKinney. *Outdoor Recreation in American Life: A National Assessment of Demand and Supply Trends*. Champaign, Ill.: Sagamore Publishing, 1999.

Corn, Paul S. "Effects of Ultraviolet Radiation on Boreal Toads in Colorado." *Ecological Applications* 8 (1998): 18–26.

Constantini, Edmond, and Kenneth Hanf. "Environmental Concern and Lake Tahoe: A Study of Elite Perceptions, Backgrounds, and Attitudes." *Environment and Behavior* 4 (1972): 209–242.

Cronon, William. "The Trouble with Wilderness, or, Getting Back to the Wrong Nature." In *The Great New Wilderness Debate*, edited by J. Baird Callicott and Michael P. Nelson, 471–499. Athens: University of Georgia Press, 1998.

———. *Nature's Metropolis: Chicago and the Great West.* New York: W. W. Norton, 1991.

Daly, Herman E. *Steady-state Economics.* 2d ed. Washington, D.C.: Island Press, 1991.

Davis, Tony. "The West's Hottest Question: In the Wake of Cerro Grande Fire, Everyone Ponders Prescribed Burning." *High Country News* 32–11 (June 5, 2000): 4–5.

De Smet, Ken D., and Michael P. Conrad. "Status, Habitat Requirements, and Adaptations of Ferruginous Hawks in Manitoba." In *Proceedings of the Second Endangered Species and Prairie Conservation Workshop. Natural History Section Provincial Museum of Alberta, Occasional Paper No. 15,* edited by Geoffrey L. Holroyd, Gordon Burns, and Hugh C. Smith, 219–221. Edmonton, Alberta, 1991.

Diller, Lowell V., and Richard L. Wallace. "Distribution and Habitat of *Plethodon Elongatus* on Managed, Young Growth Forests in North Coastal California." *Journal of Herpetology* 28 (1994): 310–318.

Dillman, Don A. "Residential Preferences, Quality of Life, and the Population Turnaround." *American Journal of Agricultural Economics* 61 (1979): 960–966.

Dowall, David E. *The Suburban Squeeze.* Berkeley: University of California Press, 1984.

Downs, Anthony. "Dealing Effectively with Fast Growth." *Policy Brief* 67. The Brookings Institution, Washington, D.C. http://www.brook.edu/comm/policybriefs/pb067/pb67.pdf, 2000 [accessed 12 January 2002].

———. *New Visions for Metropolitan America.* Washington, D.C.: The Brookings Institution, 1994.

———. "Up and Down with Ecology—The 'Issue-Attention Cycle.'" *The Public Interest* 28 (1972): 38–50.

Drost, Charles A., and Gary M. Fellers. "Collapse of a Regional Frog Fauna in the Yosemite Area of the California Sierra Nevada, USA." *Conservation Biology* 10 (1996): 414–425.

Duane, Timothy P. *Shaping the Sierra: Nature, Culture, and Conflict in the Changing West.* Berkeley: University of California Press, 1999.

———. "Human Settlement: 1850–2040." In *Status of the Sierra Nevada, Volume II: Assessment and Scientific Basis for Management Options,* Sierra Nevada Ecosystem Project, Final Report to Congress, 235–360. Davis, Calif.: Centers for Water and Wildland Resources, University of California, Davis, 1996.

———. "Recreation in the Sierra." In *Status of the Sierra Nevada, Volume II: Assessment and Scientific Basis for Management Options,* Sierra Nevada Ecosystem Project, Final Report to Congress, 557–609. Davis, Calif.: Centers for Water and Wildland Resources, University of California, Davis, 1996.

Duffy-Deno, Kevin T. "Economic Effect of Endangered Species Preservation in the Non-Metropolitan West." *Growth and Change* 28 (1997): 263–288.

Duffy-Deno, Kevin T., and Thomas C. Brill. "The Effect of Federal Wilderness on County Growth in the Intermountain Western United States." *Journal of Regional Science* 38 (1998): 109–136.

Dunlap, Riley E. "Trends in Public Opinion toward Environmental Issues: 1965–1990." *Society and Natural Resources* 4 (1991): 285–312.

Dunlap, Riley E., and Kent D. van Liere. "The 'New Environmental Paradigm': A Proposed Measuring Instrument and Preliminary Results." *Journal of Environmental Education* 9 (1978): 10–19.

Franklin, Jerry F., and Jo Ann Fites-Kaufmann. "Assessment of Late-Successional Forests of the Sierra Nevada." In *Status of the Sierra Nevada, Volume II: Assessment and Scien-*

tific Basis for Management Options, Sierra Nevada Ecosystem Project, Final Report to Congress, 627–661. Davis, Calif.: Centers for Water and Wildland Resources, University of California, Davis, 1996.

Fellers, Gary M., and Charles A. Drost. "Disappearance of the Cascades Frog *Rana cascadae* at the Southern End of Its Range, California, USA." *Biological-Conservation* 65 (1993): 177–181.

Fisher, Robert N., and H. Bradley Shaffer. "The Decline of Amphibians in California's Great Central Valley." *Conservation Biology* 10 (1996): 1387–1397.

Fite, Katherine V., Andrew Blaustein, Lynn Bengston, and Heather E. Hewitt. "Evidence of Retinal Light Damage in *Rana cascadae*: A Declining Amphibian Species." *Copeia* 4 (1998): 906–914.

Fitzgerald, James P., Carron A. Meaney, and David M. Armstrong. *Mammals of Colorado.* Niwot, Colo.: University Press of Colorado, 1994.

Foreman, David. "Wilderness Areas Are for Real." In *The Great New Wilderness Debate*, edited by J. Baird Callicott and Michael P. Nelson, 395–407. Athens: University of Georgia Press, 1998.

Frey, William H., and Alden Speare Jr. "The Revival of Metropolitan Population Growth in the United States: An Assessment of Findings from the 1990 Census." *Population and Development Review* 18 (1992): 129–146.

Fuguitt, Glenn V., and Calvin L. Beale. "Recent Trends in Nonmetropolitan Migration: Toward a New Turnaround?" *Growth and Change* 27 (1996): 156–174.

Fulton, William, Rolf Pendall, Mai Nguyen, and Alicia Harrison. "Who Sprawls Most? How Growth Patterns Differ Across the U.S." Washington, D.C.: The Brookings Institution, Center on Urban & Metropolitan Policy, Survey Series. http://www.brookings.edu/es/urban/publications/fulton.pdf, 2001 [accessed 12 January 2002].

Gallatin County Planning Board. *Zoning District Model.* Bozeman, Mont.: Gallatin County, 1996.

Gallatin County Planning Department. *Springhill Planning and Zoning District.* Bozeman, Mont.: Gallatin County, 1992.

Garreau, Joel. *Edge City: Life on the New Frontier.* New York: Doubleday, 1991.

Gebhardt, Alicia M., and Greg Lindsey. "Differences in Environmental Orientation Among Homeowners." *The Journal of Environmental Education* 27 (1995): 4–13.

Graber, David M. "Status of Terrestrial Vertebrates." In *Status of the Sierra Nevada, Volume II: Assessment and Scientific Basis for Management Options*, Sierra Nevada Ecosystem Project, Final Report to Congress, 709–734. Davis, Calif.: Centers for Water and Wildland Resources, University of California, Davis, 1996.

Green, William H. *Limdep Version 7.0.* Plainview, N.Y.: Econometric Software, 1998.

Gunn, Alastair S. "Rethinking Communities: Environmental Ethics in an Urbanized World." *Environmental Ethics* 20 (1998): 341–360.

Gunter, Valarie J., and Barbara Finlay. "Influences on Group Participation in Environmental Conflicts." *Rural Sociology* 53 (1988): 498–505.

Gustanski, Julie A., and Roderick H. Squires, eds. *Protecting the Land: Conservation Easements Past, Present, and Future.* Washington, D.C.: Island Press, 2000.

Hager, Heather A. "Area-Sensitivity of Reptiles and Amphibians: Are There Indicator Species for Habitat Fragmentation?" *Ecoscience* 5 (1998): 139–147.

Haggerty, Mark. "The Cost of Community Services in Custer County, Colorado." Tucson, Ariz.: Sonoran Institute, 2000.

———. "The Fiscal Impact of Different Land Uses on County Government and School Districts in Gallatin County, Montana." Bozeman, Mont.: Local Government Center, Montana State University, 1996.

Hamann, Betsy, Heather Johnston, John Gobielle, Mike Hillis, Sara Johnson, Lynn Kelly, and Pat McClelland. "Birds." In *The Effects of Recreation on Rocky Mountain Wildlife: A Review for Montana*, coordinated by G. Joslin and H. Youmans, 3.1–3.34. Bozeman: Committee on Effects of Recreation on Wildlife, Montana Chapter of the Wildlife Society, 1999.

Hamann, Betsy, and Gayle Joslin. "Vegetation, Soil, and Water." In *The Effects of Recreation on Rocky Mountain Wildlife: A Review for Montana*, coordinated by G. Joslin and H. Youmans, 9.1–9.11. Montana: Committee on Effects of Recreation on Wildlife, Montana Chapter of the Wildlife Society, 1999.

Hammerson, Geoffrey A. "Bullfrog Eliminating Leopard Frogs in Colorado?" *Herpetological Review* 13 (1982): 115–116.

Hargrove, Eugene C. "Anglo-American Land Use Attitudes." *Environmental Ethics* 2 (1980): 121–148.

Heimberger, Marianne, David Euler, and Jack Barr. "The Impact of Cottage Development on Common Loon Reproductive Success in Central Ontario." *Wilson Bulletin* 95 (1983): 431–439.

Herring, Hal. "Strangling the Last Best River." *High Country News* 31–7 (April 12, 1999): 6.

Hickman, Gene, Beverly G. Dixon, and Janelle Corn. "Small Mammals." In *The Effects of Recreation on Rocky Mountain Wildlife: A Review for Montana*, coordinated by G. Joslin and H. Youmans, 4.1–4.16. Bozeman: Committee on Effects of Recreation on Wildlife, Montana Chapter of the Wildlife Society, 1999.

Hine, Donald W., and Robert Gifford. "Fear Appeals, Individual Differences, and Environmental Concern." *Journal of Environmental Education* 23 (1991): 36–41.

Hirt, Paul W. "Getting Out the Cut: A History of National Forest Management in the Northern Rockies." In *Northwest Lands, Northwest Peoples: Readings in Environmental History*, edited by Dale D. Goble and Paul W. Hirt, 437–461. Seattle: University of Washington Press, 1999.

Howe, Jim, Ed McMahon, and Luther Propst. *Balancing Nature and Commerce in Gateway Communities*. Washington, D.C.: Island Press, 1997.

Ilvento, T. W., and A. E. Luloff. "Anti-Urbanism and Nonmetropolitan Growth: A Reevaluation." *Rural Sociology* 47 (1982): 220–233.

Independent Scientific Advisory Board. "Ecological Impacts of the Flow Provisions of the Biological Opinion for Endangered Snake River Salmon on Resident Fishes in Hungry Horse, and Libby Systems in Montana, Idaho, and British Columbia." Portland, Oreg.: Northwest Power Planning Council, National Marine Fisheries Service, 1997.

Jackson, Kenneth T. *Crabgrass Frontier: The Suburbanization of the United States*. New York: Oxford University Press, 1985.

Jacobs, Jane. *The Economy of Cities*. New York: Vintage Books, 1970.

———. *The Death and Life of Great American Cities*. New York: Vintage Books, 1961.

Jamison, Michael. "Whitfish-Area Growth May Be Funneling Grizzlies into Town." *Missoulian* (November 23, 1999): A1, A7.

Jennings, Mark R. "Status of Amphibians." In *Status of the Sierra Nevada, Volume II: Assessment and Scientific Basis for Management Options*, Sierra Nevada Ecosystem Project, Final Report to Congress, 921–944. Davis, Calif.: Centers for Water and Wildland Resources, University of California, Davis, 1996.

Johnson, Jerry D., and Raymond Rasker. "Local Government: Local Business Climate and Quality of Life." *Montana Policy Review* 3 (1993): 11–19.

Johnson, Kenneth M., and Calvin L. Beale. "The Recent Revival of Widespread Population Growth in Nonmetropolitan Areas of the United States." *Rural Sociology* 59 (1994): 655–667.

Johnson, Vanessa. "Rural Residential Development Trends in the Greater Yellowstone Ecosystem since the Listing of the Grizzly Bear." Bozeman, Mont.: Sierra Club Grizzly Bear Ecosystem Project, 2000.

Jones, Lisa. "El Nuevo West: The Region's New Pioneers Buoy the Economy and Live on the Edge." *High Country News* 28–24 (December 23, 1996): 1, 6–11.

Joslin, Gayle, and Heidi Youmans, coordinators. *The Effects of Recreation on Rocky Mountain Wildlife: A Review for Montana.* Bozeman: Committee on Effects of Recreation on Wildlife, Montana Chapter of the Wildlife Society, 1999.

Kelly, Lynn M. "The Effects of Human Disturbance on Common Loon Productivity in Northwestern Montana." Master's thesis, Bozeman: Montana State University, 1992.

Kempton, William, James S. Boster, and Jennifer A. Hartley. *Environmental Values in American Culture.* Cambridge, Mass.: MIT Press, 1995.

Kendall, Joan, and Bruce W. Pigozzi. "Nonemployment Income and the Economic Base of Michigan Counties: 1959–1986." *Growth and Change* 25 (1994): 51–74.

Kinney, William C. "Conditions of Rangelands before 1905." In *Status of the Sierra Nevada, Volume II: Assessment and Scientific Basis for Management Options*, Sierra Nevada Ecosystem Project, Final Report to Congress, 31–45. Davis, Calif.: Centers for Water and Wildland Resources, University of California, Davis, 1996.

Kirn, Thomas J., Richard S. Conway Jr., and William B. Beyers. "Producer Services Development and the Role of Telecommunications: A Case Study in Rural Washington." *Growth and Change* 21 (1990): 33–50.

Knight, Richard L. "Field Report from the New American West." In *Wallace Stegner and the Continental Vision: Essays on Literature, History, and Landscape*, edited by Curt Meine, 181–200. Washington, D.C.: Island Press, 1997.

Knight, Richard L., and David N. Cole. "Wildlife Responses to Recreationists." In *Wildlife and Recreationists: Coexistence through Management and Research*, edited by Richard L. Knight and Kevin J. Gutzwiller, 51–69. Washington, D.C.: Island Press, 1995.

Knight, Richard L., and Kevin J. Gutzwiller. *Wildlife and Recreationists: Coexistence through Management and Research.* Washington, D.C.: Island Press, 1995.

Knight, Richard L., George N. Wallace, and William E. Riebsame. "Ranching the View: Subdivisions versus Agriculture." *Conservation Biology* 9 (1995): 459–461.

Kondolf, G. Mathias, Richard Kattelmann, Michael Embury, and Don C. Erman. "Status of Riparian Habitat." In *Status of the Sierra Nevada, Volume II: Assessment and Scientific Basis for Management Options*, Sierra Nevada Ecosystem Project, Final Report to Congress, 1009–1030. Davis, Calif.: Centers for Water and Wildland Resources, University of California, Davis, 1996.

Krause, Daniel. "Evironmental Consciousness: An Empirical Study." *Environment and Behavior* 25 (1993): 126–142.

Land Trust Alliance. *1998 National Directory of Conservation Land Trusts.* Washington, D.C.: Land Trust Alliance, 1998.

Larmer, Paul. "Can a Colorado Ski County Say Enough Is Enough?" *High Country News* 28–3 (February 19, 1996): 1, 8–11.

Larson, David J. "Historical Water-Use Priorities and Public Policies." In *Status of the Sierra Nevada, Volume II: Assessment and Scientific Basis for Management Options*, Sierra Nevada Ecosystem Project, Final Report to Congress, 163–185. Davis, Calif.: Centers for Water and Wildland Resources, University of California, Davis, 1996.

Leopold, Aldo. *A Sand County Almanac*. New York: Ballantine Books, 1970.

Logan, John R., and Min Zhou. "Do Suburban Growth Controls Control Growth?" *American Sociological Review* 54 (1989): 461–471.

Lyon, James S., Thomas J. Hilliard, and Thomas N. Bethell. *Burden of Gilt: The Legacy of Environmental Damage from Abandoned Mines, and What America Should Do about It*. Washington, D.C.: Mineral Policy Center, 1993.

Mace, Richard D., and John S. Waller. "Demography and Population Trend of Grizzly Bears in the Swan Mountains, Montana." *Conservation Biology* 12 (1998): 1005–1016.

Mace, Richard D., John S. Waller, Timothy L. Manley, Katherine Ake, and William T. Wittinger. "Landscape Evaluation of Grizzly Bear Habitat in Western Montana." *Conservation Biology* 13 (1999): 367–377.

Mace, Richard D., John S. Waller, Timothy L. Manley, L. Jack Lyon, and H. Zuuring. "Relationships among Grizzly Bears, Roads and Habitat in the Swan Mountains, Montana." *Journal of Applied Ecology* 33 (1996): 1395–1404.

MacIntyre, Alasdair. *Whose Justice? Which Rationality?* Notre Dame, Ind.: University of Notre Dame Press, 1988.

———. *After Virtue: A Study in Moral Theory*. Notre Dame, Ind.: University of Notre Dame Press, 1984.

Marcot, Bruce G., Michael J. Wisdom, Hiram W. Li, and Gonzalo C. Castillo. "Managing for Featured, Threatened, Endangered, and Sensitive Species and Unique Habitats for Ecosystem Sustainability." In *Eastside Forest Ecosystem Health Assessment, Volume III*, R. L. Everett (Assessment Team Leader). Gen. Tech. Rep. PNW-GTR-329. Portland, Oreg.: USDA Forest Service, Pacific Northwest Research Station, 1994.

Mattson, D. J., and D. P. Reinhart. "Excavation of Red Squirrel Middens by Grizzly Bears in the Whitebark Pine Zone." *Journal of Applied Ecology* 34 (1997): 926–940.

Maxell, Bryce A., and Grant Hokit. "Amphibians and Reptiles." In *The Effects of Recreation on Rocky Mountain Wildlife: A Review for Montana*, coordinated by G. Joslin and H. Youmans, 2.1–2.29. Bozeman: Committee on Effects of Recreation on Wildlife, Montana Chapter of the Wildlife Society, 1999.

McHarg, Ian L. "The Place of Nature in the City of Man." In *Western Man and Environmental Ethics: Attitudes toward Nature and Technology*, edited by Ian G. Barbour, 171–186. Reading, Mass.: Addison-Wesley Publishing Company, 1973.

———. *Design With Nature*. Garden City, N.Y.: Natural History Press, 1969.

Meffe, Gary K., and C. Ronald Carroll. *Principles of Conservation Biology*. Sunderland, Mass.: Sinauer Associates, 1994.

Miller, James P. "The Product Cycle and High Technology Industry in Nonmetropolitan Areas, 1976–1980." *The Review of Regional Studies* 19 (1989): 1–12.

Miller, James P., and Herman Bluestone. "Prospects for Service Sector Employment Growth in Non-Metropolitan America." *The Review of Regional Studies* 18 (1988): 28–41.

Mills, Edwin S., and Bruce W. Hamilton. *Urban Economics*. 5th ed. New York: Harper Collins, 1994.

Mohai, Paul. "Men, Women, and the Environment: An Examination of the Gender Gap in Environmental Concern and Activism." *Society and Natural Resources* 5 (1992): 1–19.

————. "Public Concern and Elite Involvement in Environmental-Conservation Issues." *Social Science Quarterly* 66 (1985): 820–838.

Mohai, Paul, and Ben W. Twight. "Age and Environmentalism: An Elaboration of the Buttel Model Using National Survey Evidence." *Social Science Quarterly* 68 (1987): 798–815.

Montana Natural Heritage Program. *Montana Rare Plant Field Guide.* Helena, Mont. http://nhp.nris.state.mt.us/plants/, 2000 [accessed 12 January 2002].

Moyle, Peter B., Ronald M. Yoshiyama, and Roland A. Knapp. "Status of Fish and Fisheries." In *Status of the Sierra Nevada, Volume II: Assessment and Scientific Basis for Management Options*, Sierra Nevada Ecosystem Project, Final Report to Congress, 953–973. Davis, Calif.: Centers for Water and Wildland Resources, University of California, Davis, 1996.

Mutel, Cornelia F., and John C. Emerick. *From Grassland to Glacier: The Natural History of Colorado.* Boulder: Johnson Books, 1984.

Muth, Richard. *Cities and Housing.* Chicago: University of Chicago Press, 1969.

Myers, Phyllis. "Livability at the Ballot Box: State and Local Referenda on Parks, Conservation, and Smarter Growth, Election Day 1998." Discussion Paper, The Brookings Institution, Center on Urban and Metropolitan Policy, Washington, D.C. http://www.brook.edu/es/urban/ballotbox/finalreport.pdf, 1999 [accessed 12 January 2002].

Nelson, Ruth A. *Handbook of Rocky Mountain Plants.* Niwot, Colo.: Roberts Rinehart Publishers, 1992.

Newman, Peter, and Jeffrey Kenworthy. *Sustainability and Cities: Overcoming Automobile Dependence.* Washington, D.C.: Island Press, 1999.

Norton, Bryan G. "Why I Am not a Nonanthropocentrist: Callicott and the Failure of Monistic Inherentism." *Environmental Ethics* 17 (1995): 341–358.

————. *Why Preserve Natural Variety?* Princeton: Princeton University Press, 1987.

Noss, Reed F., and Allen Y. Cooperrider. *Saving Nature's Legacy: Protecting and Restoring Biodiversity.* Washington, D.C.: Island Press, 1994.

Noss, Reed F., Michael A. O'Connell, and Dennis D. Murphy. *The Science of Conservation Planning: Habitat Conservation Under the Endangered Species Act.* Washington, D.C.: Island Press, 1997.

Novotny, Vladimir, and Harvey Olem. *Water Quality: Prevention, Identification, and Management of Diffuse Pollution.* New York: Van Nostrand Reinhold Company, 1994.

Odell, Eric A., and Richard L. Knight. "Songbird and Medium-Sized Mammal Communities Associated with Exurban Development." *Conservation Biology* 15 (2001): 1143–1150.

Osmundson, Douglas B., and Lynn Kaeding. "Relationships between Flow and Rare Fish Habitat in the 15-Mile Reach of the Upper Colorado River: Final Report." Denver: U.S. Fish and Wildlife Service, 1995.

Peterson, Merrill D. *The Portable Thomas Jefferson.* New York: The Viking Press, 1975.

Porter, Douglas R. *Managing Growth in America's Communities.* Washington, D.C.: Island Press, 1997.

Power, Thomas M. "Ecosystem Preservation and the Economy in the Greater Yellowstone Area." *Conservation Biology* 5 (1991): 395–404.

————. *Lost Landscapes and Failed Economies: The Search for Value of Place.* Washington, D.C.: Island Press, 1996.

Putnam, Hilary. *Reason, Truth, and History.* Cambridge: Cambridge University Press, 1981.

Quartarone, Fred, and Connie Young. "Historical Accounts of Upper Colorado River Basin Endangered Fish: Final Report." Denver: Colorado Division of Wildlife, 1993.

Rand McNally. 1995 Road Atlas: Unites States, Canada, Mexico. Skokie, Ill.: Rand McNally, 1995.

———. 1986 Road Atlas: Unites States, Canada, Mexico. Skokie, Ill.: Rand McNally, 1986.

Rasker, Ray, and Dennis Glick. "Footloose Entrepreneurs: Pioneers of the New West?" Illahee 10 (1994): 34–43.

Rasker, Ray, Norma Tirrell, and Deanne Klopfer. The Wealth of Nature: New Economic Realities in the Yellowstone Region. Washington, D.C.: The Wilderness Society, 1991.

Reese, Devin A., and Hartwell H. Welsh Jr. "Habitat Use by Western Pond Turtles in the Trinity River, California." Journal of Wildlife Management 62 (1998): 842–853.

Reichert, Christiane von, and Gundar Rudzitis. "Multinomial Logistic Models Explaining Income Changes of Migrants to High-Amenity Counties." The Review of Regional Studies 22 (1992): 25–42.

Reiland, Eric W. "Fish Loss to Irrigation Canals and Methods to Reduce these Losses on the West Gallatin River, Montana." Master's thesis, Bozeman: Montana State University, 1997.

Reisner, Marc. Cadillac Desert: The American West and Its Disappearing Water. New York: Penguin Books, 1986.

Richter, Brian D., David P. Braun, Michael A. Mendelson, and Lawrence L. Master. "Threats to Imperiled Freshwater Fauna." Conservation Biology 11 (1997): 1081–1093.

Roback, Jennifer. "Wages, Rents, and the Quality of Life." Journal of Political Economy 90 (1982): 1257–1278.

Robbins Roy. Our Landed Heritage: The Public Domain, 1776–1936. Lincoln: University of Nebraska Press, 1976.

Rohe, Randall. "Environment and Mining in the Mountainous West." In The Mountainous West: Explorations in Historical Geography, edited by William Wyckoff and Lary M. Dilsaver, 169–193. Lincoln: University of Nebraska Press, 1995.

Rolston, Holmes, III. Genes, Genesis, and God: Values and Their Origins in Natural and Human History. Cambridge: Cambridge University Press, 1999.

———. "The Wilderness Idea Reaffirmed." In The Great New Wilderness Debate, edited by J. Baird Callicott and Michael P. Nelson, 367–386. Athens: University of Georgia Press, 1998.

———. "Values in Nature." Environmental Ethics 3 (1981): 113–128.

Rorty, Richard. Philosophy and the Mirror of Nature. Princeton: Princeton University Press, 1979.

Rudzitis, Gundars, and Harley E. Johansen. "How Important Is Wilderness? Results from a United States Survey." Environmental Management 15 (1991): 227–233.

———. "Migration into Western Wilderness Counties: Causes and Consequences." Western Wildlands 15 (1989): 19–23.

Ruediger, Bill. "Rare Carnivores and Higways—Moving into the 21st Century." In Proceedings of the International Conference on Wildlife Ecology and Transportation, edited by Gary L. Evink, Paul Garrett, David Zeigler, and Jon Berry, 10–16. Tallahassee: Florida Department of Transportation, 1998.

Runte, Alfred. National Parks: The American Experience. 2d ed. Lincoln: University of Nebraska Press, 1987.

Samdahl, Diane M., and Robert Robertson. "Social Determinants of Environmental Concern: Specification and Test of the Model." *Environment and Behavior* 21 (1989): 57–81.

Schmutz, Josef K., and Richard W Fyfe. "Migration and Mortalilty of Alberta Ferruginous Hawks." *The Condor* 89 (1987): 169–174.

Schuierer, Frederick W. "Remarks Upon the Natural History of *Bufo exsul* Myers, the Endemic Toad of Deep Springs Valley, Inyo Country, California." *Herpetologica* 17.4 (1962): 260–266.

Searle, John R. *The Construction of Social Reality*. New York: Free Press, 1995.

Shevock, James R. "Status of Rare and Endemic Plants." In *Status of the Sierra Nevada, Volume II: Assessment and Scientific Basis for Management Options*, Sierra Nevada Ecosystem Project, Final Report to Congress, 691–707. Davis, Calif.: Centers for Water and Wildland Resources, University of California, Davis, 1996.

Sierra Business Council. *Planning for Prosperity: Building Successful Communities in the Sierra Nevada*. Truckee, Calif.: Sierra Business Council, 1997.

Sierra Nevada Ecosystem Project, Final Report to Congress. *Status of the Sierra Nevada, Volume I: Assessment Summaries and Management Strategies*, Davis, Calif.: Centers for Water and Wildland Resources, University of California, Davis, 1996.

Sime, Carolyn A. "Domestic Dogs in Wildlife Habitats." In *The Effects of Recreation on Rocky Mountain Wildlife: A Review for Montana*, coordinated by G. Joslin and H. Youmans, 8.1–8.17. Montana: Committee on Effects of Recreation on Wildlife, Montana Chapter of the Wildlife Society, 1999.

Skidmore, Mark, and Michael Peddle. "Do Development Impact Fees Reduce the Rate of Residential Development?" *Growth and Change* 29 (1998): 383–401.

Skinner, Carl N., and Chi-ru Chang. "Fire Regimes, Past and Present." In *Status of the Sierra Nevada, Volume II: Assessment and Scientific Basis for Management Options*, Sierra Nevada Ecosystem Project, Final Report to Congress, 1041–1069. Davis, Calif.: Centers for Water and Wildland Resources, University of California, Davis, 1996.

Smith, Duane A. *Mining America: The Industry and the Environment, 1800–1980*. Niwot: University Press of Colorado, 1993.

———. *Rocky Mountain West: Colorado, Wyoming, and Montana, 1859–1915*. Albuquerque: University of New Mexico Press, 1992.

Smith, Stephen M., and David L. Barkley. "Local Input Linkages of Rural High-Technology Manufacturers." *Land Economics* 67 (1991): 472–485.

Sohmer, Rebecca R., and Robert E. Lang. "Downtown Rebound." Fannie Mae Foundation Census Note, Washington, D.C.: Fannie Mae Foundation and The Brookings Institution Center on Urban and Metropolitan Policy. http://www.brook.edu/es/urban/census/downtownrebound.pdf, 2001 [accessed 12 January 2002].

Soulé, Michael E. "Land Use Plannning and Mildlife Maintenance–Guidelines for Conserving Wildlife in an Urban Landscape." *Journal of the American Planning Association* 57 (1991): 313–323.

Stern, Paul C., Thomas Dietz, and Linda Kalof. "Value Orientations, Gender, and Environmental Concern." *Environment and Behavior* 25 (1993): 322–348.

Stiller, David. *Wounding the West: Montana, Mining, and the Environment*. Lincoln: University of Nebraska Press, 2000.

Storer, Tracy I., and Robert L. Usinger. *Sierra Nevada Natural History*. Berkeley: University of California Press, 1963.

Taylor, Paul W. *Respect for Nature: A Theory of Environmental Ethics.* Princeton: Princeton University Press, 1986.

Tilman, David. "Biodiversity and Ecosystem Functioning." In *Nature's Services: Societal Dependence on Natural Ecosystems,* edited by Gretchen C. Daily, 93–112. Washington, D.C.: Island Press, 1997.

Toole, K. Ross. *Twentieth-century Montana: A State of Extremes.* Norman: University of Oklahoma Press, 1972.

Trombulak, Stephen C., and Christopher A. Frissell. "Review of Ecological Effects of Roads on Terrestrial and Aquatic Communities." *Conservation Biology* 14 (2000): 18–30.

U.S. Bureau of Land Management. "Payments in Lieu of Taxes." Internal Report, 1995.

U.S. Department of Commerce, Bureau of Economic Analysis. *Regional Economic Information System, 1969–97,* CD-ROM. Washington, D.C., 1997.

U.S. Department of Commerce, Bureau of the Census. *County and City Data Book.* Washington, D.C.: U.S. Government Printing Office, 1988.

———. *Census of Housing. Detailed Housing Characteristics.* Washington, D.C.: U.S. Government Printing Office, 1993.

Vale, Thomas R. "Mountains and Moisture in the West." In *The Mountainous West: Explorations in Historical Geography,* edited by William Wyckoff and Lary M. Dilsaver, 141–165. Lincoln: University of Nebraska Press, 1995.

Van Liere, Kent D., and Riley E. Dunlap. "The Social Bases of Environmental Concern: A Review of Hypotheses, Explanations, and Empirical Evidence." *Public Opinion Quarterly* 44 (1980): 181–197.

Vaske, Jerry J., Maureen P. Donnelly, and Michelle Lyon. "Project Report: Knowledge, Beliefs, and Attitudes toward Endangered Fish of the Upper Colorado River Basin." Fort Collins, Colo.: Human Dimensions in Natural Resources Unit, College of Natural Resources, Colorado State University, 1995.

Wackernagel, Mathis, and William E. Rees. *Our Ecological Footprint: Reducing Human Impact on the Earth.* Gabriola Island, British Columbia: New Society Publishers, 1995.

Waller, Donald M. "Getting Back to the Right Nature: A Reply to Cronon's 'The Trouble with Wilderness.'" In *The Great New Wilderness Debate,* edited by J. Baird Callicott and Michael P. Nelson, 541–567. Athens: University of Georgia Press, 1998.

Warner, San B., Jr. *Streetcar Suburbs: The Process of Growth in Boston, 1870–1900.* New York: Atheneum, 1974.

Welsh, Hartwell H., Jr. "Relictual Amphibians and Old-Growth Forests." *Conservation Biology* 4 (1990): 309–319.

Welsh, Hartwell H., Jr., and Amy J. Lind. "Habitat Correlates of the Del Norte Salamander *Plethodon elongatus (Caudata: Plethodontidae),* in Northwestern California." *Journal of Herpetology* 29 (1995): 198–210.

White, Clayton M., and Thomas L. Thurow. "Reproduction of Ferruginous Hawks Exposed to Controlled Disturbance." *Condor* 87 (1985): 14–22.

White, Halbert. "A Heteroskedasticity Consistent Covariance Matrix and a Direct Test for Heteroskedasticity." *Econometrics* 48 (1990): 817–838.

Whitney, Stephen. *Western Forests.* New York: Alfred A. Knopf, 1985.

Williams, James D., and Andrew J. Sofranko. "Motivations for the Inmigration Component of Population Turnaround in Nonmetropolitan Areas." *Demography* 16 (1979): 239–255.

World Resources Institute. *World Resources, 1996–97: The Urban Environment.* New York and Oxford: Oxford University Press, 1996.

Wyckoff, William. *Creating Colorado: The Making of a Western American Landscape: 1860–1940.* New Haven: Yale University Press, 1999.

Wyckoff, William, and Lary M. Dilsaver. "Defining the Mountainous West." In *The Mountainous West: Explorations in Historical Geography*, edited by William Wyckoff and Lary M. Dilsaver, 1–59. Lincoln: University of Nebraska Press, 1995.

Wyckoff, William, and Katherine Hansen. "Environmental Change in the Northern Rockies: Settlement and Livestock Grazing in Southwestern Montana, 1860–1995." In *Northwest Lands, Northwest Peoples: Readings in Environmental History*, edited by Dale D. Goble and Paul W. Hirt, 336–361. Seattle: University of Washington Press, 1999.

Index

251

About the Author

Douglas E. Booth lives in Milwaukee, Wisconsin, with his wife, Carol Brill, and their two sons, Edward and Jeremy. He is an associate professor of economics at Marquette University where he teaches environmental and natural resource economics and coordinates an interdisciplinary undergraduate major and minor in urban environmental affairs. He is the author of *The Environmental Consequences of Growth: Steady-State Economics as an Alternative to Ecological Decline*, *Valuing Nature: The Decline and the Preservation of Old-Growth Forests*, and *Regional Long Waves, Uneven Growth, and the Cooperative Alternative*, as well as numerous articles. He is also a founding board member of the Driftless Area Land Conservancy, a land trust located in southwestern Wisconsin.